Communicating Security

This book analyzes the changes and tendencies expressed in the relation between army and society in Israel.

Since its inception, Israel has been defined as a nation in arms, a public space in which the security needs became central and, to a great extent, dictated the agenda and functioning of all the public arenas operating in it. The theoretical investigation is accompanied by case study illustrations of special instances related to the nexus between:

- security and society
- security and politics
- the army and the media
- the army and public relations
- security and culture
- bereavement, memory and commemoration
- social motivation to serve in the army
- the army and foreign policy.

Lebel explores the connection between the military and culture in Israel against the backdrop of globalization, individualism, liberalism, and social burn-out in the face of survival and change.

This book was first published as a special issue of *Israel Affairs*.

Udi Lebel is a lecturer and researcher at The Ariel University Center of Samaria and Sapir College.

Communicating Security

Civil-Military Relations in Israel

Edited by
Udi Lebel

LONDON AND NEW YORK

First published 2008 by Routledge
2 Park Square, Milton Park, Abingdon, Oxon, OX14 4RN

Simultaneously published in the USA and Canada
by Routledge
270 Madison Ave, New York NY 10016

Routledge is an imprint of the Taylor & Francis Group, an Informa business

Transferred to Digital Printing 2010

© 2008 Lebel, Udi.

Typeset in Sabon 10.5/12pt by the Alden Group, Oxfordshire

All rights reserved. No part of this book may be reprinted or reproduced or utilised in any form or by any electronic, mechanical, or other means, now known or hereafter invented, including photocopying and recording, or in any information storage or retrieval system, without permission in writing from the publishers.

British Library Cataloguing in Publication Data
A catalogue record for this book is available from the British Library

Library of Congress Cataloging in Publication Data
A catalog record has been requested

ISBN10: 0-415-37340-9 (hbk)
ISBN10: 0-415-58506-6 (pbk)

ISBN13: 978-0-415-37340-1 (hbk)
ISBN13: 978-0-415-58506-4 (pbk)

CONTENTS

Introduction
'Communicating Security': Civil–Military Relations in Israel
UDI LEBEL   vii

Security and Politics
1   Political–Military Relations in Israel, 1996–2003
AMIR BAR-OR   1

2   The Growing Militarization of the Israeli Political System
GIORA GOLDBERG   13

3   Civil–Military Relations and Strategic Goal Setting in the Six Day War
ARYE NAOR   31

Security and Social Strength
4   Society Strength as a Base for Military Power: The State of Israel during the Early 1950s
ZE'EV DRORY   48

5   Under the Threat of Terrorism: A Reassessment of the Factors Influencing the Motivation to Serve in the Israeli Reserves
GABRIEL BEN-DOR AND AMI PEDAHZUR   66

Security and the Shaping of Culture, Memory, Loss and Bereavement
6   The Creation of the Israeli 'Political Bereavement Model'—Security Crises and their Influence on the Public Behaviour of Loss: A Psycho-Political Approach to the Study of History
UDI LEBEL   75

7   Holocaust Survivors in the Israeli Army during the 1948 War: Documents and Memory
HANNA YABLONKA   98

Military–Media Relations

8 The Military and the Media in the Twenty-First Century: Towards a New Model of Relations
YEHIEL LIMOR AND HILLEL NOSSEK — 120

9 Three 'Travelling' Models of Politics and the Mass Media in the Context of Israeli National Security
GIDEON DORON — 147

10 Nuclear Ambiguity and the Media: The Israeli Case
YOEL COHEN — 165

11 The Media and National Security: The Performance of the Israeli Press in the Eyes of the Israeli Public
MARTIN SHERMAN AND SHABTAI SHAVIT — 182

Security and Territory

12 Competing Land Uses: The Territorial Dimension of Civil–Military Relations in Israel
AMI OREN AND DAVID NEWMAN — 197

13 Defending Territorial Sovereignty Through Civilian Settlement: The Case of Israel's Population Dispersal Policy
MATT EVANS — 214

Index — 233

'Communicating Security': Civil–Military Relations in Israel

UDI LEBEL

From the time of its establishment in 1948, and its subsequent victory in the War of Independence, it was apparent that the new state of Israel would face threats to its survival in an on-going armed confrontation with rejectionist Arab neighbours bent on its destruction. As a result, the military became not only a key symbol of statehood, with its leading figures gaining near-mythic status, but also became the largest actor in Israel's public administration sector. This was primarily due to the fact that the army's responsibilities extended well beyond the traditional aspects of security operations and touched on every aspect of daily life for Israelis—from settlement and education, to the media, immigrant absorption, transportation, and urban construction.

This phenomenon reached its acme in the wake of Israel's dramatic victory in the 1967 Six Day War. This period has been called 'the era of the generals', a time during which the man in uniform became a full working partner with the country's political legislators in a complex political–security arrangement whose imprint was felt in all the public arenas of Israeli life.

THE POLITICAL ERA: SECURITY POLICY BEYOND THE CONSENSUS

The euphoria attending the 1967 war came to an abrupt end during the 1973 Yom Kippur War—the greatest threat to Israel's existence since the War of Independence. Casualties were high. More than 2500 soldiers were killed, 7500 injured, and 301 taken prisoner, as the Israel Defence Forces (IDF) were momentarily overwhelmed by simultaneous military strikes from Egypt and Syria. Initially military intelligence bore the brunt of criticism for 'the blunder'. Blind confidence had been vested in faulty strategic and cultural conceptions. Soon, however, public opinion chose new targets, as a barrage of criticism was directed towards long-admired politicians and generals. Social movements, led by combat soldiers, bereaved parents and social activists used the war to censure state leaders, especially the prime minister and the minister of defence, and to call for their resignation.

This new perception of responsibility for military losses was reinforced after the Lebanese intervention of the 1980s, in which over 650 soldiers were killed. Whereas in 1973 state leaders were taken to task only after the guns had fallen silent, public recriminations over the Lebanese intervention occurred while the fighting was still taking place.

Indeed, through the pressure of protest movements, an investigatory commission was established which led to the dismissal of the defence minister. At the end of the 1990s, mothers of soldiers serving in Lebanon, including those who had lost their sons, organized in a protest group called 'The Four Mothers'. Their silent vigils were intended to effect a change in security policy; indeed, by the spring of 2000, owing in no small part to the activities of this movement, the IDF withdrew to the international border established with Lebanon in 1949.

Two other broadly-based social movements were active during this period: Gush Emunim (Block of the Faithful) represented settlers and their supporters in the territories of Judaea and Samaria (the West Bank), while Peace Now represented a broad spectrum of the Israeli Left who sought withdrawal of Israeli forces to the pre-1967 borders. Both movements had been intensely active in their respective causes for decades, and it appears that their impact on the formation of security policy was significant. The pressures exerted by Gush Emunim on successive Israeli governments succeeded in gaining *de facto* partnership for expanded settlement in Judaea and Samaria; IDF protection for the new settlements through an augmented military presence, routine security measures and various preventive steps designed to thwart terrorist actions, and the construction of access roads. Through the pressures of Peace Now, an opposite process occurred. The public funding by successive governments of the settlers was exposed, and a public discussion over the justification for these allocations came to the fore of the national debate.

The unique feature of the Political Model is that more and more citizens are joining social movements in order to influence security policy, engaging in an on-going dispute *with the politicians*. Operational failures and military accidents became topics of legitimate public discourse in the civilian sphere, although the security arena maintained its sacrosanct character and public claims about military ineptness and negligence became a matter of *political accountability*.

THE ANTI-MILITARY ERA

The year 1992 marked a transition from the security establishment's position of immunity from criticism to confrontation with other entities that were gaining in political strength, articulating autonomous public agendas and developing distinctive professional values. This pattern contained profound implications for the ability of the security establishment to protect itself from criticism and external intervention in its policy formulations.

This change first came to prominence through developments in the legal and media spheres. The law had recently experienced a 'judicial revolution' in which civil rights were more forthrightly defended by an activist court. Among the implications was the ability of the judicial branch to 'check' parliamentary legislation, thus intervening in the decision-making of the Israeli leadership, including army officers. The new judicial orientation gave 'right of standing' to interest groups that now began to access the Supreme Court through petitions challenging public policy they opposed.

There also emerged a 'media revolution' in which the Israeli communication system shifted from a monopolistic enterprise (one official state-operated television channel and two state-run radio stations) into a multi-channel system which included public and private stations. The new era of multiple channels turned the Israeli media into a more confrontational entity that relied upon a variety of informational sources along with traditional governmental sources.

Economic privatization was another influential development and was part of the growing business culture that slowly penetrated the public administration apparatus. The Israeli citizen became more of a client than a paternal subject of public services, aware of his rights and more demanding with regard to efficiency, transparency and accountability in service delivery.

In the political arena, both the municipal and the Knesset electoral systems were revamped to accommodate direct election of the prime minister. Even when the Israeli electoral system reverted to its earlier format, personality rather than ideological issues remained dominant. A further indication of the increasing focus on personality politics was the introduction by political parties of a system of primaries to choose their electoral candidates. Even Israel's orientations and accomplishments in foreign affairs affected citizen/military relations—for example, the peace accord reached with the Palestinians at Oslo in 1993 apparently reduced security tensions and permitted, for a limited time at least, social, economic and other domestic issues to occupy a significant place on the legislative agenda.

Israeli civil society began to increasingly confront the security establishment in an unprecedented fashion. A host of entrepreneurs, well trained in legal and media praxis, initiated civil confrontations with the military. Among their demands were curbs on military authorizations and restrictions in areas of decision-making.

There was a concomitant effort to have these particular military authorizations and powers determined by civilian bodies guided by the norms of civil society. Through the pressure of these social entrepreneurs, the army was forced to relinquish its privileged position in determining the patterns of commemoration and remembrance of the fallen; the sole right of the military to investigate itself for failed operations and training accidents; and the right to decide which officers were to be promoted to senior ranks.

These, and other developments, brought with them a degree of transparency from the military and established civilian oversight in areas where it had been lacking. As a result, facts embarrassing to the army became a matter of public knowledge: disasters and training accidents, inability to apply lessons from past experiences, corruption, sexual harassment, and a faulty organizational culture. This in turn led to a crisis in motivation among youth about to be inducted into the armed forces and a decline in the status of its officers. In response the security establishment was now required to undertake a whole slew of social, legal and media initiatives in order to protect its standing and its areas of public responsibility.

All of which necessitates the scholarly and detailed re-assessment of the relationship between the army and society in Israel provided by this work.

Political–Military Relations in Israel, 1996–2003

AMIR BAR-OR

Shortly before Israel's national elections in 2003, the chief of staff (hereafter, CGS), Lt. Gen. Shaul Mofaz, completed his military service and was appointed defence minister in Prime Minister Ariel Sharon's first government. Israel's 'Cooling-Off' Law calls for a period of one year after discharge from the army before a senior military officer can be elected to parliament. Although the law has no jurisdiction over ministerial roles, as illustrated by Mofaz's entry into the Defence Ministry, his appointment aroused widespread public criticism over the new defence minister's expected function as a 'super-CGS'. The Supreme Court also berated Mofaz for trying to get elected to parliament before the end of the legally required cooling-off period.

The attempt to reach public office by someone who 'only a few months earlier was in uniform and bore the rank of lieutenant general ... raises concern that decisions he made in the recent past within the framework of his military or security office, were influenced by his political views'.[1] This statement seems to be an additional indication of the lack of clearly defined rules in Israel regarding the division between the political and military spheres. 'For many years, no clear boundaries existed regarding relations between the military and civil authorities in Israel. In Israel's government system there was no title as commander-in-chief of the armed forces'.[2]

The turning-point in this state of affairs took place in 1976 with the passage of the *Basic Law: The Army* that was intended to define formally and explicitly Israel's political–military relations. Up to this time, the relationship had been characterized by manifest ambiguity over the allocation of authority among the prime minister, government (cabinet), defence minister, CGS, and Knesset. This *modus vivendi* lasted until the 1973 war. In its aftermath the benign vagueness of responsibility could no longer continue, especially in light of the investigating Agranat Commission that studied the war's mismanagement. The commission reached a unanimous decision regarding the nature of political–military relations: they had to be legalized and formally defined.

To fully grasp the complexity of the government's legal authority as supreme commander of the Israel Defence Forces (IDF) it must be kept in mind that political–military relations in Israel are based on the 'informal nature' of the political system and culture. This informal network developed from the lack of a precise distinction between the political and military, the absence of formal legislation regulating their relationship, and from the need to maintain workable political–military ties during Israel's first three decades.

The *Basic Law: The Army* was designed to correct the failings of the 1973 war. The law stated that the CGS is subject to governmental authority and is subordinate to the defence minister. This implies that the government, as a collective body, is the indisputable supreme commander with the right to rescind any orders issued by the defence minister – who is granted legal control of the army by government consent and whose job it is to execute government policy. Such convoluted legalistic language regarding the chain of command, and the allocation of unprecedented authority in the hands of the government and defence minister, left ample room for interpretation and did little to alter the basic rules of the political–military game. The specific situation as outlined in the *Basic Law: The Army* were supposed to clarify the chain of command vis-à-vis the government, defence minister and CGS, but the wording was sufficiently vague to leave the protagonists room for manoeuvre.

Furthermore, over the years, even partial attempts at establishing formal government supervision of the army, via professional advisory bodies, were hampered by various obstacles. Although the creation of a National Security Council in the Prime Minister's Office is mandated in the *Basic Law: The Government*, it never materialized in a way that guaranteed its success. The appointment of relatively low level, non-influential figures to this body during the Shamir (1986–1992) and Rabin (1992–1995) governments ended in failure mainly because the work style of these two decision-makers left little space for consultation.

The vacuum was filled by the army, whose proposals and political–military recommendations were generally accepted by the political echelon. The army acts according to orders from the military command – as is essential for the proper functioning of any military organization. The IDF and the CGS, in conjunction with the general staff and its various branches, execute their staff work schedule according to a smooth process. This places the CGS in an advantageous position vis-à-vis the government, the prime minister, and even the defence minister. All the attempts at setting up professional advisory boards for the prime minister and defence minister, and installing senior consultants for military affairs, have come to naught. The National Security Advisory Staff established during Ariel Sharon's term as defence minister (1982–1983) was an all-out effort to contend with the lack of an advisory board. Its failure was due to its ambitious attempt to replace the general staff.

Later efforts at creating an advisory board within the Prime Minister's Office were more limited in scope and heedful to curtail the army's main functions.

The *Basic Law: The Army* did not bring about the necessary transformation of political–military relations. The shortcomings pointed out above and the oversights that have been revealed since the law's passage rendered it almost irrelevant. The political–military relationship maintains its informal character. The ascendancy of the informal processes whose significance grew in the absence of a dominant political leadership came to expression in the army's increased strength, status, and influence over the political system despite repeated attempts at truncating it. The most significant attempt was made by Prime Minister Benjamin Netanyahu (1996–1999) who endeavoured to reshape Israeli civil–military relations. Ironically, the CGS whom he appointed, Lt. General Shaul Mofaz (1998–2002), strengthened both the army's status and his own position as the IDF's supreme commander. While Netanyahu attempted to introduce fundamental, destabilizing changes in the *modus vivendi* that had crystallized over the years, Lt. General Mofaz, who, as CGS, served three prime ministers (Netanyahu, Barak, and Sharon) and four defence ministers (Mordechai, Arens, Barak, and Ben-Eliezer), drew more fire during his term (that ended in early July 2002) than any previous chief of staff.

Following the 1996 elections, the new administration headed by Benjamin Netanyahu tried to reform Israeli civil–military relations. The first-ever direct election of an Israeli prime minister was an important factor in strengthening the new prime minister's position. Direct elections provided him with greater authority than in the past when he was only 'first among equals'. Responsibility for the army was supposed to be transferred directly to the prime minister instead of being held collectively by the government. This was intended to give the prime minister additional leverage in security matters. But Netanyahu overlooked the fact that the government's status had not formally changed and that it was still able to deliberate and decide matters of national security. The gap between the prime minister's expectations of his power and his actual performance as the *de facto* supreme commander of the IDF intensified the trend in the army toward alienation from political matters. This occurred against the backdrop of Netanyahu's criticism of a number of IDF generals for their involvement in politics during the Rabin administration.

Netanyahu believed that the army should be removed from all aspects of political decision-making. The moment he took office, he reversed the previous norm and sought to concentrate power in his own hands and sideline the CGS. Above all, he made a transparent attempt to distance high-ranking officers, who had supported the policies of the two previous governments (Rabin and Peres), from the decision-making process. This may have been the reason why Netanyahu adopted an entirely new approach towards civil–military relations and dismissed the army from the political arena. This was only the first move by the newly-installed Netanyahu government that would widen the gap between the political and military leaderships.

If the new government's aim was to narrow the senior military command's influence in the political arena, then very soon the army was removed even from discussions relating to its own role. The chief of staff and his deputy were kept out of meetings on cutbacks in the security budget, and the prime minister cancelled what used to be routine work-sessions with the CGS. Moreover, Netanyahu initiated a highly skewered presentation of the 'exaggerated' salaries of military personnel as part of a pre-planned campaign designed to finance basic changes in the IDF's priorities according to his outlook. The sense of alienation did not abate even when the new defence minister, Yitzhak Mordechai, took office shortly after completion of a long military career. On the contrary, it increased once he became a full-time partner in the government's policy of distancing itself from the army.

Even a 'positive' security initiative by Netanyahu, such as the reinstalling of the National Security Council, was seen as another attempt to sever the direct communication line between the Prime Minister's Office and the senior military command. Netanyahu's plan to establish a National Security Council in his office, as required by the *Basic Law: The Government*, could have created a new set of ground rules in civil–military relations. The council was to be headed by Maj. General (Res.) David Ivri, a former air force commander and one of the most respected figures in the national security establishment. Ivri had served in the high-profile role of director general of the defence ministry for over ten years and was now expected to usher in a major overhaul in the prime minister's capacity to oversee military operations. In addition, the National Security Council was designed to coordinate several inter-ministerial projects, such as the Anti-Terror Unit. In addition, Ivri would be directly responsible for such major areas as strategic co-operation with the United States and the Arms Control Steering Committee.

The amassing of all these roles in the Prime Minister's Office should have reduced the IDF's influence and enabled the prime minister, acting on behalf of the government, to exercise unprecedented control over national security policies. But the reforms encountered stiff resistance from Defence Minister Mordechai who succeeded in downsizing the council into a consultative forum headed by Ivri within the framework of the Defence Ministry rather than the Prime Minister's Office. The defence minister had clearly won this round. Another point of friction between the prime minister and the senior military command developed when commanders were no longer invited to political colloquiums to present their professional opinion on military matters.

Two examples are worth mentioning: First, when the cabinet discussed the Hebron withdrawal plan in 1996, the military, and especially the head of the Central Command, were kept in the dark. Secondly, before the disastrous opening of the Western Wall tunnel in the Old City of Jerusalem in September 1996, the military received no information about the timing of the opening or specific orders once the decision was made. All it received was painfully short notice to muster the troops. The fact that military figures were no longer 'in the game' consigned them to the awkward position of having to provide military solutions for political contingencies that they were not consulted on in the first place.

In light of the worsening relationship between the prime minister and the army after the Western Wall tunnel fiasco, when blame was placed on the army, and the IDF became, in effect, a political punch-bag, distrust between the different sectors soared to its highest level since the 1967 war. Some political analysts claimed that the prospect of a putsch in Israel was on the rise because of the combined effects of the deep credibility gap and the direct election of the prime minister. This analysis, as expected, sparked a heated public debate that exposed the government's inept handling of relations with the army and other security services.

But public criticism had little impact on the prime minister's management of civil–military relations, which worsened as the 1999 election campaign approached. A minor incident mushroomed into a major clash between the prime minister and CGS, who was now seen as a growing threat to the prime minister's political future. When Netanyahu, as the state's supreme authority on security matters, cut short the CGS's delivery of a routine report during a government session, criticism was levelled at the prime minister for interfering in the proper funtioning of the government. To recall, after the 1973 war the Agranat Commission had warned that proper decision-making by the government on security matters depended on the free flow of information. By obstructing the government from receiving up-to-date information from the army's best-informed soldier, the prime minister, who has no status in the *Basic Law: The Army*, had been in the wrong.

Not surprisingly, a backlash against Netanyahu erupted, emanating from anonymous voices within the military establishment and surfacing in the media. In vitriolic language the prime minister was criticized for mishandling his relations with the IDF high command and for upbraiding the top brass on public occasions such as the graduation ceremony at the National Security College in the summer of 1996.

The cumulative effect of the continuous marginalization of the army led to a further exacerbation and polarization of relations between the prime minister and the CGS. The prime minister targeted the brunt of his criticism at the chief of staff, Lt. General Shahak who, more than any other figure in the IDF, was identified with the previous government's support for the Oslo peace process. Netanyahu's brazen disregard of Shahak's military expertise was in line with his constant whittling down of the CGS's stature and authority and attempt to discredit the general.

Netanyahu brushed aside the CGS and replaced him with a general who was considered a more professional and less political officer – Shaul Mofaz. Defence minister Yitzhak Mordechai, was also replaced toward the end of the administration. At this point Netanyahu established the National Security Council within the framework of the Prime Minister's Office. If the council can be considered an improvement in civil–military relations, although it failed to play a significant role in national security decisions, then Netanyahu's behaviour toward the IDF general staff and his co-option of the role of supreme commander without the required legal backing should be seen as a negative, dangerous development in the fragile, complex relationship between the political and military sectors in Israel.

Over the years, senior IDF military commanders acquired almost mythic admiration and professional respect from the political leadership. The government and defence minister granted them near total freedom of action, even if it meant the gradual reduction of the civilian authority's involvement in military affairs. It is natural, then, that in the course of time the CGS has become a very influential figure indeed in the political arena.

Mofaz replaced Lt. General Shahak after a stormy episode of prime minister–CGS relations and after beating out a rival who had better prospects of getting the job. Expectations for Mofaz were modest. He assumed the role during a relatively quiet period and planned on being the 'Peace CGS' by devoting most of his time and energy to building up the army in a plan entitled – 'IDF 2000'.

Netanyahu appointed Mofaz chief of staff in 1998. The following year a new government came to power headed by Ehud Barak, who also appointed himself as the new defence minister. The Barak government, too, was short-lived, and after a trouncing at the polls it handed over the reins of power to Ariel Sharon. Prime Minister Sharon headed a national unity government at a time of worsening conditions in the Israeli–Palestinian conflict. After Sharon's ascension, Lt. General Mofaz precipitated incidents that created a crisis in civil–military relations. Simmering tension between Mofaz and the political leadership reached a boiling point in the conflict with the Palestinian Authority (PA).

If the main reason for appointing Mofaz to CGS had been to prepare the IDF for the twenty-first century, then it soon became apparent that he was on the high road to becoming the most political CGS in Israel's history. In retrospect, very few CGS's managed to stay aloof from political identification during their tenures. The role of CGS as 'the highest command role in the army' is explicitly defined in the *Basic Law: The Army*. The CGS is the commander of the army and not the commander-in-chief of the army; in other words, he is subordinate to the government. But, since the CGS also serves as the government's senior military advisor (not enshrined in the law), this function emerged as one of the main sources of conflict between Mofaz and his last two civilian bosses, especially during the renewed confrontation with the Palestinians.

Mofaz's command went smoothly under the Netanyahu government, excluding one incident when the CGS expressed reservations over the government's restraint after a Hizbollah-launched Katyusha rocket attack in the north. However, once Barak was elected prime minister and took on the additional role of defence minister, Mofaz found himself increasingly in dispute with the government. At first the two men reached a tacit understanding: the CGS would handle military affairs without interference by civilians, and the prime minister would manage the state without military opposition. But, in reality, the army received orders from the political level on state matters that ran counter to the IDF's professional opinion.

Within the army Mofaz's position was strong and secure. Minimal involvement from the prime minister at the outset of Barak's administration granted the CGS ample room for manoeuvre without having to provide superfluous explanations. But later he was estranged from state affairs and presented with *faits accomplis*, such as the May 2000 pullout from Lebanon, major defence cutbacks, and the prime minister's relentless disparagement of the senior staff command; an open breach, characterized by mutual animosity, erupted between Mofaz and Barak.

At the same time, and against the advice of fellow senior officers, Mofaz rushed headlong into a clash with the Supreme Court, perhaps in the belief that he could influence the bench. For the first time in the history of the state, one of the CGS's appointments was turned down by a Supreme Court ruling. The court had intervened in the promotion of a brigadier-general convicted of sexual harassment, but the CGS stubbornly insisted on going through with the promotion for professional reasons. The Supreme Court's willingness to accept the victim's plea (a female soldier) to block the brigadier's advance exposed the army to excoriating social criticism over its insensitivity to normative changes in sexual conduct. In another case, the Supreme Court stopped short of intervening in the CGS's decision to promote an officer charged with questionable judgement during a military operation.

After the 2001 elections, Ariel Sharon assumed power and placed a full-time defence minister in the seat next to him. This presented a new series of difficulties before the CGS, who for a year and a half had enjoyed almost absolute freedom as commander of the army. This happened just as the IDF was beginning to respond aggressively to the Palestinians' terror campaign (the al-Aqsa Intifada). The army may have known how to suppress the complex challenge of terrorism, but the newly-instated Sharon administration dithered endlessly before deciding on a *modus operandi*. A list of misunderstandings about the new game rules at the political level, and between the politicians and the experienced chief of staff, characterized the early stages of containing Palestinian terror.

The government accepted almost all of the CGS's recommendations for terminating the confrontation by toppling the PA and expelling Arafat.[3] If the political echelon harboured reservations, then most, if not all of them, were agreed over the way the CGS handled the Sharon government's curtailing of his authority. Moreover, the government's decision to extend Mofaz's term by another year (to four years), and its approval, without the defence minister's say, of the CGS's nominations for the general staff, worked to enhance Mofaz's strength in his last year of command and afforded him greater freedom to speak his mind and perform his duties. Mofaz now realized that he had the power to advance or frustrate affairs of state. For example, when he expressed his professional reservations over President Clinton's 'bridging plan' during negotiations with the Palestinians, his statements caused a loss of public support in Israel for the American proposal. When Sharon assumed the office of prime minister, Mofaz's declaration that the PA was 'a den of terror' appears to have exceeded a purely professional estimate and penetrated the realm of political opinion. The CGS's statement may have been seen as a warning signal to the new government.[4]

Above all, further events in the last year of Mofaz's service proved that he overstepped the boundaries of 'professional estimate' when he announced that parts of the seam area (the 1967 border) would become closed-off military areas – an act that had far-reaching political consequences. The prime minister, who was abroad at the time, immediately responded that the Israeli government alone was the supreme commander of the army. The prime minister and his close associates were heard to say: 'Mofaz thinks he's running the state', or, 'in Israel it's not the army that has a state, but the government that has a military establishment subordinate to it'.[5] Nevertheless, this altercation was quickly pushed aside after the events of 11 September 2001. The stage was set for a battle of wills between the CGS and the defence minister.

The next tangle with the civilian authority was the CGS's public criticism on 13 October 2001, in an official military announcement, of the government decision to pull out of PA territory in Hebron. According to the IDF statement, a pullback at this time was liable 'to create a security danger that would make it difficult to safeguard civilians and IDF personnel. This will continue as long as the PA takes no steps to counter terrorism'.[6] In this case, the

> Chief of Staff Lt. Gen. Shaul Mofaz overstepped his jurisdiction and clearly strayed from what may be considered acceptable conduct. It is one thing for the chief of staff to express his [professional] opposition at a cabinet meeting to a proposal by the prime minister or defence minister. Such a statement would have probably leaked to the press but this would have been no fault of his. But it is an entirely different story when he issues a public statement through the IDF spokesperson criticizing

a decision of his civilian superiors. This borders on insubordination, and is unacceptable.⁷

Mofaz's reaction did nothing to calm the crisis; in fact, it only exacerbated the already tense relationship between the defence minister and the CGS. 'I admit that the wording of the second part of my statement was not well drafted, but it was not my intention to announce that I opposed the decisions of the political echelon', Mofaz admitted. He said that his role 'was only to make recommendations and render professional assessments. I come to no one with complaints in this matter and accept full responsibility'.⁸ The defence minister was very close to firing the CGS but settled for dishing out a stern reprimand.

Even this relatively mild response failed to keep the lid on Mofaz, who again let fly with his opinion of the government's policies. The crisis came to a head in April 2002 during Operation Defensive Shield when the government decided to isolate Arafat. The CGS declared that in the army's view Arafat should be expelled from the PA. The public regarded this 'as casting doubt on the wisdom of a government decision, [and had] the effect of undermining its authority'.⁹ Moreover, according to the army's assessment, that was also given public expression, four to eight weeks would be needed to complete the operation. This was another broadside to governmental authority. Mofaz continued to avow that his own handling of the affair was correct and that he was required to express his professional opinion, which, unlike military actions, was not subordinate to a higher authority. But, in effect, it indicated that the CGS had forgotten the difference between a public servant appointed by the government and a person elected by the public to fulfil a political role. In contrast to elected officials, the CGS's authority is not derived from the public will but is subordinate to the body that appointed him, and he is required to adhere to the accepted rules of the democratic system.¹⁰ Mofaz was the first CGS, according to Levi, to promote a new perspective of the CGS's role. Mofaz saw himself as a public servant, not only as a government appointee; therefore he had no compunctions over going public and expressing his differences with the government.

The CGS appeared to have difficulty in fathoming the rules of the democratic game. In his relations with the government he consistently upset it, criticizing and trying to change its decisions by methods more in line with those employed by elected politicians than by appointed office holders. At the same time, according to the definition of his role, he was supposed to be the guardian of democratic values in Israeli society. Paradoxically, in the name of democratic values he became the adversary of a group of reservists that refused to serve in the occupied territories. Mofaz asserted that such a phenomenon was unacceptable in Israel since unwillingness to serve and obey orders could weaken the pillars of democracy. This was the same CGS who threatened to resign, not over his disagreement with government decisions, but over the possibility of having to call soldiers to appear on the witness stand before a UN investigating commission in the wake of the IDF's operation in the Jenin refugee camp during Operation Defensive Shield in April 2002. Mofaz's readiness to resign over this matter 'justified all those who shun discipline and leave their role without doing what is called for, when a legal order is not to their liking'.[11]

Lt. General Mofaz saw his role as that of commander in chief of the army. This perspective stemmed from his limited familiarity with the *Basic Law: The Army*, and from his misunderstanding of the political aspects of the CGS's role in Israel's democratic political system. His public statements, along with an official letter he sent to the Supreme Court were signs of a major rupture in the historical, informal 'game rules' that had characterized political–military relations. This may have stemmed from Mofaz's' lack of experience and inability to discern who the supreme commander of the army was: the IDF senior staff or the government of Israel.

CONCLUSION

The two cases dealt with in this work are recent examples illustrating the complexity of civil–military relations in Israel in the absence of formalized rules of conduct. They also reflect the attempts of the two echelons to force the other's hand even though it is absolutely clear that the army is required to obey the political leadership. The power struggle is the result of two parallel phenomena: the army's growing influence over government decision-making in security matters, and the government's attempt to narrow the senior command's influence on its decisions.

The main causes of this can be traced back to the long and arduous process that brought the army to a dominant position on national security issues. Paradoxically, the military's enormous leverage appeared as a threat to the very political system that abandoned the front lines to the army's responsibility. This was the state of affairs up until the summer of 1996 when a new government came into power.

Two studies were published in the mid-1990s by members of the inner political and military circles. Yehuda Ben-Meir, a former deputy foreign minister, claimed that although Israel's elected government still retains incontestable control over the IDF, research shows that behind the scenes the army is fully in charge of its own affairs.[12] Maj. General. (res.) Israel Tal also discovered that despite nominal civil control of the military, the IDF has in fact been transformed into an independent, self-directing institution whose autonomy and influence exceeds the state's original designs.[13]

This situation challenges the principle canonized by Israel's first prime minister and defence minister, Ben-Gurion, in a document sent to Lt. General Yigal Yadin upon his appointment as the IDF's second chief of staff in 1949. Ben-Gurion stated that,

The army determines neither the policies, administration, nor the laws in the state. The army does not even determine its own structure, missions, modes of operation, or peace treaties. The army is nothing more than the executive arm for the defense and security of the State of Israel. Organizing the army ... [is] the sole responsibility of the civilian authorities who form the government, the Knesset, and the voters... The army is unconditionally subordinate to the government.[14]

Ben-Gurion wielded his authoritative powers vis-à-vis the senior military staff, and completely changed the game rules in a way that left no doubt where the centre of decision-making stood. This move reflected his basic concept that the overall management of military matters in a democracy, such as Israel, should be in the hands of the democratically elected political authority. When Ben-Gurion served as both prime minister and defence minister relations between the political and military spheres were maintained on the basis of his leadership, personality and vision, rather than according to formal legalized guidelines.

This relationship can be defined as civil supremacy. Civil supremacy was justified because it served as a basic value in the construction of the political–military relationship on the eve of statehood and in the early years of national independence. In Ben-Gurion's view, civil supremacy implied more than the political leadership's participation in determining military policy in times of war and peace or in contributing to political thinking and orientation.[15] Civil supremacy, according to Ben-Gurion, meant the total involvement of the political sphere in all aspects of military and wartime activity, even in real time situations, in order to serve the political view loyally and consistently. In his view, the ability to dictate decisions that sometimes ran counter to the professional judgement of military commanders was the necessary condition for the wisest and most effective way of managing the military system. In retrospect, Ben-Gurion's term in office was the only time in Israel's history when the political leadership had civil supremacy over the IDF.

NOTES

1. A. Oren, 'The Attorney General's Passivity', *Ha'aretz*, 20 May 2003.
2. M. Hofnung, *Democracy, Law and National Security in Israel*, Aldershot, 1996, p. 188.
3. A. Benn, 'The Army Dictates, the Political Level Consents', *Ha'aretz*, 8 August 2002.
4. Y. Limor, 'Beginning his Extended Tenure', *Ma'ariv*, 2 April 2001.
5. A. Benn, 'The Army Dictates, the Political Level Consents', *Ha'aretz*, 8 August 2002.
6. Military Spokesperson Announcement, 14 October 2001.
7. Y. Ben-Meir, 'A Crisis in Civil–Military Relations', *Jerusalem Post*, 15 October 2001.
8. A. O'Sullivan, 'Mofaz Apologizes Publicly for Criticism', *Jerusalem Post*, 16 October 2001.
9. H. Zadok, 'The Censured CGS Returns to His Bad Habits', *Yediot Achronot*, 7 April 2002.
10. A Oren, 'Skylight or Pinhole', *Ha'aretz*, 8 February 2002.

11. A. Oren, 'Gaza Dilemmas', *Ha'aretz*, 15 May 2002.
12. Y. Ben-Meir, *Civil–Military Relations in Israel*, New York, 1995.
13. I. Tal, *The Few Against the Many*, Tel Aviv, 1996.
14. D. Ben-Gurion, *Yichud Vi'Yiud*, Tel Aviv, 1971, p. 82.
15. Y. Harkaby, *War and Strategy*, Tel Aviv, 1990, p. 526.

The Growing Militarization of the Israeli Political System

GIORA GOLDBERG

Israel is a garrison state. It is also a western democracy. How is such a combination possible? Does it make Israel a military democracy?[1] The fact that Israel preserves its democratic character at a time when the required security level is increasing is rather surprising. Apparently we are talking about especially strong democratic roots, which curb the strong military influence on Israeli society. Another explanation that can be adopted in connection with this paradox is that Israeli democracy does not have real liberal roots and its political behaviour does not tend towards democracy, but only the formal structural foundations are characterized by a democratic tendency. Meaning, it is easy to preserve a formal-structured democracy in the presence of increasing militarism.

One of the ways to review the conflict between the democratic elements and Israel becoming a garrison state is by investigating the penetration of militarism into politics. This problem can be dealt with in several ways. One of them is to examine the policies taken and evaluate the weight of the military forces in the decision-making process. Another way is to examine the positions taken by the upper echelon of the army, retired generals, in the political system. The assumption is that generals who served in the army for decades will not change their way of thinking and acting immediately upon entering politics. The military mind will continue to characterize them and will have a critical influence on political outputs.

Uri Ben-Eliezer is one of the proponents of the belief in the military role expansion process that has taken place in Israel and that this process was not connected 'with modernization and nation-building, not even with military coups and the army's direct political intervention, but with militarism and war'.[2] He views the penetration of retired officers into politics as 'another non-formal mechanism of role expansion in Israel'. When Ben-Eliezer examined the orientation of the retired officers who went into politics he found that 'they view politics as the continuation of their military service by other means, and not vice versa'.[3]

He is not inclined to accept the traditional viewpoint, that the recruitment of retired officers into politics is a safety valve against their becoming a junta that would threaten the democratic government. Ben-Eliezer did not measure the phenomenon of officers who are parachuted into politics over a long period of time. He claims that the phenomenon

> was a route which confirmed and even strengthened the idea of the link between the army, society and politics and the cultural insight regarding the existence of a common denominator according to which it is legitimate for the army to have political influence on matters of war and peace; all of this, of course, in a way that will not endanger the political leadership and Israel's formal democratic order.[4]

He sums up his claims of the army's role expansion as follows:

> While Israel is actually changing and becoming a society with signs of neo-liberalism, and there are those who will say that there is also a clear civilian tendency emerging, it is doubtful whether these changes are sufficient to change cultural patterns which place the army and possible military solutions at the centre of all policies, and to create a counter-balance to the army's power and political involvement, or in fact, to its expansion into politics. In the absence of weighty anti-militarist forces the institutional arrangements, which link the army and politics and Israeli society, must be viewed not as a softening mechanism, which permits Israeli democracy to function and prevents military coups, but as a form of infrastructure which could, in the future, form an obstacle to a political compromise, without any connection to its intentions and the extent of the other side's intentions to establish real peace with Israel.[5]

Moshe Lissak, one of the most prominent researchers of civil–military relations in Israel, refers to the 'militarization of the civilian sector' and distinguishes between its influence on national security and other spheres. He does not accept the claim of Ben-Eliezer and Kimmerling[6] concerning the military character of Israeli society.[7] Lissak's important insight concerns the character of the militarization process 'even if a certain degree of "militarization" does exist in the political area, this does not necessarily imply significant and consistent penetration into other areas'.[8]

Stuart Cohen raised a different argument against Ben-Eliezer's main claim concerning military role expansion, according to which the army's standing in Israeli society has been decreasing in recent years: 'Approximately fifty years after its establishment, the IDF finds itself in a position that it is unaccustomed to, and which it has to fight against on several fronts, the mounting erosion of its public image'.[9]

Cohen divides the reasons for this into local and general factors. The conventional wisdom views it as a product of war weariness. Cohen adds two additional local factors: the meagre achievements of the army from an operational aspect and the extensive social–cultural change, mainly in the ideological sphere, which finds expression in undermining the myth of national symbols. The general factors are reflected in 'the negation of the traditional position of military service as the highest acknowledgement of citizenship', in 'the revolution that took place in the well known meaning of the identity of professional military personnel, who are described today (and who describe themselves) more and more as professional people employed by the army' and in 'the public's right to re-examine the military norms and to pass judgment on military values'.[10]

Cohen claims that

> These expressions of military role expansion in Israel reached their peak at the end of the seventies but since then an opposite trend is taking place ... a general trend is recognized of a reduction in the IDF's role at the institutional level ... the reduction process—despite being in its infancy, in many instances—is expanding, and its signs can be seen in various fields of public life in Israel.[11]

Underpinning this process, which Cohen illustrates by settlement, immigration and education, are three processes: the weakening of the state apparatus, changes in security thinking and the professionalization of the army.

Ben-Eliezer and Cohen are not arguing between themselves, but it is possible to refer to their claims as representing two approaches. Ben-Eliezer establishes military role expansion, while Cohen stands for military role extraction. Ben-Eliezer examines the policies adopted and concludes that the military perception permeates Israeli politics and is taking it over. Cohen emphasizes the increasing public criticism of the army as proof of his main argument.

The main argument of this research is that a process of the penetration of retired officers into Israeli politics is taking place. The most prominent researcher dealing with the militarization of Israeli politics is Yoram Peri. In his book *Between Battles and Ballots*, he analyzed and measured the phenomenon of the penetration of retired officers into politics.[12] Peri supplies a number of explanations. The structural explanation refers mainly to the aspect of the supply of retired officers. The functionalist explanation deals more with the aspect of the demand for retired officers. Peri calls the third explanation 'exchange of power and prestige' between the veteran leadership and the officers, with its main point being the interest of both parties.

The research period under study here dates from the establishment of Israel in 1948 until the end of 2002. The fifty-four years will be divided into five different periods according to decades. The first period begins with the establishment of the state in the middle of 1948 until the 1950s. Thereafter come three periods of a decade each: the 1960s, 1970s and 1980s. The fifth, and last, period includes the 1990s and the first three years of the twenty-first century.

The phenomenon of the militarization of politics is composed of a few elements. The first refers to the retired officers serving as ministers. A measurement was made of the rate of retired officers in each government that existed in Israel, taking into account the size of the various governments. Consideration according to the period of time of each government gave a result that fluctuated between 0 and 100 for each period.

While the first element does not take into account the ministries dominated by retired officers the next two elements do. The second element refers to the position of prime minister. Calculation of the percentage of time in which a retired officer served as prime minister supplied the result—which also fluctuated between 0 and 100 for each period. The third element refers to the position of minister of defence and a similar calculation was made to that of the previous element.

The fourth element refers to the period of time that retired officers headed political parties in Israel. A measurement was made in relation to the rate of retired officers amongst party leaders. The calculation was made by taking into account the size of each party. The calculation led to a result which fluctuates between 0 and 100 for each period.

The fifth element moved away from national politics and refers to local politics, when retired officers serve as the mayors of the three large cities—Jerusalem, Tel Aviv and Haifa. Each city was given an equal weight and the calculation was made according to the period of time in which retired officers headed these cities. The importance of local government stems from its having a clear civil character. Namely, the intention is to examine the expansion of retired officers not only in obvious security positions such as the minister of defence and the prime minister, but also in less obvious civil positions. Tel-Aviv, with its cosmopolitan characteristics, symbolizes more than others the element of a non-military civic culture.

The retired officers are those who were appointed as ministers after they reached one of the three highest ranks in their military service: brigadier general (a rank existing only since 1968), major general and lieutenant general. Twenty-three officers fit these two conditions. Nine of them were lieutenant generals, nine major generals and five were brigadier generals. Most of the chiefs of staff—nine out of sixteen—belong to this group. Almost half—eleven out of twenty-three—came to their ministerial posts via left-wing parties, eight via right-wing parties and four via centre parties. These four generals from the centre are closer to the left than the right. There is also a clear tendency in this group towards the left. Almost a third of the members of the group—seven—changed their party affiliation over the years. In terms of Israeli politics we are talking about a rather high replacement rate. Five of them entered the government prior to their serving as Knesset members. These may be characterized more than the others as 'paratroopers'.

Three-quarters of the retired officers who were elected to the Knesset became ministers. This is a very high rate. The rate amongst women who reach the government is only 15 percent. This gap between retired officers and women attests to the enormous differences in the power of the two groups. The share of Ashkenazim in the group of retired officers who entered the government is very high. Only four of them—17.4 percent—are from an Oriental background. Almost three-quarters of the retired officers who became ministers were born in Israel.

Five of the twenty-three retired officers who served as ministers took up their ministerial posts immediately after their military service without being Knesset members when they joined the government. Three of them were chiefs of staff (Haim Barlev, Ehud Barak and Shaul Mofaz). The other two were Ezer Weizman and Effi Eitam. Another nine were appointed as ministers immediately upon their being elected to the Knesset, or a few months later. The other nine served in the Knesset for a few years until they entered the cabinet. Efraim Sneh was the quickest in this group (two years), while Binyamin Ben-Eliezer was the slowest (eight years). More than 60 percent did not go down the conventional political route and, in effect, leapt into the political arena without political or party preparation.

RETIRED OFFICERS AS MINISTERS

The first retired officer to become a minister was Moshe Carmel from Ahdut Ha'avoda. In November 1955 Carmel was appointed minister of transportation. After the 1959 elections Carmel was no longer minister but Moshe Dayan from Mapai was appointed minister of agriculture. The range of membership of retired officers in government was very small and stood at 2.4 percent in the first period. Dayan continued to be the only retired officer in the government until 1961 when Yigal Alon from Ahdut Ha'avoda was appointed minister of labour. Upon Dayan's resignation in 1964 Alon remained as the only minister who came from the senior officer echelon, but in the middle of 1965 he was joined by his party colleague Carmel as minister of transport. In June 1967, on the eve of the Six Day War, Dayan replaced Eshkol as minister of defence. The number of retired officers in the government increased to three. Carmel did not return to the government after the 1969 elections. He was replaced in the position of minister of transportation by another retired officer—Ezer Weizman, who left the army in order to immediately join the government. The range of membership of retired officers in the government increased in the 1960s from 2.4 percent to 10.8 percent.

In the summer of 1970 Gahal resigned from the government. As a result Weizman ceased to serve as a minister and the number of retired officers dropped to two. In 1972 Haim Barlev was appointed minister of trade and industry, a short time after he completed his term as chief of staff. With his appointment the number of retired officers in the government was again three. After the Yom Kippur War there was an increase in the number of retired officers. There were five retired officers in the government formed after the 1973 elections. Yitzhak Rabin (minister of labour) and Aharon Yariv (minister of transport), both from the Labour Party, joined Dayan, Alon and Barlev. All five officers came from the ranks of the Labour Party. In Rabin's government, which was formed in June 1974, there were four officers, after Dayan left the government following his failure as minister of defence on the eve of the Yom Kippur War. Alon served in Rabin's government as foreign minister. In February 1975 Yariv resigned from the government and the number of retired officers in the government dropped to three.

After the 1977 elections the number of retired officers in the government again stood at three. Weizman was minister of defence; Dayan was foreign minister; and Ariel Sharon minister of agriculture. In October 1977 two ministers joined the government from the centre party Dash—Democratic Movement for Change. Yigal Yadin as deputy prime minister and Meir Amit served as minister of transport and communications. Once more the number of retired officers in the government was five, but three resigned quickly one after the other: Amit in 1978, Dayan in 1979 and Weizman in 1980. The range of retired officers in the government increased from 10.8 percent in the 1960s to 15.9 percent in the 1970s.

Following the 1981 elections Sharon was promoted to minister of defence, a position he held until February 1983. Mordecai Zipori from the Likud became minister of communications. Yadin retired from politics. The number of retired officers remained at two. After the 1984 elections a National Unity Government was formed which contained five retired officers. On the right there was only one minister (Sharon as minister of trade and industry). On the left, on the other hand, there were four retired officers, three of them from the Labour Party: Rabin as minister of defence, Barlev as minister of police, Mordecai Gur as minister of health (until October 1986 and minister without portfolio from April 1988), and Weizman who represented the new party, Yahad, as minister without portfolio. After the 1988 elections Weizman served as science minister. The range of membership of retired officers in the government stood at 15.3 percent in the 1980s—a very slight drop in comparison to the 1970s.

After the dissolution of the National Unity Government and the departure of the Labour Party in 1990, Rafael Eitan joined the government as minister of agriculture and later on Rehavam Ze'evi also joined as minister without portfolio. Together with Sharon, who was now minister of housing, the number of retired officers stood at three. Eitan resigned at the end of 1991 and Ze'evi at the beginning of 1992. In the left-wing government headed by Rabin, formed after the 1992 elections, there were two retired officers at the beginning—Rabin himself, who headed the government and also served as defence minister, and Ben-Eliezer who was housing minister. At the beginning of 1994 Sneh joined as minister of health and in July 1995 Barak joined as minister of the interior. Rabin's assassination in November 1995 reduced the number of retired officers to three. Barak was then made foreign minister.

There were four retired officers in the government Benjamin Netanyahu formed in June 1996: Sharon was minister of infrastructure and from October 1998 also foreign minister; Avigdor Kahalani, the leader of 'The Third Way' was minister of interior security; Eitan was minister of agriculture and the environment; and Yitzhak Mordecai was minister of defence until his dismissal in January 1999. With the formation of a left-wing government headed by Barak in July 1999 the number of retired officers in the government increased to five: Barak was prime minister and minister of defence; Mordecai, the leader of the Centre Party, was minister of transport (until his resignation in May 2000); Amnon Lipkin-Shahak, also from the Centre Party, served at the beginning as tourism minister and after Mordecai's resignation also as minister of transport; Ben-Eliezer was minister of communications and from October 2000 also housing minister; and Matan Vilnai—a new minister from the Labour Party—was minister of science, culture and sport.

In Sharon's government, formed after the 2001 elections, there were five retired officers: Sharon; Ze'evi (who was murdered in October 2001) was tourism minister; Ben-Eliezer was minister of defence; Sneh was minister of transportation; Vilnai was minister of science, culture and sport. In April 2002 Eitam, the new head of the Mafdal—the National Religious Party— joined the government and became minister of infrastructure in September 2002. In October 2002 the National Unity Government broke up and the Labour ministers resigned from the government. Instead of Ben-Eliezer, Sneh and Vilnai, Shaul Mofaz joined the government as minister of defence. The number of retired officers dropped to three. The rate of membership of retired officers in the government between the years 1990 and 2002 stood at 15.4 percent. This is a slight increase in comparison to the 1980s, but, in fact, since the 1970s there has not been a significant change.

RETIRED OFFICERS AS PRIME MINISTERS

Until June 1974 no retired officer had served as prime minister. Israel's fifth prime minister, Yitzhak Rabin, was the first retired officer to reach the position. He served in his post for three years between 1974 and 1977. In 1992 he again returned to the post and served until his assassination in November 1995. The second retired officer to become prime minister was Barak. He served in the position until he lost the elections in 2001 to Ariel Sharon—the third retired officer to serve as prime minister. Since 1999 retired officers have served in the most important political position. In 2001 and 2003 both candidates for prime minister were retired officers.

There is no doubt that there is a clear increase in this period in the level of penetration of retired officers into the top government positions. In addition to the three retired officers who were prime ministers, another nine presented their candidacy for the position (such as Mordecai and Ben-Eliezer) or were considered as candidates for prime minister (such as Dayan and Weizman). A dozen from amongst the twenty-three retired officers tried to compete for the most senior political position.

RETIRED OFFICERS AS DEFENCE MINISTERS

Until June 1967 no retired officer had served in the position of defence minister. Moshe Dayan was the first of the military men to take this post. He served in the position for seven years (until 1974). Three years later Ezer Weizman was appointed defence minister and he was the second retired officer who served as defence minister. Weizman held this position for three years. The next in line was Ariel Sharon who served as defence minister from 1981 to 1983. The fourth retired officer to serve as defence minister was Rabin, who was defence minister for the entire six years of the National Unity Government between 1984 and 1990. From 1992 until his death in 1995 he held the two main posts—prime minister and defence minister. This combination was Ben-Gurion's creation and Eshkol carried it on from 1963 to 1967.

Yitzhak Mordecai was the next retired officer who served as defence minister (1996–1999). Barak was the sixth retired officer who held the position (between 1999 and 2001), serving as prime minister at the same time. After the 2001 elections Ben-Eliezer began to serve in the position of defence minister and was the seventh retired officer who reached this position. He was appointed after defeating two other retired officers—Vilnai and Sneh—in a vote that took place in the central committee of the Labour Party. After Ben-Eliezer's resignation in October 2002 Mofaz from the Likud was appointed defence minister. Three months earlier Mofaz was still serving as chief of staff. There were retired officers, such as Weizman, whose transition period was shorter than three months, but not to the position of defence minister, but a more junior post. Mofaz recorded the shortest time period between completing his service as chief of staff and being appointed as defence minister. For Mordecai, while never reaching the position of chief of staff, approximately a year passed until he was appointed defence minister. Dayan, the first chief of staff to become defence minister, gained the post after nine years. For Rabin sixteen years passed (though six years after he left the army he became prime minister) and for Barak four years. Mofaz—the first chief of staff to be recruited by the Likud—is the best example of a defence minister blurring the boundaries between the political and the army echelons.

The increase in the share of retired officers amongst defence ministers is more prominent than amongst prime ministers. While only three of the eleven prime ministers (a little more than a quarter) were retired officers, eight of the thirteen defence ministers (a little more than 60 percent) were retired officers. In fact, recently retired officers dominated this position which until 1967 had been unmistakably civilian.

In the decade since the 1992 elections it is hard to find prime ministers and defence ministers who are not retired officers. Over this entire decade, the two positions were not held by retired officers for interim periods only. The first, between November 1995 and the 1996 elections, when Peres, who replaced Rabin, served as prime minister and defence minister. The second was after Mordecai was dismissed by Prime Minister Netanyahu at the beginning of 1999 from the position of defence minister and replaced by Moshe Arens until the 1999 elections.

During the rest of the time retired officers served as defence ministers and except for Netanyahu's three years as prime minister (1996–1999), as the prime minister as well. Since 1999 the trend has increased even more. Retired officers completely control the two senior posts—prime minister and defence minister. Barak, Sharon, Ben-Eliezer and Mofaz are the four retired officers who held these posts in these four years. The phenomenon took root so strongly that it does not matter what sort of government we are talking about. The retired officers' control of the two senior posts existed under a left-wing government (1999–2001), under a national unity government (2001–2002) and under a right-wing government (from November 2002).

Prime ministers Rabin and Barak served as defence ministers as well. Ben-Gurion and Eshkol did this in the 1950s and 1960s. This changed for a short period of two years when Ben-Gurion resigned in 1953 (when Moshe Sharett was prime minister and Pinhas Lavon, and afterwards Ben-Gurion, served as defence minister). On the eve of the Six Day War Dayan was appointed defence minister and Eshkol continued to serve as prime minister. For fifteen continuous years there was a separation between the holders of the two positions until Rabin took the position of defence minister in 1992. Peres continued with this for a few months until the 1996 elections. For the entire time Barak served as prime minister he also served as defence minister.

An interesting fact is that five of the seven prime ministers who came from the Labour Party served as defence ministers at the same time. Only Sharett and Golda Meir were not defence ministers. On the other hand, none of the four prime ministers who came from the Likud took the position of defence minister. Amram Mitzna, the leader of the Labour Party in 2002, was of the opinion that the prime minister should also serve as defence minister.[13] There is a basic difference between civilian leaders—Ben-

Gurion, Eshkol and Peres—who also served in the two positions at the same time and between retired generals such as Rabin and Barak who did this.

RETIRED OFFICERS AS PARTY HEADS

Until 1974 no Israeli party had been headed by a retired officer. The Labour Party was the first to appoint a retired officer as its leader. This was Rabin, who beat Shimon Peres in the vote in the party's central committee on his way to the top of the party. He led the party until his resignation on the eve of the 1977 elections. In these elections two new parties appeared that were led by retired officers.

Yigal Yadin founded the centre party Dash, which won fifteen Knesset seats (out of 120) but dissolved before the next elections in 1981. Ariel Sharon founded the Shlomzion Party, which received two seats and immediately after the elections was swallowed up into the large Herut party headed by Menachem Begin. The three retired officers who led parties in the 1970s did not last—Rabin gave up the leadership, Yadin resigned from politics and Sharon joined a larger party whose leadership he took over only in 1999. When taking into account the periods of time and the size of the parties, the range of the control of retired officers over the parties in this decade is close to 18 percent.

In the 1980s not one retired officer succeeded in leading a veteran party but four new parties were founded by retired officers. Prior to the 1981 elections Dayan founded a centre party called Telem that received two seats and came to an end with Dayan's death in the same year. Prior to the 1984 elections Weizman founded a centre party called Yahad that won three seats, and prior to the 1988 elections merged with the Labour Party. On the eve of the 1988 elections two right-wing parties were founded by retired officers. Rafael Eitan founded Zomet and Rehavam Ze'evi founded Moledet. Each of them received two mandates. The range of control of retired officers over parties decreased in the 1980s from 18 percent to 1.5 percent.

In the period between 1990 and 2002 there was an enormous increase in the control of retired officers over parties. While only one new party was founded that was led by a retired officer (Avigdor Kahalani who founded The Third Way which received four seats in 1996 but failed to gain any in the 1999 elections), the large parties were taken over by retired officers. In 1992 Rabin returned to lead the Labour Party and he did this until his death in 1995.

Peres inherited the job from Rabin. In the primaries held in 1997 Barak won as head of the party, with one of his three rivals being a retired officer (Sneh). Barak held the post until his defeat in the 2001 elections and after that another senior retired officer—Ben-Eliezer—at the end of 2001 won the primaries against Avraham Burg. From 1992 onwards only retired officers won the primaries for the head of the Labour Party.

In the 2002 primaries two retired officers participated—Ben Eliezer and Mitzna—and one politician who was not a retired officer (Ramon). The two retired generals won 93 percent of the votes. Mitzna won by a majority of 54 percent. In all four primaries held by the Labour Party retired generals defeated civilians: Rabin in 1992, Barak in 1997, Ben-Eliezer in 2001 and Mitzna in 2002. The power of the retired generals increased so much that in 2002 the real contest was between two retired generals. On the two previous occasions the main challenger was a civilian politician (Peres in 1992, Beilin in 1997 and Burg in 2001). In 2002 both the winner and the runner-up were retired generals.

In 1999 a retired officer, Ariel Sharon, won control of the Likud for the first time. In the National Religious Party Eitam became the first leader to come from the officer echelon. He did not compete in the primaries but was crowned by the party's leadership. Zomet was headed by Eitan until its dissolution following its failure in the 1999 elections. Ze'evi headed Moledet until his murder in 2001. Since 2002 three of the veteran historic parties—Labour, Likud and the National Religious Party—have been led by retired officers. The range of the control of the retired officers over the parties increased in the fourth period to 40 percent. The rise from the 1980s (when it was 1.5 percent) to the next period (40 percent) shows how strong the position of the retired officers are in party politics.

The strengthening of the retired generals' standing in their parties created a situation where, in the two most recent national elections prior to those of March 2006, only retired generals competed for power. In 2001 Barak and Sharon competed and in 2003 Mitzna and Sharon. Sharon's challenge in 2003 became possible after he beat Netanyahu in the primaries in November 2002. More than anything else, this victory underlined the strengthening of the retired generals. Netanyahu appointed Sharon as his deputy after he lost to Barak in the 1999 elections. Prior to the 2001 elections Netanyahu was deterred from competing for prime minister against Barak, despite the fact that at the time Netanyahu's chances of beating Sharon in the Likud primaries were enormous. In the two years that passed Sharon succeeded in changing the power relationship and the younger Netanyahu, who was considered a charismatic leader, was defeated by the elderly Sharon.

RETIRED OFFICERS AT THE HEAD OF LARGE CITIES

In 1973 a retired officer was elected as head of one of the large cities for the first time—Tel Aviv. This was Shlomo Lahat from the Likud who served in the position until his voluntary resignation on the eve of the 1993 elections. In those elections a politician who was not a retired officer, Ronnie Milo, beat the retired officer that the Labour Party placed opposite him— Kahalani. Five years later, in 1998, the job returned to another retired senior officer. Ron Huldai from the left beat the right-wing candidate Doron Rubin, also a retired officer. In Haifa Mitzna took over as mayor in 1993, and was re-elected in 1998. The range of control of retired officers over the three largest cities was zero in the first two periods, it grew to 20 percent in the 1970s, climbed to 33 percent in the 1980s and reached a peak of 44 percent in the most recent period. The city that contributed the most to this upward swing is Tel Aviv, widely regarded as the capital of anti-militarism in Israel.

THE INDEX OF MILITARIZATION OF POLITICS

In order to get a more general picture of the range of militarization of politics over time, an index of the militarization of politics has been designed. When calculating the index equal weight was given to each one of the elements of militarization of politics. The index ranged between 0 and 100. In the first period the index stands at only 0.5. In the 1960s it was 7.2. In the 1970s there was an enormous increase when the index reached 30.8. In the next decade, the 1980s, the upward trend was halted and the index dropped slightly to 26.0. Despite this, in the final period the index leapt to a peak of 45.7. This increase reflects in the clearest way the militarization process within Israeli politics.

The expanded role of the retired officers reached not only the arenas covered by the general index, but others as well. In recent years other government branches have been taken over by retired officers. Danny Yatom was the head of the Intelligence Service, Ami Ayalon was the head of the Interior Security Agency, Yakov Turner was the commissioner of police, Uzi Dayan was head of the National Security Council, David Ivri was Israel's ambassador to the United States and Amos Yaron was the director general of the Ministry of Defence. Even the presidency—a ceremonial office—has followed this pattern. Up until the election of Chaim Herzog in 1983 the presidency was held by civilian leaders. Herzog served in the position for ten years. Ezer Weizman replaced him in the post and served as president until his resignation in 2000. For seventeen consecutive years the position of president was filled by retired officers.

WHY DO RETIRED OFFICERS SUCCEED?

The Increase in Inter-party Competitiveness

The multitude of officers in politics is explained by the increase in inter-party competitiveness. Up until 1973 there was a multi-party system with a dominant party. Such a party system is characterized by low competitiveness. The transition to a multi-party system without a dominant party, which began in 1973, caused an enormous increase in competitiveness.

This was expressed in the first change in government in the history of Israel (1977) and in the creation of the two-bloc structure in 1981.

The main struggle between the two largest parties is for the centre voters who decide the fate of the elections. The two large parties try to hunt the votes of these voters. The right tries to push the Labour Party to the left and the left attempts to return to the centre by cultivating a centrist image. One way of creating this image is by promoting retired officers into senior political posts. The officers are not seen as being significantly leftist.

Their military experience helps them to create an authoritative, tough and uncompromising image. This is the main reason that the number of retired officers on the left is larger than on the right. After the left placed retired officers in political positions, the right responded by courting retired officers and integrating them into the government and the Knesset, even though its needs are different from those of the Labour Party.

A good example of the Labour Party's acute need for a leadership composed of retired officers is the four primary campaigns that were held in the last ten years. In 1992 Rabin beat three civilian candidates: Shimon Peres, Israel Kesar and Ora Namir. In 1997 Barak defeated Sneh and a couple of civilian candidates—Yossi Beilin and Shlomo Ben-Ami. In 2001 Ben-Eliezer defeated the civilian candidate—Avraham Burg. In 2003 two retired officers competed (Ben-Eliezer and Mitzna) and a civilian candidate—Haim Ramon. For the fourth time the Labour Party members preferred a retired officer, this time Mitzna, as the party leader and candidate for prime minister. The electoral victories of Rabin in 1992 and Barak in 1999 strengthened the trend of electing a retired officer in order to take control of the government. The main argument for this preference is the electoral appeal of the retired officers amongst the general public. While Rabin, Barak and Ben-Eliezer had a powerful image and were not considered as being clearly on the left, Mitzna, who is left wing, defeated the centrist Ben-Eliezer. The conclusion could be that the expansion of retired generals in the Labour Party has been institutionalized to such a degree that even the electoral need of electing a centrist candidate has been weakened.

A Lowering of the Ideological Mentality

Historically Israeli political leaders were not seen as managers or as policy-makers but as promoters of ideology and the initiators of historic changes. As the years passed, the ideological mentality weakened and began to be replaced by a pragmatic orientation, according to which leaders are perceived first and foremost as efficient managers. The parties did not succeed in adapting themselves sufficiently to this big change and they are still offering citizens, though in a lesser way, leaders who continue to promote distinct ideologies. The last two civilian candidates for prime minister—Peres and Netanyahu—are typical ideological leaders. While Netanyahu does have the signs of a modern politician based mainly on a marketing and communications outlook, he is basically motivated by ideological motives. Peres and Netanyahu reflect the ideological and historical rivalry between the left and the right.

The retired officers supply what the public wants by their being free of pure ideological perceptions. The first of them, such as Alon and Carmel, had clear ideological orientations. Those who came after them, however, developed a pragmatic orientation. The source of this orientation is that their employment as senior officers forced them to cope with the forces of reality, to abandon the past and to deal the whole time with solving problems. The military system does not expect serving officers to develop ideological positions. Accordingly, they reach politics equipped with the resources required by a large part of the public, mainly by the younger generations.

The manipulative use that the parties make of retired officers lowers the number of demands from party politicians. This pragmatic orientation causes most of the retired officers to hold centrist positions. Almost 40 percent—nine of the twenty-three—of the retired officers who served in the government were members at a certain times of parties that defined themselves as centrist: Yadin, Amit, Yariv (who went from Labour to the Democratic Movement for Change), Dayan, Weizman, Ben-Eliezer (first elected to the Knesset in 1984 on the Yahad list headed by Weizman), Kahalani, Mordecai and Lipkin-Shahak. This is a much higher than usual proportion of party leaders who came from centre parties. Half of the ministers who at a certain stage belonged to centre parties were retired officers, while the general proportion of officers amongst the ministers is much lower.

Dislike of Party Politics

Israel experiences to an extreme extent what western democracies undergo—a process of dislike of party politics amongst a large part of the public, mainly the young. This phenomenon is stronger in Israel because of the high level of penetration of politics into society. Traditional politicians are viewed by the public as being self-interested and corrupt. Anti-politics is the most suitable name for this feeling. Opinion polls taken since the end of the 1980s show that this aversion to politics is growing stronger every year.[14] The level of trust in parties dropped from 21 percent in 1995 to 11 percent in 2001, and the level of trust in the Knesset dropped from 41 percent to 14 percent over the same years.[15] Yuli Tamir, a philosophy professor who served as minister of absorption in Barak's government describes it thus: 'One of the prominent expressions for the erosion in the standing of Israeli politics is the demonstrative contempt for politicians. The Israeli politician is perceived as being a person without values, without knowledge, hypocritical, not speaking the truth and very often corrupt.'[16] The retired officers are perceived as the antithesis of party politicians. Their contribution to the state over decades is the opposite of the obsessive concern of the party leadership with satisfying narrow interests—party and personal. The officers are seen as honest and having the ability to act. The fact that they were managers of huge public systems helps them greatly in winning public support. While politicians are apt to indulge in rhetoric, the retired officers are not men of words, but of deeds. The dislike of party politics is encouraged by the media, which is apt to mock 'the old politicians'. An additional advantage of the retired officers is reflected in their youth in comparison to other politicians at their level.

Not only is a large part of the public disgusted by party politics. A similar process is developing amongst the various elites—from academia, the arts, media, the law and business—that in the past were recruited into the political system. Recently the tendency of their members to enter politics has fallen. As a result, a gap has been created which has been filled by the military elite, and the retired officers' ability to expand into politics is growing stronger. In an article written after Mofaz joined the government in November 2002, Dan Margalit claimed that 'It's not the expansion of officers into the political system which is worrying, but ... why aren't prominent people coming from the education, medical, and business systems'.[17]

The Increase in the Salience of Security

While Israel has not had a full-scale war since 1973, its security problems have not ended. Since then there have been only small wars, but the public's involvement in them has been greater than in the past. The two intifadas, which broke out in 1987 and 2000, were guerrilla wars mainly involving terror against civilians. The direct threat to the lives of civilians increased in comparison to the era of the major wars in which the IDF was involved, but not on the home front.

The Oslo Agreement had a very temporary influence in terms of reducing the security threat to civilians. In 1996 a wave of terror broke out which had considerable influence on the public. The Gulf War (1991) was a war that consisted mainly of a large threat to the public with the minimal involvement of the army. From the aspect of civilians the military threat has increased rather than being reduced, despite the fact that from the military point of view the tendency is the opposite. The sense of a lack of security among the public is growing and it calls for strong and authoritative leadership. Since the recruitment of the political leadership depends mainly on the public, the demand for retired officers in the political system is on the rise.

The Personalization of Politics

A decrease in the ideological mentality described above reinforces the personal basis in politics. The electoral confrontation is not just between parties, or between party blocs, but between people. In the past the weight of the personal factor was small, but it began to grow from the 1970s. The personalization process in Israeli politics is reflected in three prominent changes: the reform of local elections that mainly involves a transition from proportional representation to a method where the mayor is chosen directly by the public.

The second change was similar in character, but more moderate. In the 1990s direct elections for the prime minister were introduced whereby the public, rather than the Knesset, decided. The third change is connected to the power relations within the political parties. It began in the method of selecting candidates for the Knesset and the prime minister. The internal party democratization process became stronger in the 1990s until the primaries were institutionalized, mainly in the two large parties.

The relative advantages of the retired officers are not on the ideological side, but in their personal attributes. The personalization process of politics was expressed in the search for leaders with abilities suited to running a country. The retired officers knew how to take advantage of this situation in order to expand into the political system. The parties courted them and the public proved time after time that it is interested in having retired officers controlling the government.[18]

CONCLUSIONS

It can be argued that, despite the expansion of the militarization of politics, it is still better to have a situation where retired officers gain a lot of political power over a situation where the army itself will influence government policy. From this aspect the problematic situation in Israel is better than that existing in a country such as Turkey. The retired officers entering politics are not acting in an organized manner. They are individuals in various parties, generally opponents of each other. Neither are the retired officers prone to create factions based on military service inside the parties. Generals in the same party do not automatically cooperate. Sometimes they even compete with each other, such as Barak and Sneh in 1997, or Ben-Eliezer and Mitzna in 2002. An exciting example is Sharon and Weizman. In 1967 they both pressured the government to initiate a war against Egypt, but in the political arena they did not cooperate. In the Begin government formed in 1977 Sharon served as minister of agriculture and Weizman as minister of defence.

While Weizman moved in a dovish direction and supported concessions to Egypt in return for a peace agreement, Sharon was much more sceptical and was one of the leaders of the hawkish bloc in the government. Barak, when serving as a minister in Rabin's government, was less enthusiastic than Rabin about the Oslo process and the political agreements with the Palestinians. In the primaries campaign in the Labour Party in 2002 there was a prominent gap between the central position of Ben-Eliezer and the leftist outlook of Mitzna on the questions of foreign affairs and security.

Another factor which contributes to the softening of the dangers in the process of militarization of politics is the amount of time that passes between the end of a military career and the start of a political career, or the beginning of serving in senior political positions. The shorter the time, the bigger the risk to the civilian character of politics. Of the four retired generals who were the most influential from 1999, two of them entered political positions a very short time after their retirement from the army—Barak and Mofaz. The two others—Sharon and Ben-Eliezer—advanced more slowly. Ben-Eliezer ended his military service about twenty years ago and Sharon thirty years ago. The longer the civilian period in their lives, the more the military mind will presumably become blunt and its influence decrease.

Israel is the only western democracy where retired generals have so much political power. The increasing militarization of Israeli politics is not in contradiction to democratic processes that take place in society. The role of the Supreme Court, the State Comptroller and the mass media is on the rise. Legislation ensures that the rights of the individual are expanding. The political processes are more open and transparent. Criticism of the political system, politicians, and even the army, is increasing. The state penetrates less and less into the lives of its citizens.

The militarization of politics does not prevent all these processes, and they can grow even under a leadership emanating from the army. The retired generals who enter senior political posts never question these processes. When talking about domestic policy as a rule it is impossible to identify any influence from their military past. They are not socially more conservative than political leaders who did not come from the army. Neither are they significantly different from other politicians on matters of foreign affairs and security. The three prime ministers who made the biggest breakthroughs towards peace and compromise were actually retired generals—Rabin, Barak and, most recently, Sharon.

This anomaly calls for a deeper clarification in the future. Cohen stipulated the functional contraction process of the army in the expansion of the peace process.[19] And indeed, the end of the peace process that began with the rise of the right in 1996 and reached its peak when the second intifada broke out in September 2000, was amongst the factors that explain the increase in the militarization of politics. How is it possible that the processes of militarization of politics and the de-militarization of society are taking place at one and the same time? Will a balance be kept that can ensure the apparently opposing interests of the two sides? Can military democracy survive? Can Athens and Sparta exist at the same time?

NOTES

1. This term was used by Yoram Peri, *Between Battles and Ballots*, Cambridge, 1983, p. 286.
2. Uri Ben-Eliezer, 'From Military Role-Expansion to Difficulties in Peace-Making: The Israel Defence Forces 50 Years On', in Daniel Maman, Eyal Ben-Ari and Zeev Rosenhek (eds.), *Military, State and Society in Israel*, New Brunswick, 2001, p. 141.
3. Ibid., p. 149.
4. Uri Ben-Eliezer, 'Do the Generals Run Israel? The Military–Political Linkage and the Legitimacy for War in Nation-in-Arms', in Hanna Herzog (ed.), *A Society in Reflection*, Tel Aviv, 2000, p. 245.
5. Ibid., p. 261.
6. Baruch Kimmerling, 'Patterns of Militarism in Israel', *European Journal of Sociology*, Vol. 34 (1993), pp. 196–223.
7. Moshe Lissak, 'Uniqueness and Normalization in Military–Government Relations in Israel', in Maman *et al.* (eds.), *Military, State and Society in Israel*, p. 410.
8. Ibid., p. 412.
9. Stuart A. Cohen, 'Israel and her Army', *Democratic Culture*, Vol. 4–5 (2001), pp. 9–10.
10. Ibid., pp. 10–11.
11. Stuart Cohen, 'The IDF and Israeli Society: Towards a Functional Contraction in the Army's Role?', in Moshe Lissak and Baruch Kney-Paz (eds.), *Israel Towards the Year 2000*, Jerusalem, 1996, pp. 217–218.
12. Yoram Peri, *Between Battles and Ballots*, Cambridge, 1983, pp. 101–129.
13. *Ha'aretz*, 15 November 2002.
14. Yohanan Peres, 'Most Israelis are Committed to Democracy', *Israeli Democracy*, No. 1 (February 1987), pp. 16–19; Ephraim Yuchtman-Yaar, 'The Israeli Public and its Institutions', *Israeli Democracy*, Vol. 3, No. 3 (Fall 1989), pp. 7–11; Yohanan Peres and Ephraim Yuchtman-Yaar, *Trends in Israeli Democracy*, Boulder, 1992.
15. The details were taken from the Knesset's web-site: http://www.knesset.gov.il.
16. *Ha'aretz*, 10 November 2002.
17. *Ma'ariv*, 5 November 2002.
18. Muli Tsafrir, 'IDF Retired Officers in Israel's Political Parties Primaries 1977–1997', MA thesis, Bar-Ilan University, 1998.
19. Cohen, 'The IDF and Israeli Society', p. 232.

Civil–Military Relations and Strategic Goal Setting in the Six Day War

ARYE NAOR

In his ground-breaking work on civil–military relations Samuel P. Huntington summed up the changes in the pattern of the relationship between political leaders and professional military commanders. According to his analysis, the Korean War broke the previous pattern which had been based on the separation of powers, that is to say a dichotomy between the two echelons that left politics exclusively to the politicians. But the Korean War 'aroused public interest in, and indignation over, foreign policy; it stimulated opposition, partisan and otherwise, in Congress; it exhausted the political influence of the Joint Chiefs ... It was also the first time that public resentment of the conduct of a war contributed to the ousting of the party in power'.[1]

The same could be said about the Six Day War and civil–military relations in Israel with two big differences. First, the political involvement of military commanders on the one hand, and political influence and public pressure on strategic decision-making on the other occurred during the crisis that preceded the war. Even the change of power took place before the first bullet was fired. Prime Minister Levi Eshkol had no political choice but to relinquish his post as defence minister to Moshe Dayan, who at that time was one of the leaders of Rafi, an opposition party, and to give two cabinet seats to opposition leader Menachem Begin and Joseph Sapir, chairman of the Liberal Party.

This article analyzes the crisis in civil–military relations before the war and its influence on the setting of war targets and on the conduct of the war, the greatest military victory in Israel's history.

ESHKOL AND HIS GENERALS

At the beginning of 1967 the Israeli intelligence community presented an optimistic estimate to prime minister and minister of defence, Levi Eshkol.

According to that estimate, no full-scale Arab–Israeli war could be anticipated before 1970. No war could be launched against Israel without Egyptian participation; and Egypt had to rehabilitate its army after its draining intervention in the Yemen civil war. Military intelligence estimated that the completion of that process could not be foreseen prior to 1970, hence Israel could expect at least three more years of quiet, so desperately needed for economic recovery. Eshkol listened carefully to the analysis, made by the head of military intelligence, Major General Aharon Yariv and adopted by the Israel Defence Forces (IDF) chief of the general staff, Lieutenant General Yitzhak Rabin. 'Say, perhaps you are wrong?', he asked simply.[2]

Eshkol had served in World War I like his great predecessor, David Ben-Gurion, but during Israel's War of Independence he was in charge of mobilization, military manufacturing and also dealt with civil–military relations. He helped Ben-Gurion in subjugating the military echelon, the Supreme Command in particular, to the political leadership. Known for a long time as a man of compromise he succeeded in calming the political pressure in the armed forces and in finding a common language and division of power between the civil and military spheres.[3] However, he was never considered to be one of inner circle of the security establishment. The economy, rather than the battleground, was his main interest. Shortly after the end of the war he returned to building the economic infrastructure of Israel, and served as Israel's minister of finance for eleven years before he succeeded Ben-Gurion as prime minister and minister of defence.

Eshkol and the general staff were critical of each other. Eshkol criticized Rabin for press interviews, which the Syrians interpreted as threats, and consequently ordered him to refrain from unauthorized public statements.[4] Earlier he noted that some military reports to him were incorrect.[5] In his eyes, Rabin was politically immature, if not imprudent. Hana Zemer was editor-in-chief of the daily newspaper *Davar*, owned by the *Histadrut* trade union and favourable to the Labour government. She was a personal friend of Eshkol, and heard him expressing the view that he did not absolutely trust Rabin.[6] Some members of Eshkol's cabinet also questioned Rabin's competence, and Moshe Dayan, still in opposition, accused him of bearing personal responsibility for the crisis that broke out in May 1967. According to Dayan (though when he became defence minister he had a different explanation), the crisis resulted from Rabin's order to the Air Force to fly over Damascus.[7] That order was interpreted by the Soviets as a direct threat against their main ally in the region, on the back of Rabin's anti-Syrian statements.[8] On the other hand, Rabin was critical of Eshkol's caution, which he interpreted as hesitancy, rather than prudence.[9]

When the Israeli–Egyptian crisis broke out in mid-May, Rabin's deputy was Major General Ezer Weitzman, former commander of the Air Force. Eshkol liked him personally, but disregarded his candidacy for the top military position. He wanted a more level-headed, cautious man for that job; hence after Rabin collapsed during the May 1967 crisis, he called Major General Haim Bar-Lev from his leave and appointed him deputy chief of staff.[10] Even if he did not mean to do so, he thus drove a wedge between the top generals which may have had significant consequences.

Eshkol became prime minister and minister of defence following the resignation of David Ben-Gurion in June 1963. In subsequent years the generals respected Eshkol and appreciated the public backing he usually gave them, as well as his arms policy and the success he had in the US in this regard. However, most of them still admired Ben-Gurion, who ever since his resignation had been very critical of his successor, had spoke publicly against his decisions, and had belittled his leadership. Mapai (Labour), the ruling party of the time, was torn from within and finally there was a split. Ben-Gurion and his followers, Moshe Dayan among them, formed an independent list for the coming elections, Rafi.

In particular Ben-Gurion and his Rafi followers portrayed Eshkol as being unable resist foreign pressure and therefore unfit to serve in the defence ministry. Beyond that, they regarded him as someone who disregarded proper government, truth and justice; who could not make up his mind whenever a difficult, tough decision was needed; in short, one who could not match Ben-Gurion, his predecessor. A book with jokes about Eshkol and his leadership qualities was distributed all over the country. At a time of economic recession this discrediting of Eshkol permeated the Israeli elite. In the general elections in November 1965 Eshkol won very impressively, with forty-five seats while Ben-Gurion's, Rafi list gained only ten.

This de-legitimization process was influential in shaping military–civil relations. Not only did most senior officers admire Ben-Gurion, on the Rafi list there were also two former chiefs of staff (Moshe Dayan and Zvi Zur), as well as a former director-general of the ministry of defence (Shimon Peres), and other former defence-establishment officials. Deeply rooted in the establishment, they all had good reputations. Their opinion of Eshkol was expressed and intensively covered by the press. The formal expression reached wide segments of the population, and the influential *Ha'aretz* daily gave them an effective platform. Alongside the formal channels of communication were the informal ones, perhaps even more influential with regard to servicemen. Friday night meetings at private homes with friends, common across Israel at the time, resulted in political discussions in which officers in active service could listen to their former commanders, in an informal policy network. Listening to their criticism of Eshkol, especially with regard to his leadership capabilities, members of the IDF general staff were influenced by the participation in this on-going campaign of senior figures in the defence establishment, such as Dayan, Peres, Zur and Major

General Chaim Herzog (who was not elected to the Knesset in 1965, but was still active in Rafi's efforts).

As long as Eshkol and the Supreme Command officers agreed on national security issues, the influence of the illegitimacy campaign was latent. When differences of opinion arose the political attacks played their part in the negative attitude toward the premier, questioning his capability to lead the nation in the most difficult time it had known since the 1948 War of Independence. Members of the general staff interpreted the prudent, cautious way in which Eshkol managed the crisis as weakness, indecisiveness and anxiety. As the crisis continued voices expressing a desire for the strong leadership of Ben-Gurion could be heard in political circles (including members of Eshkol's cabinet), as well as in the national press.[11]

From the standpoint of the generals these expressions were a false yearning, since Ben-Gurion opposed opening fire by Israel, in spite of the military arguments, which were known to him. Rabin went to visit 'the old man' (Ben-Gurion) and listened to his sharp criticism of the brinkmanship strategy, the mobilization of the reserve forces and the danger of isolation. It was after this visit that Rabin collapsed. Ben-Gurion's opinion was based on the presumption that Israel could not wage a war without the backing of at least one of the world's great powers.[12]

Eshkol's management of the crisis was based on the same strategy, and aimed at achieving an understanding with US President Lyndon B. Johnson that would ensure political backing during the war and the rehabilitation of the IDF after the war, as well as the supply of sophisticated weapons, especially aircraft, that France had already embargoed.

At the same time, the diplomatic campaign conducted by Eshkol and his foreign minister, Abba Eban, across the globe were meant to legitimize unilateral activities by Israel, should international efforts to re-open the Straits of Tiran at the Red Sea (closed by Egypt on 22 May 1967) fail. In the end the premier was successful; however, many generals, politicians and media figures continued to doubt his ability to govern in such a crucial time. In his memoirs Rabin made clear the attitude that developed inside the general staff: Eshkol was 'depressed', his cabinet was unable to make the necessary decisions under the adversity of the situation.[13]

The different approaches of Eshkol and his generals were revealed also in the debate on the place of military issues in national priorities. The premier held a Clausewitzian view that war is an instrument of policy; hence in case of conflicting considerations policy overrides operative military aspects of war.[14] For this reason he wanted to wait for international legitimacy before opening fire. The generals saw it differently; believing that if Israel were to wait there would be a danger of a three-front simultaneous war, which might be catastrophic. In order to ensure victory IDF commanders wanted to fight Egypt first, without a delay, and the closure of Tiran was a satisfactory *casus belli* in their eyes.

Thus they approached Eshkol on the morning of 23 May, after the Egyptian blockade had been announced, with a clear opinion that Israel must act immediately. Yariv warned of an attack by all the Arab countries, because he believed that Arab leaders would interpret ongoing Israeli diplomatic steps as a demonstration of weakness that could create an opportunity to annihilate the Jewish state. Weizman held the same opinion. Rabin said that the IDF must either take Gaza as a bargaining chip or destroy the Egyptian army; either way the war should open with a surprise attack on their air force. Then, he added, perhaps Israel should fight Syria and Jordan as well.[15]

Shortly before his meeting with the senior generals, the premier was approached by the US administration with a friendly letter in which Israel was promised half-tracks, spare parts for tanks and economic aid. President Johnson also criticized the UN withdrawal from the Sinai, declared that Israel had a right to free navigation in the Straits of Tiran, and announced that the US, the UK and Canada proposed jointly to the Security Council to call for preservation of the status quo.

Six days earlier, while the generals interpreted Nasser's moves as a demonstration and propaganda, Eshkol expressed his opinion that war was inevitable. He did not change his view on this matter. The analysis he heard from the generals could only strengthen his feeling that war was the only option for Israel. On the other hand he had his policy considerations, to which political ones were added in a cabinet meeting called later on 23 May. For various reasons some members were against pre-emption, and Eshkol himself was reluctant to wage a war without consensus in his own cabinet. He finally agreed that Foreign Minister Abba Eban would travel to Washington to clarify the US position. An American 'green light' could be politically important and a source for legitimacy. Eshkol found himself on the horns of a painful dilemma. On the one hand he had to explain to world leaders and public opinion why Israel must act immediately and unilaterally, and on the other hand he had to explain to Israelis why they should not act unilaterally, at least for the time being.[16]

On 27 May there was a deadlock in the cabinet discussions: nine members, including Eshkol, were in favour of a pre-emptive first strike, and nine opposed it. Eshkol, still looking for internal consensus, did not use his prerogative to win the vote. Rather he decided to continue with the discussion later that day. When the cabinet reconvened, a message from President Johnson persuaded Eshkol that Israel had to give the US more time to resolve the crisis diplomatically. The decision taken on 28 May was thus to continue the military stand-off. Aware of the political pressure and the growing public dissatisfaction, Eshkol wanted to explain the international background and the political implications to his generals. The meeting was scheduled for the evening, following a live radio speech to the nation.

This speech was the worst mistake Eshkol made during the whole crisis. An aide of his corrected in handwriting a word in the printed text without notifying him. Eshkol, who suffered from poor eyesight, could not read the handwriting of his aide and faltered. The whole nation was listening and this mistake was interpreted as proof of incompetence. The political reaction to this was out of all proportion and was used as a convincing argument to remove the prime minister from his other post as the minister of defence.

'REBELLION IN THE AIR'

As mentioned earlier, the essence of Eshkol's concept of national security was not different from that of David Ben-Gurion. Eshkol was also very reluctant to wage a war without the backing of at least one of the great powers. From 17 May, two days after the beginning of the crisis, he was sure that a war was inevitable.[17] On 27 May he even proposed to the cabinet to finalize its long deliberations by a decision to launch a pre-emptive strike, waiting no longer for the international convoy to break the Egyptian blockade in the strait. At that time there were many inside the cabinet opposed to this. Nine ministers—Eban, Sapir and Aran of Mapai; Shapira, Warhaftig and Burg of NRP (Mafdal); Barzely and Bentov of Mapam; Kol of the Independent Liberals—voted against the proposal, while nine were in favour—Eshkol, Shapira, Yesha'ayahu, Gevati, Sasson and Sharf of Mapai; Allon, Carmel and Galili of Ahduth Ha'avoda).

At that time only two members of the cabinet were former generals—Allon and Carmel. Eshkol and Galili had a deep involvement in the defence establishment. All four of them voted in favour, but could not achieve a majority.[18] In the eyes of the general staff Eshkol failed to deliver the goods. Eshkol tried his best to persuade the generals that he had to take into account the international situation, but once he changed his own mind his credibility among the generals was further reduced.

The generals, waiting for the premier at headquarters, were anxious. The decision taken by the cabinet meant that the inevitable war would start in circumstances significantly worse than the conditions that already existed. In particular they were concerned for the prospects of pre-emptive air strikes, without which the number of predicted Israeli losses would be terribly high and the chances of a clear victory doubtful. The political crisis and the impact of Eshkol's radio speech added to the feeling of helplessness among the Israeli public. Many generals felt that Israel might even lose a war without any fighting taking place.

As such, the discussion quickly turned in a bitter clash between the generals and the premier and, as one general later admitted, 'a feeling of rebellion was in the air'.[19] Rumours of unrest among high ranking officers quickly spread, adding to the political unrest and anxiety among politicians. The men in uniform must have paid attention to the fact that minister Yigal Allon (a general in the 1948 War of Independence), who accompanied Eshkol to the meeting, kept silent when they criticized the cabinet decision and its strategic effects. At that time he was a candidate for the defence portfolio should Eshkol yield to political pressure. Allon did not defend Eshkol; nor did Rabin.

The atmosphere in the room was tense from the beginning. Eshkol told the generals that he had changed his mind on an immediate strike—a result of a secret message from President Johnson, who had earlier told Eban: 'Israel will not be alone unless it decides to go alone ... Give me more time.'[20] Eshkol could not ignore this presidential plea. The 'hawkish' group inside the cabinet disintegrated and the decision was to continue waiting. If necessary, Eban was authorized to travel again to Washington.

The generals seemed to lose their manners while expressing their reaction to the premier and his message to them and to the nation. Brigadier General Israel Lior, Eshkol's aide de camp, wrote a summary of the discussions.[21] It reveals the difference between the grand-strategic perspective of the political echelon and the tactical perspective of the operative echelon. The summary opens with Eshkol's explanation for the cabinet decision:

> The danger is still there and we must continue our stand-by. The closure of the straits is [internationally] considered as an act of aggression, and there is an international willingness to resolve that problem. At the moment we use our brains, not just our force. Perhaps IDF generals do not feel at ease with it, but you have to remember that we were just a hairsbreadth far from a decision to act yesterday. Meanwhile things happened on the international arena, which dictate restraint and wait ... I received a top-secret message from the US president. He told me the Russians had told him that Israel was preparing an attack on the Arabs, and they, the Russians would assist the Arabs in case of war. If the US calmed Israel they would have done the same with the Arabs. The president promised that the US, Britain and other countries were acting to ensure the freedom of navigation in the strait. Lastly he warned us that a pre-emptive strike would cause a disaster. In light of all this it would be politically, diplomatically and perhaps even morally illogical to open fire. We must restrain for two or three more weeks. The cabinet approved of that almost unanimously. I understand that it might cause some disappointment among the commanders, however political and military maturity should dictate our behaviour. We must let the Powers prove their capabilities.[22]

Reading these words of prudence, one cannot find there any sign of the weakness or depression that Rabin described in his memoirs, written some twelve years afterwards. On the contrary, Eshkol was sure of himself, and believed that there was an overriding consideration to stay on the alert without opening fire at that time. Eshkol argued this when answering the criticism of a young division commander, Major General Ariel Sharon, who disregarded the diplomatic context and harshly accused the government of damaging 'the deterrence power of Israel', by not giving the IDF an order to attack. 'We are capable of destroying the Egyptian army; however, should we give up on the navigation issue we would open way to the cessation of Israel. All this lobbying, including the maritime act, presents us as weak. We present ourselves as a helpless nation. We have never degraded ourselves that much before.'

Eshkol was offended by these blunt words. 'I do not share this view', he said. But still he had to listen to some other criticisms. The Northern Command's head Major General David Elazar (chief of the general staff in the 1973 Yom Kippur War) presented the generals' mode of thinking. He opened by saying that there was no doubt that the IDF must obey the government. However, there was an operative 'decisive datum' that should be taken into consideration:

> The decisive datum is that the IDF must be the first to operate its Air Force. The IDF would not win, should the enemy achieve air supremacy; and if we did win it would pay deadly price. Consequently the government is requested to return to the IDF its deterrent power. This could be achieved only if the government allows us to act [now] and not at a time when acting might be impossible. It is not automatic that we can wait for any delay of yours. We cannot wait until the end of time, because by then our force may run out.Elazar was one of Eshkol's favourites on the general staff. He listened carefully to this rising commander, who emphasized the operative conditions for victory—conditions that Eshkol never disagreed with.[23]

Head of logistics, Major General Matityahu Peled, added the economic perspective to the operative argument. He argued that it was beyond the economic capacity of Israel to have all its reserve forces mobilized for a long period of time, 'Is this the intention of the Government?' he asked rhetorically.

Central Command head, Major General Uzi Narkis, tried to assure the premier that the IDF was ready and could win. 'We are stronger than ever and the Arabs are just a soap bubble'. The real problem that the government faced, he added, was not in its relationship with the general staff. 'We can be talked with', unlike 'the youngsters' who would not believe the generals should they tell them Israel was not going to launch a strike.

Eshkol replied with a disposition on the meaning of deterrence in the context of a defensive concept of national security. 'We need a long breath, we need patience', and 'the very meaning of deterrence is long breath'. He went on to explain his concept of just war,[24] while he objected to a preventive war (as opposed to a pre-emptive strike). According to Eshkol,

> Deterrence does not mean that we must act, that we must strike—and that's it. I believe that a deterrent power means also capability to wait to exhaust all the other possibilities. I have never thought that the presence of a large Egyptian army near the border means we shall rise and destroy them. Only if there were good reasons for that it would be justified. You have got more jets and tanks, in order to win should it be necessary. You have not got all that in order to tell us: now we can destroy the Egyptian army—so let's do it. We have been educated against the concept of a preventive war, and now you ask me to give you a chance to blow up the Egyptian Air Force.

The tone Eshkol used, even more than his arguments, contradicted the position he held in the cabinet deliberations. For a person who proposed to the cabinet to open fire it was almost incomprehensible that he adopted quite the opposite position only thirty-six hours later. The explanation for this behaviour is that in the meantime he was persuaded that Israel must give President Johnson an opportunity to find a non-military diplomatic solution. And if they failed, a war would not be illegitimate, hence diplomatic backing and arms supply to rehabilitate the IDF would be attainable. Beyond this rational attitude he had also an ideological barrier, based on the concept of just war, contradictory to the mode of thinking expressed by the generals.

As Lior remembered, Eshkol was weary after the long cabinet deliberations, the exchange of messages with Johnson, the political debate and the unsuccessful radio speech. However, he went on, giving the worried, furious generals a piece of his mind: 'It should be remembered that the destruction of the Egyptian army couldn't be final. The Egyptian army would be rehabilitated [by the Soviets]. Israel [also] cannot recover without external help ... The government must have a comprehensive view, taking into consideration issues of blood-saving, arms supply and the damage to military machinery'. Thus he presented the generals with a wider meaning of the concept of planning than they were used to, that is to say, a concept that takes into consideration national and international political variables and gives them a decisive weight. In other words, the war everybody in the room was talking about should have been a continuation of policy, in a Clausewitzian sense; and international politics must be considered very seriously as part of the process of policy-making and agenda-setting. Above all, if there were any chance of preventing a war by an international solution to ending the blockade, Eshkol believed it was his duty to act accordingly. 'IDF generals', he said, 'should understand the place of the political echelon and they should not let their feelings of dissatisfaction turn the scales.'

With his sharp political instincts, Eshkol might have sensed the threatening meaning of the tense atmosphere. By calling on his audience to 'understand the place of the political echelon' he softened the tone of his rebuke, trying to use understatement to calm the atmosphere, though the message remained clear: the political echelon will make the decisions, and the military commanders must obey, whether they like it or not.

Rumours about the confrontation must have reached Ben-Gurion. On 29 May he called a press conference, criticized Eshkol and added that the government should not engage in war unless Israel had international backing. All the newspapers in Israel published his opinion. In discussions with senior military figures Eshkol did not mention the political difficulties he had, and used only policy arguments. However some members of the general staff had conversations with political leaders in government and in opposition, in which opinions were exchanged with regard to the government policy and the defence portfolio. Quite typical were the meetings of Rabin with Mapam leader Ya'akov Hazan, and that of Weizman with Eshkol, in the presence of Justice Minister Ya'akov Shimshon Shapira. Both took place on 1 June, only hours before the nomination of Dayan as defence minister.

Rabin met with Hazan at the request of the latter, who wanted to know his opinion of Moshe Dayan.[23] Thus the chief of the general staff was invited by a political leader to either approve of, or oppose, the nomination of his civilian superior. In the eyes of both of them there was nothing wrong in the participation of a top IDF general in the political process. Hazan spoke indirectly, asking Rabin if he had 'evaluations' of his 'capability to work with one man or another as defence minister'. In the circumstances it was clear enough that Rabin's position might have been decisive, since Mapam was very critical of Rafi for a variety of political and ideological reasons. Rabin was indirect too. He said he had no personal preference. 'Be it Eshkol, Dayan or Yigal, I don't care', he said, thus legitimizing Dayan as a candidate for the portfolio. He did not report to Eshkol on this meeting.

A different attitude was expressed on the same day by General Weizman. He was Dayan's brother-in-law (their wives were sisters), but Weizman did not want Dayan as the head of the defence establishment, nor was he satisfied with Allon. Without previous notice Weizman entered Eshkol's private office, and shouted, with tears in his eyes, 'The country is being destroyed, everything is being ruined! Eshkol, just give an order and the IDF will fight and win the war. What do you need Dayan for? Who needs Allon? We have a powerful army, waiting only for your order. Give us the order and we shall win and you will be the victorious Prime Minister!'

In his memoirs, Brigadier General Lior describes the whole scene as highly emotional. Justice Minister Shapira, who was having lunch with Eshkol at the time burst into tears, and when Weizman left Eshkol's private office, he tried to remove his general's badge from his uniform. 'I don't remember exactly what happened afterwards', wrote Lior, 'it was a scene quite difficult to describe with words.'[24]

The emotional atmosphere can explain such events. IDF generals were deeply involved in politics because of a sincere belief that 'everything was being ruined'. It was not an attempt to overthrow the government. Rather they wanted to influence the decision-making process, which they believed was completely mistaken, and which endangered the very existence of Israel. According to Weizman 'there have been difficulties [among the generals] in making the decision, how much time should be given to the government to exhaust the chance of political solution of the crisis', and he immediately added that he did not mean to say that anyone ever thought of acting in contradiction to the decisions made by the cabinet, 'only as a recommendation'.[25]

However, there was an attempt by the military to manipulate national security policy, even though it was done out of good intentions and patriotic motivation. In any case, Weizman's intervention came too late. By this time Eshkol realized he had no real choice but to give the defence portfolio to Dayan. There can be no doubt that the generals influenced public opinion as well as political leaders. The lobbying against the waiting policy was political in its results, even if the generals had no political goals. Thus the general staff became an actor in the political arena, and a powerful pressure group. They wanted an order to pre-empt and contributed to the decision by Eshkol to hand over the defence ministry to Dayan, a former chief of the general staff and now the first general in Israel's history to become minister of defence.

UNINTENDED CONQUEST

Looking at the results of the Six Day War, Mordechai Bar-On raised the question of whether Israel had a 'dormant wish' to conquer the West Bank, given the disproportional reaction of the IDF to the Jordanian provocation on the first day of hostilities.[26] As mentioned earlier, Rabin said to Eshkol that there was a possibility of fighting the Jordanians and the Syrians after a battle with Egypt was won. In an interview given after the end of the war Rabin said it had developed, on the Jordanian front, 'on the basis of its own logic'. The chief of the general staff identified that logic: a defeat of Jordanian forces in the West Bank led to the capture of the 'natural border of the Land of Israel—the Jordan'.[27] Does it mean that the logic of the military reflected that of the politicians?

The truth of the matter is that even if a 'dormant wish' existed in the hearts of some high-ranking military and political officials, it had no influence on policy-making, agenda-setting or the determination of the war objectives. When the war broke out Israel had no intention of occupying the West Bank. In fact political leaders and military commanders did their best to limit the war to the Egyptian front, while keeping their eyes open to any option that might emerge on the Syrian front as well. On the morning of 5 June Eshkol sent a message to King Hussein of Jordan, through General Odd Bull, the chief UN observer, clarifying that Israel had no intention of attacking his kingdom: 'We shall not initiate any action against Jordan', it read, 'however, should Jordan open hostilities we shall react with all our might, and the king will have to bear the full responsibility for the consequences.'[28]

As Avi Shlaim has correctly observed, 'had King Hussein heeded Eshkol's warning, he would have kept the old city of Jerusalem and the West Bank'. This conclusion is based on the fact that 'no one in the cabinet or the general staff had proposed the capture of the Old City before the Jordanian bombardment began'. And even then Israel was reluctant to advance into that holy part of the Jewish patrimony. As General Uzi Narkis noted, the Mapai leadership wanted no change in the territorial status quo and thus turned down all his suggestions to attack. When the Jordanian bombardment persisted he was ordered by Defence Minister Dayan to adopt a defensive approach and to encircle Jerusalem before a possible advance of Jordanian armoured forces coming from the east, without entering the Old City, since 'we don't need that Vatican'.[29]

However, the battle had its own 'logic'. Some forty-eight hours later Dayan stood at the Western Wall and read an emotional declaration. This time he did not mention the Vatican. Rather he associated himself with Jewish history and Jewish faith. 'We have returned to our holiest places', he declared, 'so as not to abandon them forever.'[30] More than a calm, rational change of mind, Dayan's words reflected a change of mood in the Israeli consciousness, caused by the reunion with the land of the Bible. This change played a major role in the decision-making process of the cabinet when the war was over. Did it also play a significant role in the management of the war?

The hard fact is that when the war ended on 10 June Israel was the occupying power of the West Bank and the Gaza Strip. As General Gazit (first activities coordinator in the administrated territories) has written, formal legal preparations had been made and the necessary documents had been published a long time before the crisis. However, nothing was arranged apart from the legal formalities. Israel preferred to manage a rolling war, that is to say, whose objectives would be determined on the basis of contingent battle developments and on-going intelligence input.[31]

A first-hand observation of this 'tactization of strategy'[32] was expressed by Colonel Yitzhak Hofi (later an acting chief of the general staff and a head of the Mossad), who was chief of operations during the Six Day War. In a rare press interview about Dayan and his approach, Hofi gave an example of this kind of reasoning. He criticized Dayan for the frequent changes of mind, which looked quite bad from the perspective of the chief of operations, and was interpreted as 'instability'. One minute Dayan ordered that there be no advance to the Suez Canal, and immediately afterwards issued a contradictory order; one minute he gave the order to occupy Jenin and then he issued an order not to occupy it. 'Tens of times we had to change operational orders which had already been sent', noted Hofi, 'more than once we turned back forces that had been already sent to their mission, and then we sent them again [to the same mission]. This was a continuous instability during the whole war.'[33]

An historian who compares this retrospective criticism of Dayan with the head-on attack on Eshkol at military headquarters can conclude that either the officers were too busy fighting the war, or that they saw Dayan as one of them and as such his 'instability' was not considered a serious argument against him. One can only speculate what their reaction might have been had Eshkol, not Dayan, changed orders so frequently as defence minister.

The real problem in the management of the war was systematic rather than personal. Had Israel planned its war objectives in accordance with its other national goals, the minister of defence could not have altered operative changes as a result of his change of mood. On the Jenin front Israel had a serious problem, resulting from the bombardment of its main northern air base in Nir David. There could have been more than one military option to silence enemy fire: for example, an artillery or air attack, commando raids. The decision made finally on the ministerial level to occupy the town and its surrounding areas cannot be disconnected from other decisions regarding parts of the West Bank. Perhaps the final decision to conquer the whole West Bank can demonstrate the supremacy of tactics and contingent developments, together with changes of mood and consequent changes of war objectives.

On the afternoon of 6 June, the Ministerial Defence Committee decided that the IDF would capture the West Bank.[34] The cabinet was reluctant to take the whole West Bank, and did not approve of an offensive that would sweep Hussein's army out of the area. Accordingly, in late afternoon the general staff issued a correction to the *Nachshonim 2* operation order, stating that the 'IDF will capture the West Bank up to the hillock'. The order that followed the instructions of the cabinet lasted for less than five hours. At 22.40 hours Israeli intelligence reported that King Hussein had ordered all his troops to withdraw from the West Bank and cross the Jordan eastwards. Hence the IDF corrected its operation order once again and set a new war objective: 'the IDF will capture the West Bank and safeguard the descents to the Jordan'.[35]

This has been one of the most significant decisions made during Israel's history, made without any serious attempt to anticipate its strategic results and their influence on national goals. Was it in Israel's interests to destroy completely the 1949 armistice lines, which had international legitimacy, and replace them by cease-fire lines, thus returning 'the Palestine question' in all its aspects back to the UN? Was it really in the best interests of Israel to become the occupying power of the area, rule the Palestinians regardless of their aspirations, thus pushing them forward towards nationalism, self-determination and international recognition? In other words, was it really in the best interests of Israel to replace the Jordanian option by a Palestinian one?

Reading the memoirs of politicians and military figures involved in the decision-making process one cannot find any sign of long-term thinking and strategic planning, either before the occupation of the West Bank or immediately following hostilities. The intelligence services could, and should, have supplied the political echelon with evaluations, but they did not. The general staff could, and should, have supplied staff work, but they did not. Retrospectively it seems that Israel's future was shaped by tactical principles and evolving opportunities, rather than any long-term planning.

Strategically it might have been wrong, as indeed it has turned out. A military victory such as this can dialectically result in negative outcomes, giving a new meaning to the Hegelian *List der Vernunft* (cunning of reason), as noted by military historian Martin van Creveld: 'In retrospect, the smashing victory of 1967 was probably the worst thing that ever happened to Israel'.[36] Better management of the war; better use of the professional staff's work; and sound strategic advice from the general staff could have revealed this in advance.

It should be reiterated that from a professional military perspective tactics can determine the fate of a campaign and should never be underestimated. However, a military victory can lead to negative historical results. Senior military officers should take care of the military aspects of the war, and in so doing the role of tactics is crucial in their considerations. Political leaders should concern themselves more with the historical processes, the dialectical outcomes that can fundamentally change the nature of the military results. They have to anticipate what other people cannot foresee, and act accordingly. They have to realize the *Zeitgeist* while its appearance is still unclear to others. They must see what will be the outcomes of the decisions they will have to make tomorrow, resulting from the decisions they make today in response to the aftermath of the decisions they made yesterday. This is a difficult task, and leadership will always be difficult. Therefore some of their crucial decisions, perhaps the most consequential ones, are made by gambling with history.[37] This is a good reason to assist them with a system of decision-making, based on professional staff-work that will minimize uncertainties and clarify the meaning and consequences of all decisions. In the absence of such a system military officers influence the content of policy-making much more than they should.

This is not just a policy-making issue, concentrating on the quality of advice given to leaders.[38] It is also an issue of democracy and the proper relationship between the political and military echelons.[39] In the absence of such staff-work taking place in the prime minister's office or the cabinet secretariat, the military has too much influence on the government and national grand strategy. A typical result is the recurring failure to learn from experience;[40] hence the influence of the military mind on government decision-making can be error inducing.[41]

An empirical example of this can be seen in deliberations chaired by Eshkol on 6 June 1967, the second day of the war. In light of the reports of victories on several fronts, the premier asked some of the ministers who had participated in the discussion in his office to 'consider new definitions of security and diplomatic trends and to formulate a programme that would ensure Israel a respectable place in the Middle East with lasting peace and secure borders'. He formulated a list of problems that would have to be solved: Israeli–Egyptian relations; the status of Sinai and the Gaza strip; freedom of passage in the Gulf of Aqaba and the Suez Canal; the status of the West Bank; the status of the Old City of Jerusalem; the problem of the demilitarized zones in the north; the water problem; the problem of refugees and of the Arab population in the occupied territories.[42]

Eshkol covered the main problems and also showed a willingness to embark on totally new paths, but he could have done it only intuitively. A central planning body, which did not exist, was needed to define the decision-making problems, present possible options for action, thoroughly analyze their pros and cons, and assist leaders in deciding on the preferred options. In asking for 'new definitions' Eshkol was really asking for a status report, which should be the primary responsibility of a professional policy staff. Professional knowledge, prior training, personal and institutional experience and integrative ability of individuals from various sources are required for this task.

Preparation of a status report is similar to a military intelligence evaluation. The evaluator is meant to distance himself from his own prejudices and personal preferences and evaluate the various options on the basis of the information and knowledge at his or her disposal. However it should be noted that that kind of staff-work cannot be considered a part of the duties of the military general staff. Much more consideration is needed of ideological, moral, historical, political, social, economic and international aspects of history-shaping decisions. The military and intelligence agencies do have to enrich staff-work by supplying their outputs to the planning machinery as input; no more, no less.

On the other hand, in the absence of the necessary staff-work, political leaders face an impossible task in making history-shaping decisions. Because of their tendency to interpret reality in a manner that serves their ideological perspective and political interests, political leaders are bound to find this difficult. As a result they tend to base their decisions on either their own personal experience and intuition, or the opinion of the general staff, which necessarily depends on operative and tactical perspectives. This is how Israel found itself at the end of the sixth day ruling the West Bank and digging in along the east bank of the Suez Canal. These were very impressive military achievements. The first one raised Palestinian resistance; the second was the reason for the War of Attrition and later the 1973 Yom Kippur War. The dialectics of history turn a clear victory on the battleground into a danger to the victor's future. With the case of the Six Day War we learn that to the victor belong all the risks.

NOTES

1. S.P. Huntington, *The Soldier and the State: The Theory and Practice of Civil–Military Relations*, Cambridge, MA and London, 1957, p. 387.
2. Author interview with Mrs Miriam Eshkol, 31 December 2001.
3. Y. Rosental (ed.), *Levi Eshkol—The Third Prime Minister*, Jerusalem, 2002, pp. 218–222.
4. E. Haber, 'Today War will Break Out': The Reminiscences of Brig. Gen. Israel Lior, Aide-de-Camp to Prime Ministers Levi Eshkol and Golda Meir, Tel Aviv, 1987, pp. 146–147.
5. A letter from the Prime Minister and Minister of Defence to the Chief of the General Staff, 8 December 1964; Rosental, *Levi Eshkol—The Third Prime Minister*, p. 447.
6. H. Zemer, 'Before Television', in A. Susser (ed.), *Six Days—Thirty Years, New Perspectives of the Six Day War*, Tel Aviv, 1999, p. 240.
7. Brig. General A. Brown, *Moshe Dayan and the Six Days War*, Tel Aviv, pp. 17–19.
8. Z. Schiff, 'May 1967—The General Staff in the Eyes of Eshkol's Government', in Susser (ed.), *Six Days—Thirty Years*, pp. 192–196.
9. Y. Rabin, *Service Book*, Tel Aviv, 1979, Vol. 1, p. 170 (original Hebrew text of Rabin's *Memoirs*).
10. On Bar-Lev's return and appointment see C. Gai, *Bar-Lev—A Biography*, Tel Aviv, 1998, pp. 118–126.
11. A first-hand, vivid report of the political mood is given by S. Nakdimon, *Towards Zero Time*, Tel Aviv, 1968.
12. Ben-Gurion Diary, 22 May 1967; Y. Rabin, *The Rabin Memoirs*, Berkeley, 1996, pp. 73–75. For a different explanation of Ben-Gurion's position see S. Aronson, 'Israel's Nuclear Programme, the Six-Day War and Its Ramifications', in E. Karsh (ed.), *Israel: The First Hundred Years, II, From War to Peace?*, London, 2000, pp. 83–95.
13. Rabin, *Service Book*, Vol. 1, p. 170.
14. C. von Clausewitz, *On War*, trans. and ed. M. Howard and P. Paret, Princeton, 1976, p. 605.
15. Haber, 'Today War will Break Out', pp. 164–165.
16. Rosental, *Levi Eshkol—The Third Prime Minister*, p. 532.
17. Author interview with Mrs. Eshkol.
18. Rosental, *Levi Eshkol—The Third Prime Minister*, p. 540.
19. Schiff, 'May 1967—The General Staff in the eyes of Eshkol's Government', pp. 195–196.
20. R.B. Parker (ed.), *The Six-Day War—A Retrospect*, Gainesville, FL, 1996, pp. 208–209.
21. Haber, 'Today War will Break Out', pp. 194–198.
22. Haber, 'Today War will Break Out', p. 154.
23. Haber, 'Today War will Break Out', p. 155.
24. Eshkol's thoughts mirrored those of Michael Walzer, *Just and Unjust Wars*, New York, 1977.
25. Nakdimon, *Towards Zero Time*, p. 243.
26. Haber, 'Today War will Break Out', p. 203.
27. Author interview with Ezer Weitzman, April 1998.

28. M. Bar-On, *Smoking Borders, Studies in the Early History of the State of Israel*, 1948–1967, Jerusalem, 2002, p. 386.
29. M.A. Gilboa, *Shesh Shanim, Shisha Yamim*, Tel Aviv, 1969, p. 229.
30. A. Shlaim, *The Iron Wall: Israel and the Arab World*, New York and London, 2000, p. 244.
31. Brown, *Moshe Dayan and the Six Days War*, p. 64.
32. Dayan speech at the Wall, *Kol Yisarael*, 7 June 1967.
33. A. Naor, 'The Six-Day War and its Aftermath: A Case for Professionalism in Policy Planning', in D. Korn (ed.), *Public Policy in Israel: Perspectives and Practices*, Lanham, MD, 2002.
34. Y. Harkabi, *War and Strategy*, Tel Aviv, 1992, pp. 587–588.
35. E. Rosen, 'Dayan said Untruth' (an interview with Titzhak Hofi), *Ma'ariv*, 22 September 1991.
36. Brown, Moshe Dayan and the Six Days War, pp. 64–65.
37. Ibid., p. 65.
38. M. van Creveld, *The Sword and the Olive: A Critical History of the Israeli Defence Force*, New York, 1998, p. 199.
39. Y. Dror, 'Israeli Gambles with History: The Lavi Combat Airplane and the Peace Process with the PLO', in H.J. Miser (ed.), *Handbook of Systems Analysis, Cases*, London, 1995, pp. 239–268; Y. Dror, *The Capacity to Govern: A Report to the Club of Rome*, London, 2001, pp. 151–157.
40. A. Wildavsky, *Speaking Truth to Power: The Art and Craft of Policy Analysis*, New Brunswick, 1996.
41. Huntington, *The Soldier and the State*, p. 61.
42. C. Hood, *The Art of the State: Culture, Rhetoric, and Public Management*, Oxford, 1998, pp. 38–39.
43. C. Perrow, *Normal Accidents*, New York, 1984.
44. Haber, 'Today War will Break Out', p. 241.

Society Strength as a Base for Military Power: The State of Israel during the Early 1950s

ZE'EV DRORY

This paper explores the societal factors which impact upon the capability of the Israel Defence Forces (IDF). The nature of a nation's social fabric may both weaken and enhance its military potential and performance. In order to explore this nexus, military and social developments during the early 1950s are selected as a case study of the reciprocal influences occurring between these two spheres.

SOCIETY AS A FACTOR OF NATIONAL STRENGTH

'The doctrine of national security' presumes an ideational and principled basis for guiding national undertakings in different, and varied, areas. Its role is to assure national security in the short and long term by drawing on national potential.

This approach, which examines the security doctrine from a broad perspective, includes a number of variegated themes: a definition of state objectives; available state resources; and the geo-strategic environment in which it operates. The broad basis for a powerful security establishment resides in the leadership's ability to draw upon the state's social, demographic, economic and technological resources, as well as to actuate its political and military capacities through their proper mix and coordination.

MILITARY RESILIENCE

Military resilience derives from the capacity of a nation to realize its potential from all the power components that are available. These include the physical, economic, engineering and human resources, as well as the organizational capacity to build military formations which can mobilize the greater, and best, part of the population for the purposes of safeguarding the security of the nation; military formations, which contain the best quality military equipment in sufficient quantities to defend and secure the defence of the nation; the ability of military commanders to orchestrate the weapons at their disposal in the right place and at the right time, both during periods of declared war and between wars, while maintaining a deterrent capacity. In long wars, and clearly in hostile situations, border clashes and continuous terrorist activities, the importance of the same resources increase.

From the moment Israel was established and compulsory conscription was implemented, a debate began over the advantages and disadvantages of a large people's army, as opposed to a small and professional military force. Manpower quality, as well as the national consciousness and loyalty of inductees, became the central components in the strength of a people's army. Strategic analysts and military leaders ascribed great importance to morale and the fighting spirit.

As the role of industry and technology grew in the military sphere, there was an increased need for proficient and skilled manpower in the military campaigns. The modern battlefield presented demands for qualitative manpower which could cope with the complexity of the war machinery on the battlefield.

One of the decisive components in national defence capacity is the human factor, the power of society, both quantitatively and qualitatively. For example, quantitatively, an optimal number of the state's population should be conscripted for military service as compensation for the state's numerical deficiency in manpower. Qualitatively, questions associated with the human potential touch on education, technological levels, and the ability to integrate advanced systems and operate them. In-depth and broad discussions on the issue of security, society and Israeli security doctrine may be found in two recent publications by Avner Yariv, *Politics and Strategy in Israel* and Israel Tal, *National Security*.[1]

SOCIETY'S IMAGE IN THE 1950s

The wave of immigration in the early 1950s doubled the population of Israel. In less than four years, from 1948 to 1953, the number of citizens grew from 700,000 to 1,484,000. This demographic change brought with it difficult economic and social challenges.

There were two principal sources of immigration: one was survivors of the Holocaust, homeless and bereft of family, scarred in body and spirit by war and the concentration camps. The second was Oriental Jews from the Eastern Mediterranean and North African countries, whose cultural and traditional background was different and clashed with the cultural tradition of the country's Jewish inhabitants. Moreover, the majority of immigrants had little formal education and lacked economic resources and a business/employment background, factors which hindered their ability to become integrated into the country's economy.[2]

THE STRUCTURE AND COMPOSITION OF THE IMMIGRANT POPULATION

From the establishment of the state on 14 May 1948 until the end of 1951, 700,000 immigrants arrived in the country. In 1948, 102,000 arrived, in 1949, 240,000, in 1950, 170,000, and in 1951, 175,000.[3] This was mass immigration both in absolute terms and in relation to the size of the existing population. The population grew at an annual rate of 20 percent during these years of mass immigration and within three and a half years doubled. By the end of 1953, the Israeli population had reached 1,484,000 inhabitants.

Approximately 80 percent of the population growth was due to immigration and the remainder was a result of natural growth. The immigration waves brought with them newcomers from different countries with foreign cultures, customs and languages. Some upheld traditional religious values, while others distanced themselves from any traces of religion and Jewish tradition. So large and varied an immigration in such a short period of time created difficult problems which had an impact upon the formation of the character of Israeli society for many years to come.

In 1948, the majority of immigrants (86 percent) were of European origin but after that Jews from African and Asian communities were more numerous. In 1951, 71 percent of the immigrants were Asian- and African-born. This change in the composition of Israel's immigrants brought about considerable changes in the social fabric and structure of the Jewish population in the country.

The educational level of the immigrants in the 1948–1951 period was considerably lower than that of the veteran population. Among new immigrant males over 15, only 16 percent had completed high school as compared with 34 percent of the veteran population. Among those of Asian and African origin, who constituted half the immigrants, only 8.5 percent had received high school education.[4] The social and economic gap between the new immigrants and the veteran population grew quickly, generating friction and bitterness even in these initial years of immigration.

Mass immigration included different social strata and varied ethnic and cultural elements. It was an encounter between worlds which clashed in their outlooks but whose common denominator was the Jewish religion and the desire to reach the land of Israel. This desire was due to a mixture of push and pull factors. There were those who were driven by ideological and national motivations. But there were also many for whom Israel was a refuge and a shelter. The new immigrants arriving after the War of Independence were, by and large, refugees who immigrated to Israel under the necessity of circumstances, unlike earlier immigrants who were motivated by ideals and a pioneering ideology.

Most of these post-1948 immigrants were bereft of all material possessions. They were sent to settlements on the country's periphery where conditions were difficult, as well as to transit camps and collective settlements on the frontier. Many did not find appropriate employment for many years. On top of these absorption challenges was the danger faced from external terrorism and insurgency which struck at morale and had negative implications for the IDF and security policy in general.

THE IMPLICATIONS FOR SECURITY

The doubling of the population in the first years after the founding of Israel affected security considerations in several ways. Only through a critical population mass, numbering two to three million, could Israel be secured. This rise in the population contributed to the basic resources of national security. In an age of total war, in which the entire population is mobilized, and certainly when the armed forces are based on military reserves, the size and strength of the population impacts directly on national security. At the same time, in the era of modern warfare, where population and vital strategic sites in the heart of the state are legitimate targets, the resilience of the population becomes a security asset or burden during periods of continuous violent conflict.[5]

The strength of the state is also measured by the resilience of its frontier residents. During a period in which the defence burden is placed primarily on the frontier settlements a relatively greater weight was placed on the national security aspect of the frontier challenge. The identification of the population with the state and its goals turned the entire nation into a *de facto* army. The resolution to withstand the daily security problems, not only in times of war, constituted a significant part of the power of the state. The level of education and the technological capability of society had an immediate impact upon the security and military capability of the state.

Immigrant absorption, and the doubling of the population, had conflicting influences on the formation of Israeli society in the early 1950s. It had decisive bearing for state security in two main areas: the first pertained to problems of security on the immigrant agricultural settlements and transit camps, particularly those situated along the borders; the second concerned the human and qualitative composition of the combat units during these same years.

THE NEW SETTLEMENT—PROBLEMS IN ROUTINE SECURITY MEASURES

The War of Independence did not solve the problem of the integration of the young Israeli state into the Middle Eastern region. Its very existence was rejected by the Arab world, and its borders were not recognized as international boundaries but as cease-fire lines only. The Israeli leadership saw the territorial problems and the problem of refugees which the Arab states put forward as part of a grand strategy to destroy the Israeli state.[6]

Nevertheless, the political and military leadership did not foresee war with the Arab states in the near future. Their true concern was the fragile situation along the borders. Problems of infiltration, theft and, more than once, murder, reduced morale and damaged national security.[7]

After the War, hundreds of thousands of Palestinian refugees lived in temporary camps situated along the borders of the state and in Arab countries, waiting for the opportunity to return to their homes. Arab states, with the exception of Jordan, placed the onus of responsibility for the refugee problem on Israel, and refused to work for a permanent solution to the refugee crisis in their own territory.

The Israeli position with regard to the refugee issue was in effect that of 'an exchange of populations'. The refugee problem for both sides would be solved through their integration into the countries to which they had moved. The Israeli leadership held up the example of the solution to the refugee problem in the wake of World War II, when more than a million refugees were integrated into the countries where they were situated at the end of the conflict and began a new life with the assistance of the host countries and the United Nations.

To fill in and close, even partly, the newly drawn-up cease-fire lines, to seal them against border intrusions, was a primary and vital component in the dispersal of settlements during the first years. The settlement policy was designed not only to solve the housing problem of the new immigrants but even more to respond to two worrisome facts reflected by the settlement map. The first concern was that only 10 percent of Israel's land was cultivated by Israeli farmers. The second concern was that most of the Jewish population was concentrated in the central coastal plain between Gadera and Hadera.

The government proclaimed the following objectives: dispersion of the population; settlement in the frontier areas and in vital locations as defensive belts; and also borders. In addition, there would be an effort to create an agricultural infrastructure to supply the basic food needs of the population.

THE CONCEPT OF TERRITORIAL DEFENCE

The security concept, which for many years stood behind the settlement effort, was called 'territorial defence'. This term was used to characterize the military conception for securing borders and settlements. The system relied principally upon the residents of the frontier settlements. The security establishment provided military training and equipment for local defence needs and linked the individual locations to IDF forces in the area. The territorial defence system of the IDF served as an additional instrument in the war against enemy infiltration, in addition to its strategic objective— a defensive shield and initial trip-wire, a territorial warning system against enemy forces as well as a cover in the absence of strategic depth.

The integration of 'territorial defence' in the war against infiltrators during the summer of 1949 was an attempt to integrate all the forces involved in the struggle against incursions: the IDF, the police forces, settlement agencies, and the settlers themselves. In the following years, settlers would continue to participate in many operations aimed at curbing, and preventing, border infiltrators.

Increasing infiltration activities in the early 1950s, however, placed the settlers in dire straits. This led to a decision to expand the activities of the territorial defence network within the framework of the war being waged against border incursions.[8] The decision to involve new immigrant settlers in guard duty activities somewhat improved counter-infiltration efforts. The settlers underwent basic training in the use of firearms and took part in guard duty, which in turn raised the self-confidence of the population.

Nevertheless, the process of organizing and training settlement residents and preparing them for military missions in the war against infiltration was slow and complicated. Only after 1954 was significant progress made in this area.[9] The public institutions had exaggerated expectations of the collective settlements' abilities to cope with infiltrators and other security problems.

The establishment of immigrant moshavim (agricultural communities) as a security belt and as part of the security conception was of course a necessity at the time. Nevertheless, the socio-economic reality and the deteriorating security situation brought about by escalating infiltration and hostile activity often converted the asset into a security burden. In fact, the territorial defence system was neglected by the IDF, particularly toward the end of 1955, when the army was preparing itself for preventive war.[10]

The problem of infiltration became Israel's central security problem in these years. In the first fifteen months after the War of Independence, 134 people were killed and 104 injured by infiltrators. Driving on the roads was dangerous, especially at night. Driving to Beersheba after dark was avoided and cars could only travel to Eilat in coordinated convoys under the protection of the IDF.

The battle over the frontier was in fact a struggle over the state's borders. The fear was that the unstable and temporary cease-fire lines would be annulled or changed in the face of local circumstances and international pressure. Israel's leadership widely believed that the facts on the ground would in the end determine the state's borders. Any compromise or neglect of the boundary line would bring about a situation of a pregnable border, leading to the return of the refugees and the renewed settlement of Arab villages abandoned during the War.

When the data on terrorist and sabotage activities provided by the defence establishment for these years is examined, it presents a gloomy picture, not only because of the activities connected to infiltration, theft and robbery but also because of the security threat to the life of the settlers. The constant threat faced by frontier residents did not allow them to organize their lives normally and certainly severely impeded the possibility, for tens of thousands of new immigrants sent to the frontier settlements, of integrating their families into the young state.[11]

ABANDONMENT OF THE FRONTIER SETTLEMENTS—THE LOSS OF SECURITY

A 1953 report on Arab infiltration into Israel stated that the impact of these incursions was identical to those of irregular fighting. It was stressed that among the immigrant settlements the incursions had brought about a war atmosphere and desertion. It had also caused heavy damage to the country's economy and imposed the heaviest burden on the agricultural settlements in Israel.[12]

Infiltration activities not only caused loss of life and limb but also inflicted heavy economic and moral damage. The damage to property and the economic toll were serious, but the worst impact was on the components of national security, on personal safety within the state's borders.

The army and the police had to establish a security system which would routinely safeguard every frontier settlement. The settlements were not able to sustain the security burden by themselves and needed additional support in the form of manpower, funding and military and police forces. Constant infiltration activities instilled fear and even panic in many settlements. The feeling of insecurity spread to settlements situated well within the borders. There were numerous occurrences of people leaving the settlements and sometimes immigrant settlements folded; the abandonment of an entire settlement was a recurrent phenomenon.

The settlements in the Jerusalem corridor also suffered severely from the incursions and security burden, and many inhabitants left. Many other settlements along the state's borders and in areas distant from the centre of the country were harmed by the departure of large numbers of families, sometimes approximating 50 percent of the total families on the settlements.

Frontier settlements, which were to serve as a security belt for the state, became security burdens, hindering rather than expediting, routine security measures.[13] Already in 1949, the war against the infiltration phenomenon led to the formation of a Frontier Corps under the command of General David Shaltiel. The Corps received instructions to undertake defensive and offensive actions against the infiltrators.[14]

The Frontier Corps was a failure even before it came into existence. The dispute between the IDF and the civilian police force over funding and the poor quality of manpower allocated to the Corps led the IDF to disavow any responsibility for the entire affair and the enterprise was discontinued in August 1950. There were additional attempts by the police force to set up a Border Guard during these years, but lack of cooperation from the army again contributed to the project's non-realization in the early 1950s. In July 1953, the Border Guard was established and received formal and practical authorization to safeguard the borders. The Corps was reorganized under the command of Pinchas Koppel.

The IDF continued to have responsibility for safeguarding the borders for many years to come. However, it had not been trained to contend with infiltration and encountered difficulties in preventing incursions despite the numerous ambushes and patrols conducted along the borders. Thus the IDF viewed the Border Guard as the body which would help in this difficult undertaking.

David Ben-Gurion, Israel's first prime minister, was greatly concerned with the adverse influence which infiltration and hostile activity had along the borders. The fear that settlements would be abandoned as a consequence of sabotage actions and murders bothered him very much and he regarded it as a danger to the state's very existence.

In 1952–1953 extensive efforts were invested in strengthening the defence capabilities of the frontier settlements but it became apparent that Israel had not found satisfactory responses to the infiltration activities. In 1955 Ben-Gurion stated: 'We have formulated means for securing routine security measures after much searching and many false starts. We did not have the necessary tools and what we had was not suitable for the job. In addition, the course chosen was not correct.'[15]

It was Moshe Dayan who, as head of Southern Command in the early 1950s, prescribed the stringent military policy to counter infiltration:

> The Arabs ... cross over to reap crops which they have sown in our territory, they, their wives and their children, and we open fire on them ... We repeatedly have them enter minefields and they return minus a hand and foot ... and I don't know any other way to secure our borders. If we allow shepherds and harvesters to cross our borders, then tomorrow the State of Israel will have no borders.[16]

During the struggle against infiltration it was Dayan who, as IDF chief of staff between 1953 and 1956, formulated the policy of retaliation and spearheaded its implementation. The oppressive influence of the security problems on the immigrant settlements was an essential factor in the failure to settle new immigrants in the early 1950s. Yet it was an additional, albeit important, element among all the factors which brought about the failure of the absorption policy.

The personal and social problems of the new immigrant population on the moshavim contributed to the instability and weakness of those very locations which, in addition to all their other problems, could not maintain the added burden of defence. New immigrant moshavim situated along the borders in the frontier regions tended to disintegrate at a greater rate than those moshavim which were removed from such daily threats and anxieties.

IMPLICATIONS FOR THE STRENGTH OF THE IDF

Following the cease-fire agreements of 1949, the IDF underwent changes. Demobilization, the reorganization of the army, and the general deterioration of military spirit impacted on all areas. Many officers left military service and returned home, some exhausted by years of duty far from their family and some for ideological reasons. In his book *Pinkas Sherut* (Service Record), Yitzhak Rabin writes: 'Palmah commanders began to release themselves from army service not only of their own free will but also because they had no desire to cope with the ill wind directed toward them'.[17] Many commanders did not seek an army career and regarded their army service as a one-off mission. They were convinced that the cease-fire agreements would lead to a peace process and thus army service was no longer perceived as a challenge.

Beyond these factors, the army was busy reorganizing general headquarters, as well as developing a basic instructional system for senior commanders. The IDF was not prepared for a period of 'no peace and no war', and preferred to ignore the infiltration problems and to pass them on to the police and other bodies.

At the end of the war, the IDF numbered 100,000 soldiers, many of whom were about to be demobilized and were worried about adjustment to civilian life. Within a year of the war's end, the IDF numbered 35,200 soldiers, including 7,780 in the standing army and 27,424 in compulsory service. The induction of new immigrants into army service during the first years after the war projected the situation of the entire society on the image of the army and its capabilities.

The socio-economic problems and education level of the new recruits became the army's central concern and the source of its weakness. Battle units received youth whose Afro-Asian origins stamped them as 'second-class citizens', immigrants and residents of development towns and distressed areas. Very few native-born served in these units, and most of those who did were commanders.

Intelligence Unit, Department 3, which in its new framework was also responsible for reporting on morale and the mood in the army, is instructive on these issues:

> The tension in activities declined, black market dealings between soldiers and Arabs grew ... an unhealthy atmosphere is taking root within the army which needs to be remedied. On all the fronts, instances of soldiers selling equipment and supplies have multiplied and this must be regarded

as a sign of moral debilitation and a weakening of the guard, and hence of the soldier's financial distress.[18]

Discussions by senior officers were devoted to the problems of immigrant absorption and the ability of the army to cope with the available manpower which constituted the backbone of the IDF—the fighting units. In a discussion with the prime minister and minister of defence, David Ben-Gurion, in April 1950, IDF generals raised doubts and resentment in light of the difficulties which they had to face.[19] The head of Northern Command, Josef Avidar claimed that a change of direction was needed in order to build up the fighting ability of the IDF:

> The situation today is as follows: soldiers who arrived as volunteers from abroad and have now served for a year and a half have not attained, at least part of them have not attained, a level whereby they could be considered soldiers who could carry out those duties which we wish to assign them, that would bear the esprit which is necessary for battle when the occasion demands.[20]

The hard fact according to General Avidar was the inability to select suitable soldiers for even squad courses—the smallest army unit. Essential factors, such as a lack of knowledge of Hebrew, no rudimentary school education, and a difficult family and economic situation constituted the grounds for incompetence and low motivation. The underlying value system of the veteran Israeli society and Zionist ideology were foreign to these soldiers. The new immigrants were concerned with the basic economic problems of their family and by personal and social problems. The central problem, as put forward by the commanders, was the lack of native-born commanders in the ranks of the IDF:

> You will not find among the instructors and commanders native-born Israelis ... If the head of a squad who will lead a platoon tomorrow teaches the soldier Hebrew and shows him the ways of the country—something which we have to force him to do, this will only be carried out under one condition—that the squad leader and the platoon leader will be with their platoon. But what kind of squad or platoon leader is that?[21]

The command backbone of the field unit, of the level of the squad and platoon commander, constituted the weak point in the entire system of the fighting units.

The conscription cohorts for 1950–1952 averaged 6,000 inductees per year. The number of high school graduates per annum was about 600. Out of these 600, a high percentage never served in combat units. Some of them were directed to Nahal service and others to professional units which required a knowledge of Hebrew and a high school education.

The issue of morale and recruiting quality manpower continued to concern senior commanders during these years. The National Security Planning Branch in the Planning Division of General Headquarters conducted studies among IDF units to determine the quality of the armed forces. Among the topics examined were the level of education of the soldiers, their command of Hebrew, their social education (membership in youth movements, etc.), their service in Gadna, and their service in the Hagana.

In addition, the average health condition of every unit, the average age, family status, and job situation of the soldier, as well as family welfare problems, were recorded. Various surveys also checked the country of origin of the soldiers in each unit and the number of years they had been in the country. The place of residence of the soldier had great significance too—soldiers were enumerated in units according to moshavim and kibbutzim, cities and towns and transit camps.

The questionnaires also asked soldiers about the extent of their satisfaction with the unit, the quality of food and sanitation, their opinion of their commanding officers, the degree of concern and attention paid by the commander to his soldiers, their health situation and social welfare. An examination of the manpower data and the education level of the field units for the years 1950–1953 confronted IDF commanders with very difficult human and command problems.

Examination of reports containing the composition of compulsory recruits for the 1930–1933 cohort years uncovers interesting data in the following categories: educational attainment, command of Hebrew, IQ test, physical fitness, and family status.[22] Report data show that 21.1 percent of the compulsory service conscripts were native-born Israelis. An additional 16.8 percent of conscripts had arrived before 1947. The remainder, 62.1 percent, arrived between 1948 and 1951. Among this inductee population, 6.5 percent were illiterate and almost all of these (96 percent) were new immigrants; 72 percent had an elementary school education and 19.8 percent had a high school education; 60 percent of those with a high school education were born in the country or arrived before 1947; 45 percent of the inductees could read and write Hebrew, most of them native-born or immigrants who arrived before 1947; 43 percent could only speak the language and 11.7 percent could not read, write or speak Hebrew. These absorption difficulties found expression in two primary forms:

1. In the group which is being absorbed: through non-identification with cultural values and non-cooperation, aggressive behaviour, poor work efficiency, health, and so forth.
2. In the absorbing group, through the undermining of existing values, a feeling of social insecurity, prejudices against the persons being absorbed, and so forth.[23]

The document points to practical implications of immigrant absorption from Oriental countries on morale and trust in the military ranks. It cites evidence of violent brawls, disrespect, lack of initiative, a negative attitude towards the army, expressions of distrust towards military institutions, and non-participation in many educational and social activities. This damage inflicted upon military idealism and morale, might, according to personnel in the Manpower Branch create a large group which would suffer from deprivation and possess low morale, which could harm the fighting quality of IDF units.

The attempt to deal with these problems also raised simplistic suggestions such as the establishment of special training units comprised of Oriental Jews which would isolate them from other soldiers with the intention of nurturing an ethnically homogenous command staff. These commanders might then constitute a communicative link from the cultural vantage point between 'Western' officers and the deprived Oriental Jews. Suggestions to establish special training and instruction camps were rejected as senior commanders did not see nine months of special training as the solution to the creation of a command staff of Yemenites, for example, who were qualified to lead mixed platoons. The idea appeared to be invalid and contrary to the ideal of the integration of the exiles as expressed by army commanders.

The army establishment sought to comprehend the way of thinking, the desires and feelings of the Oriental Jewish soldiers in order to make their integration process easier. Who would be the best instructors and what would be the most efficient methods of instruction that would make these soldiers part of the culture and internalize the value system that the IDF commanders sought to impart to them? The fear of establishing units along ethnic lines was great and it was even regarded as dangerous should the experiment fail.

In tests for officers native-born candidates had higher test results than others, even though results for their initial psychometric grading produced no country-of-origin distinctions. While 30 percent of native-born candidates obtained a 'good' grade and 14 percent a 'passing grade', only 5.2 percent of Oriental Jewish candidates had 'suitable grades' and 6.4 percent 'passing grades'. Approximately 88 percent of the Oriental candidates did not pass the entrance exams for the officer's course and thus the way was blocked in those years for developing a cadre of officers of African and Asian origin. The process of socialization and integration of Oriental Jews into the military required many more years and extensive changes in the Israeli educational system, as well as in the overall integration into Israeli society of Oriental immigrants. Integration into the IDF command echelons changed from a slow and gradual process in the 1960s to a large-scale measure of success in the 1970s, the results of which can be seen even today.

According to the conception that was the basis of manpower policy, people with little education were sent to the infantry brigades, whereas those with an education were sent to headquarter units. At the headquarter units, there was a demand for personnel with reading and writing abilities in Hebrew and a high school education. As a result of this policy, the dropout rate during basic training in infantry brigades was 35 percent and by the end of the platoon training period the dropout rate had reached about 55 percent. Battalion commanders demanded that unsuitable recruits be dropped not only because they did not train but because they got in the way and in effect did not allow the companies to undertake their training exercises. Commanders' complaints and the inability of units to operate during these years led to the ejection of hundreds of soldiers who in effect did not serve in the armed forces.

The problem which confronted IDF commanders was also faced by Israeli society as a whole and demanded, first and foremost, a long-term investment in Hebrew language education. The IDF was requested to harness itself to civilian areas in order to convey to soldiers, who would be citizens of the state following their demobilization, basic values in the areas of Zionism, geography and the history of the country beyond knowledge of Hebrew, mathematics and basic education. These same soldiers would enter the ranks of reserve units upon demobilization, and the army understood the important contribution which the reserves made to the country's security. Together with the long-term vision, the IDF had to provide an immediate solution on the operational level of the field units. The many problems in the area of instruction and training and in routine security activities required a response.

FAILURES IN THE OPERATIONAL ARENA

As discussed above, the central security problem confronting Israel in the early 1950s was infiltration. The rise in infiltration resulted in increased efforts to organize the settlements for defence and combat against infiltrators. These activities were only partially successful on the kibbutzim and fortified strongholds manned by Nahal, while frontier settlements, which were populated by new immigrants, could not shoulder the security burden. Many settlements were abandoned and the damage was not only material but also a heavy blow to morale.

As such, Israel began to adopt a policy of retaliation. During the 1950s the IDF did not have the means, or the manpower, to seal the borders hermetically in order to guarantee security. Passive defensive measures along the borders required considerable manpower and exhaustive efforts of the regular army observation posts, patrols and ambushes along the borders, with no guarantee that they would succeed in fulfilling their mission. Thus, the object of the policy of retaliation was to stop infiltration activities while trying to impose the responsibility for coping with the phenomenon and combating infiltrators on the Arab states where they were based.

From the early 1950s, IDF units were sent on punitive and revenge missions against the villages located along the borders, but many of these sorties ended in failure and humiliating withdrawal. Units would set out for their objective but not carry out the mission. Infantry units would withdraw at the first volley fired by the Arab village guards. Some units could not find their objective, navigation was faulty, and there was a notable lack of motivation and combat leadership. Increasingly, the IDF learned to live with military failures in the frontier war against the Syrians, Jordanians, and the infiltrators from the Gaza Strip. This led to an undermining of the operational ability of the IDF and concern for Israel's deterrent capability.

During the course of 1953 IDF units failed in almost all the military operations conducted against Palestinian villages in the West Bank. These failures added to the long list of unexecuted missions, as well as falsified reports. In his memoirs, Moshe Dayan wrote:

> Many missions assigned to our forces during this period were not carried out. If they penetrated a village and encountered a guard, or were discovered, this often brought about a withdrawal of the force. Preparations were not sufficient; intelligence information was not updated. Even our elite units, trained for special actions, such as the parachute brigades, exhibited shameful laxity, and many of our actions ended in failure.[24]

On 26 January 1953, a company from the Givati Brigade attacked Palma Village, beside Kalkilya. The attack failed and the company returned without carrying out its mission. On 28–29 January 1953, a reduced battalion from the Givati Brigade set out on an additional attack against the same village. And again they retreated after village guards, soldiers from the Jordanian National Guard, humiliatingly routed the attacking force. That same night, fighters from the parachute brigade attacked the Jordanian village of Rantis, and there, the Jordanian National Guard as well as local villagers succeeded in driving the Israeli force away.

There were numerous other examples of missions that ended in failure due to incompetence, a lack of organization or motivation. Anyone examining the operational reports for 1953 and the beginning of 1954 cannot but be impressed by the number of sorties which were not carried out at all, that failed during the first phases of the attack and did not in any way attain the military objectives set by the command echelon.

The continuous failures of the IDF infantry units to carry out their missions led to the appointment of Colonel Yehuda Wallach, head of the Infantry Branch in the Adjutant General Branch/Training Department as chairman of a committee whose task was to investigate the problem. His report, dated 17 April 1953, cited many points of failure in the assignment of manpower and the quality of the commanders in the infantry units.[25]

The inspection and critique were conducted for all infantry battalions, reconnaissance companies, squad-training schools, Nahal battalions, instructional bases at command and headquarter level. The report pointed out that soldiers from the lowest levels of the IDF were allocated to the infantry units. In addition, within a short time there was 'leakage' from these units of those soldiers who exhibited a higher performance level.

As a result of the drop-out rate 'there is no company which preserves its framework for more than a few months. The "veteran companies" in the battalions are simply what is left of 4–5 companies which have been depleted. The companies remaining are simply "leftovers" in the quantitative *'but also the qualitative sense'* (emphasis in the original).The quality of that manpower replacing 'drop-outs' was poor: As the report explained:

> While good soldiers were squeezed out—soldiers with a record of disciplinary problems on their bases or at different facilities are placed in brigades. Soldiers punished for possession of hashish, criminals and thieves ('graduates of the prison system'), pimps, and the like are from time to time sent as reinforcements—on an individual basis to the battalions.[26]

The report cited health problems which did not permit the stabilization of a training unit for a long period of time. In addition, emphasis was given to the difficult and numerous welfare problems for which no solutions were found and which constituted the main factor for disciplinary problems, absenteeism and desertion. The report also pointed out shortcomings in the brigade's training programmes and the unsuitability of the instruction given. Many platoons in the infantry units were commanded by sergeants due to a lack of officers.[27]

At the end of 1953 and the beginning of 1954 no improvement occurred in infantry battalions. The head of the Infantry Branch continued monitoring and reported on the matter in highly worrying terms.[28] The inspection team concluded that at the operational level there was no confidence in the soldiers in times of danger. 'It is possible to do a lot with these soldiers but it is impossible to rely upon them', the report stated.

Nevertheless, the report points to initial indications of native-born soldiers arriving in infantry units. At the end of 1953, these regular units were made up of about 20 percent native-born Israelis. Or as the author of the report put it: 'It is likely that IDF combat units will cease to be exclusively composed of "blacks"'.

The matter of mastering the Hebrew language was still a difficulty. Welfare problems continued to be the central cause of the lack of motivation and functioning of the infantry units, while absenteeism was the principal disciplinary problem. About 80 percent of disciplinary problems pertained to absenteeism, the reasons for which resided in the soldiers' welfare background.

'In private conversations and through observation of privates I received the impression that the characteristic traits of the vast majority were: 1. Apathy, 2. Lack of ideas, 3. An extreme tendency to hold personal grudges and to satisfy personal needs.' The report mentions problems with the command staff as a central cause for the ineffectiveness of the units. The low quality of the squad chiefs was the weak link in the chain of command.

> Currently, the squad leader courses do not produce a command stratum with a uniform educational level. ... Today, most of the good soldiers don't want to be squad leaders, and the superior stratum among the new recruits generally seeks out more respectable and easier duties than squad leader. The stratum of sergeants and company sergeant majors in the IDF do not have that standing which would constitute them as 'the backbone of the army'.

The evaluation of the officer class in the IDF, coming at the end of the report, is also negative, and points to fatigue and apathy. It cites a lack of motivation because of unawareness of the objectives and goals. There are signs of anxiety and severe doubts about the combat capability of units under their command. There is criticism of organizational shortcomings and the lack of ethical behaviour and honesty in the army.

As the situation along the borders continued to worsen and the danger of war was in the offing, the quality of the IDF, which was based principally on the infantry, continued to bother the political leadership. Despite rapid improvement in specialist units, like parachutists, the prime minister was sceptical and anxious about the operative capability of the combat units.

After Operation Sabha on the Egyptian border on the evening of 2–3 November 1955, an operation in which the infantry forces of the parachute units, Golani and Nahal overran the positions of Sabha and Wadi Siras, David Ben-Gurion asked to meet with the forces' commanders. At the meeting scheduled on 7 November 1955 in Jerusalem, the prime minister interrogated company commanders who had taken part in the battle about manpower issues and the morale of the combatants. His questions repeatedly focused on the quality of the soldiers, the composition of the combatant population, with an emphasis on the Oriental soldiers and their operative capability.[29] Despite the decisive victory in the Sabha operation, in which the Egyptians lost more than eighty combatants, sustained dozens of wounded and surrendered prisoners of war, in comparison to six Israelis killed and thirty-seven wounded, Ben-Gurion's tough interrogation left the infantry soldiers with a feeling of wariness and uncertainty.

CONCLUSIONS

This article examined two areas—the defence doctrine relating to settlement along borders and the factors which impacted upon the unit commands in the regular army and the operational capability of the IDF during these same years. An accurate analysis of the data of the immigrant Israeli society during these years offers a bleak picture. The majority of immigrants were young, conscripted into the armed forces even before they had settled down in their new country and established themselves socially and economically.

Absorption and integration into the state and society required time and means which the state was not able to provide. Immigrants who were drafted justifiably placed personal and family problems as their highest priority. The army, which was also in a process of evolution, change, and organization after the War of Independence, was preoccupied with numerous other concerns, most notably preparation for 'a second round' of hostilities against Arab armies.

In the same period, a territorial defence system was built whose purpose was to solve the problem of the absence of strategic depth and territorial deterrence against a possible Arab attack. The defence establishment and the IDF sought to achieve this by training new immigrants living on the frontier settlements alongside the kibbutzim and the Nahal fortified strongholds.

The process of organizing the settlements for the war against infiltration was not successful, especially in those immigrant settlements located along the frontier. The failure to get new immigrants to build a 'defensive shield' was a fundamental error and the material, as well as the moral, damage brought about by the abandonment of the frontier settlements not only harmed the security of the entire state but also undermined the balance of deterrence towards infiltrators and their political masters. There was no security or settlement value in sending immigrants to frontier settlements.

With respect to the strengthening and improving of the operational capability of the IDF, there was a harmful impact on the level of the conscripts. The army had no alternative; it had to induct and train these young people and place them in combat units—resulting in the utter failure of many IDF actions against Arab villages along the border.

The senior command, which sought to circumvent the problem of deficiency in operational fitness of the field units, found a solution in the establishment of an elite cadre, Unit 101, under the command of major Ariel Sharon. In effect, the solution offered by the IDF in the establishment of this unit, and afterwards in its amalgamation with the parachutists' unit, allowed for the management of security problems by means of a select group of combatants—residents of kibbutzim and moshavim imbued with conviction, confidence and a high level of operational capability.

The parachutists developed their own doctrines and methods. It was the operational capability of the parachutists that allowed the IDF to carry out its security missions during this period and to begin the required radical overhaul of all the field units.

Many more years were required to absorb immigrants into Israeli society and to bring about the accompanying improvement in army standards. Undoubtedly, as the years passed, there was a gradual improvement in both the command structure and the field units of the IDF. Military service itself constituted a central part of the process of absorption and socialization and was a central factor both for the individual and for the entire society.

NOTES

1. Avner Yaniv, *Politics and Strategy in Israel*, Haifa, 1994; Israel Tal, *National Security: The Few Against the Many*, Tel Aviv, 1996.
2. Dan Horowitz and Moshe Lissak, *From Settlement to State*, Tel Aviv, 1977, p. 293.
3. M. Sicron, *Immigration to Israel, 1948–1953*, Jerusalem. See also M. Sicron, *Mass Immigration: Its Dimensions, Characteristics, and Influence on the Israeli Population Structure in Immigrants and Transit Camps*, Jerusalem, pp. 31–52. For statistics, see Jewish Agency, Department of Immigrant Absorption, 1959.
4. Sicron, *Mass Immigration*, p. 43.
5. Tal, *National Security*, p. 17.
6. David Tal, *Israel's Day-to-Day Security Conception: Its Origin and Development, 1949–1956*, Beersheva, 1998.
7. Benny Morris, *The Birth of the Palestinian Refugee Problem*, Tel Aviv, 1986.
8. Letter from Lieutenant-Colonel Harsina, Operations Branch of the General Staff entitled 'Security Guidelines for Planning Agricultural Settlements and their Location', February 1953.
9. State Archives 22/2393, 10 February 1955. Report from General Headquarters/Intelligence Branch on 'Fortification of Frontier Settlements', Central Zionist Archives (hereafter, CZA) S-15/9786.
10. Tal, *Israel's Day-to-Day Security Conception*, pp. 52–56.
11. Ibid.
12. Morris, *The Birth of the Palestinian Refugee Problem 1947–1948*.
13. Morris, *Israel's Border Wars 1949–1956*, p. 126.
14. Letter of David Shaltiel to the Minister of Defence, September 1949, CZA 150/86.
15. See 'Session of the State Committee', 28 December 1955, Labour Party Archives 26/55.
16. See meeting of the Mapai Secretariat with its Knesset faction, 18 June 1950, Labour Party Archives 1/11/3.
17. Yitzhak Rabin, *Pinkas Sherut*, Tel Aviv, 1979, p. 84.
18. See AZ file 104/51/56, 6 June 1949 and file 169/56/580, June 1949.
19. Education and Morale in the IDF, GHQ Discussion, 6 April 1950.
20. Ibid.
21. Ibid.
22. AZ. file 55/65 312, Composition of Inductees into Compulsory Service, 11 March 1951.
23. AZ. file 702/60 115, Research on the Problem of Military and Social Absorption of Oriental Immigrants, Adjutant General Office/GHQ, 6 March 1952.
24. Moshe Dayan, *Milestones: Autobiography*, Jerusalem, 1976, p. 121.
25. AZ 63/55, file 35, Report on a Visit to Infantry Units, Colonel Yehuda Wallach, 17 April 1953.
26. Ibid.
27. Ibid.
28. AZ, Report of Colonel Wallach, Moral Survey and Operational Capability of Infantry Brigades in the IDF, 1954.
29. AZ, 204/21, file 6031, meeting with company commanders who carried out the Operation at Nitzana, Jerusalem, 11 July 1955.

Under the Threat of Terrorism: A Reassessment of the Factors Influencing the Motivation to Serve in the Israeli Reserves

GABRIEL BEN-DOR and AMI PEDAHZUR

Discussion of the various aspects of relations between the military and society in Israel has been widespread in social and political science research for many years.[1] The changing character of these relations and, in particular, the weakening of the nation's army reserve,[2] has attracted special attention recently.[3]

The developments of the last twenty years have raised a number of questions, among them vital issues at the heart of Israel's national security perceptions. A crucial postulate is that, because of the country's small population, the Israeli military cannot continually maintain its full capacity. Thus, in the case of emergency or war, a small conscript and professional army is expected to defend the front lines and hold back an enemy advance for the time needed (about 48 hours) to deploy the remaining (hundreds of thousands of) reserve soldiers constituting the main force of the military.[4] This concept, which has proven efficient throughout Israel's military conflicts, is now a matter of concern due to the growing number of citizens no longer taking part in reserve service. Therefore, the very essence of Israel's security concept is under investigation here. Does Israel still have a large enough reserve army for the actual defence of its borders in times of emergency? In addition, what are the factors which affect the size of this force?

The outbreak of terror during the Al-Aqsa Intifada since 2000 has forced Israel to issue immediate draft orders for the first time in almost two decades. Although the threat of terror is in itself considered an important contributor in a soldier's motivation, many of the reservists called up experienced such orders for the first time in their military careers. This has enabled the testing of established notions under circumstances which have not existed for two decades. This study looks into the factors which explain motivations among Israeli reservists to report for duty prior to Operation Defensive Shield in April 2002. This military action was a response to the wave of Palestinian suicide terrorism during the preceding months. These findings will be compared to motivational levels and attributes that had been measured two years earlier.[5] This study examines the motivations of Israeli reservists to report for service, and asks whether these motivations have been affected by the recent developments in terror and security.

THE RESERVES IN ISRAEL

The notion of a 'nation-in-arms' is exemplified in Israel by universal conscription for both men and women, with appropriate exemptions (as determined by the minister of defence) accorded to minorities (Arab citizens are exempt altogether from compulsory service) and certain religious sectors of the majority Jewish population (e.g., ultra-Orthodox Jewish men studying full time at religious academies and religious women in general, except for those who elect to perform some type of national service). Universal service has been a matter of faith in the Israeli national ethos, and has been almost totally unquestioned for decades. However, this is now beginning to change.

The Israeli army consists of three organizational structures: an army of conscripts, based on compulsory and almost universal military service for those aged 18–21; the army reserves, mostly males (although female service in the reserves has increased in the last decade), who have completed their compulsory service; and a professional army made up of career soldiers. Reserve soldiers serve in combat, logistic and service units, and actually make up 65 percent of all Israeli Defence Forces (IDF) combat units. Reserve combat units, when called to active service, perform various security assignments in addition to military training and maintenance of combat skills.

From the age of 35, reserve combat soldiers are transferred to logistic units, away from the battlefield. In essence, a Jewish Israeli male who has completed his compulsory military service may remain in the reserves until he is approximately 51 years old, and in total usually devotes five to six years of his life to military service. All types of reserve units are summoned once a year for a period that, on average, lasts 36 days for soldiers and 42 days for officers.[6] During emergency periods, such as a state of war, Israeli reservists may spend several months in service.[7] In these situations, reserve forces are conscripted by emergency governmental orders which dispense with the usual 60-day notice, and are effective immediately. These forces may be fully mobilized within two to three days. Emergency orders are subject to governmental decision and Knesset approval within two weeks of issue. During April 2002, large-scale use of such orders was approved for the first time since the 1982 Lebanon War, although they mostly applied to a limited number of strategic forces.

In recent years, however, the compulsory nature of the Israeli army has begun to break down, resulting in less universality and a growing tendency of some citizens to avoid service. According to Yoram Perry, the IDF has been suffering from a negative balance in the size of its reserve force for a number of years, implying that the number of soldiers dropping out of the reserve army before their official discharge age has increased at a faster rate than the proportion of new soldiers recruited to the conscript (compulsory draft) army. A study conducted by the IDF revealed that, if given a choice, most reserve soldiers would not report for duty. This finding stands in sharp contrast to the findings of a similar study conducted more than 25 years ago, in 1974, showing unwillingness to serve only among 20 percent of reservists. A survey conducted towards the end of the 1990s demonstrated that, out of eleven potential reserve soldiers, only two actually reported for duty.[8]

These changes in the number of reservists actually showing up for service suggest two complementary trends. First, although conscript laws and military regulations remain the same, there is less acceptance of these regulations by the public and little willingness by the state to uphold the laws and regulations by means of punishment.[9] Second, service in the Israeli reserves is consequently dependent to a greater extent on motivational factors more commonly associated with volunteer forces. Studies conducted earlier, primarily in the US, suggest several factors influencing reserve personnel motivation.

A first group of factors relates to the personal characteristics of the individual soldier. It is argued that these determine the individual's tendency to enlist for military service and to carry it out in full. Such an approach would suggest that militaries screen their applicant pool for individual qualities which encourage high retention.[10] It has been determined by Grissmer and Kirby, for example, that lower educational levels and lower aptitude were among the strongest predictors of army reservists leaving before the end of their preliminary training. Studies also found that recruits who were white, older, and female have been found to have higher attrition rates.[11] Studies also demonstrate that, compared to older or married reservists, younger unmarried reservists were less likely to remain in long-term service.[12] However, other findings might suggest that age and marital status have a different effect. Reservists in the US army who were married and mobilized were found to have a much higher propensity to leave the service, mainly due to the unfavourable attitude of the spouse.[13]

Another group of factors influencing motivation is concerned with the various commitments a soldier has which may compete with his or her commitment to the military. These are sometimes referred to as competing commitments. This logic suggests that certain civilian commitments, such as job and family responsibilities, will take precedence over a commitment to reserve service. The potential conflict between the requirements of civilian life and reserve service revolves around difficulties such as work schedules and responsibilities, and competing organizational loyalties. As civilian work is generally a more significant income provider, reservists are likely to put more weight on the potential danger to their jobs than they would on the benefits of reserve service. An important aspect of this approach may also involve other commitments, such as to a spouse or family member. The relatively lengthy period of reserve service makes changes in lifestyles and responsibilities almost inevitable, increasing the potential for a conflict of interest. Research carried out in the US has shown that conflicts with both spouse and with employer were important factors in the decision to discontinue reserve military service.[14]

In Israel, competing commitments have also been highly relevant, especially during periods of extended service due to military hostilities, including not only wars and post-war periods, but even the first Palestinian uprising—the first Intifada (1987–1993). Combat soldiers, including reservists, who are most important in times of emergencies, bear the major burden. Therefore, these reservists are more likely to experience conflict. Non-combat units serve for much shorter periods. The army determines who is called up, how often, and for how long, and these decisions are based on military need rather than on any considerations of fairness. The 1973 Yom Kippur War was quite lengthy by Israeli standards and involved long post-war periods of reserve service.[15] All areas of civilian life: academic studies, the workplace and the family, were acutely affected, leading to feelings of dissatisfaction and discrimination among those who served for longer periods, mostly combat soldiers.[16] Consequently, the most active combat soldiers experienced a sense of lack of consideration by army authorities, which led to a strong decline in motivation.

Social conditions often accentuated in 'patriotism theories' have dominated Israeli research for many years[17] but have also been relevant in the American context. In the context of the US reserves, 'patriotism theories' assume that time devoted to reserve service is a normal benefit, providing positive feedback from an effort which is not financial.[18] In general, Israeli discourse regarding patriotism emphasizes the notion of 'nation-building' and defence. Therefore, the main factor influencing willingness to serve in the reserve army is related to a commitment to the collective.[19] As the perception of the security situation becomes more threatening, the identification with the collective and the individual's willingness to protect it increases accordingly.[20] In addition, a citizen's identification with the core values of the collective will also increase his willingness to serve in combat units.[21] In Israel, as the nation has matured, other considerations have come into play, gradually replacing a motivation to serve based on feelings of commitment to the collective. Ben-Dor has found that Israeli society has become involved in the process of a search for 'normality'. The peace process of the 1990s also affected the gradual elimination of the siege mentality which had previously prevailed. There have been essential changes in the social sphere as well.²² As globalization has evolved, Israel has become part of the Western world and subject to similar social processes. However, in contrast, since the start of the new century, there has been a change in the Israeli security climate following the outbreak of the Al-Aqsa Intifada in September 2000, causing a regression in the normalization process, and the political and social discourse has become increasingly patriotic.

Finally, while many studies list a variety of factors which are external to the military organization, several scholars also stress endogenous factors such as organizational or institutional policies and practices, which may affect the expectations, satisfactions, and motivations of reserve soldiers. These have highly relevant ramifications for both voluntary and compulsory reserve forces. Soldiers' experiences within the reserve unit lead to significant hypotheses. Attrition may be affected by factors such as attachment to the unit, reliance and confidence in officers, and a perception of unit commanders as helpful.²³

In contrast, incentives which might reinforce the reservist's motivation to remain in the forces may include the quality of supervision, and the level of satisfaction with various aspects of the job.²⁴ Civilian literature which deals with the strong connection between job characteristics and job retention may be relevant to such an approach. In the context of the Israeli reserve forces, two factors would appear to be salient: the commitment of the soldier to other members of his unit with whom he may have served for years, and the amount of satisfaction he feels regarding his treatment by army authorities.²⁵ Research indicates that a significant factor in maintaining a high level of motivation when called up to the reserves is whether or not the soldier belongs to a stable and organic unit of soldiers who have been serving together for long periods of time. These units tend to develop an 'extended family' sense of comradeship, and the reserve soldier knows that if he evades service, this will have an effect on his close friends.²⁶ Reserve service in organic combat units fosters the perception of 'community experience', entailing a strong feeling of mutual dependence among soldiers in the unit. This is especially true during a war, or during authentic combat activities.

The organizational reshuffling which has taken place in the IDF has had important consequences in terms of motivation to serve. Over the years, the IDF has undergone many changes aimed at increasing its efficiency, as would be expected of a modern army still faced with security challenges. The motto 'small but smart', coined by Chief-of-Staff Dan Shomron in the 1980s, implied that fewer citizens were being called up for military service. In the conflict between the notion of a people's army and the need for organizational efficiency, the IDF chose to implement the latter with a programme designed to reduce the burden of reserve duty.²⁷ Hence, the reduction in reserve duty served to accommodate feelings expressed by reserve soldiers and tried to alleviate the crisis in the motivation to serve.

RESERVE SERVICE MOTIVATION IN THE FACE OF TERROR—OPERATION DEFENSIVE SHIELD, 2003:

In order to assess the various motivations for service, telephone interviews were conducted with 503 Israeli reservists.[28] This representative sample of reservists, and the study questionnaire, duplicated an earlier study of reserve service motivation in Israel.[29] The findings of this study and comparisons with earlier research suggest that crisis situations, exemplified in Israel by the prolonged threat of terrorism and the consequent military operation launched to deter it, actually enhance the motivation of reservists to show up for service.

In our 2002 sample, Israeli reservists displayed more willingness to continue their service in the reserves, showed a higher satisfaction with the service itself, were more willing to devote time and effort, and showed a preference for combat (as opposed to administrative) service. In addition, findings also indicated less inclination to avoid service by contacting liaison or mental health officers (the most common ways of avoiding service), and found that the legal threat of jail service for those refusing to serve influenced their decision to serve to a much lesser extent.

However, an examination of the various factors contributing to, or interfering with, motivation showed that the same factors which seem to influence reservists during peaceful periods are also those most dominant during times of crisis. In fact, not only were the same factors relevant in both studies, but the examination of motivation conducted in March 2002 actually showed that war and crisis further enhance the motivational factors which are active in peacetime.

What are the factors that affect a reserve soldier's motivation in times of crisis (but not solely during these periods)? Most important, it seems, are factors rooted in the military organization itself. This is surprising in itself, as motivation in crisis situations is often attributed to social solidarity and cohesion, sometimes referred to as a 'rally round the flag' effect. However, it seems that it is not this social cohesion which motivates soldiers, but rather inter-organizational cohesion and behaviour. Thus, the most important influence on motivation found was that of communal relations within the soldier's own unit. The closer the unit, and the closer the individual soldier feels to the unit and his/her colleagues and friends in the unit, the more motivated he/she is likely to be.

Also important (although only in fourth place when compared to other factors) is the way a soldier perceives his/her treatment by the military as an organization, and by his/her immediate commanders. Soldiers whose commanders offered an 'open door' and a 'listening ear' are more likely to be motivated than soldiers who feel they are ignored. During peacetime, this should be of no surprise. But the strong connection measured in a crisis situation should underline the importance of inter-organizational relations precisely when motivation is most important—during a war.

Second in importance in its impact on a soldier's motivation are the various commitments which compete with military service. These include responsibility to family and friends, and concerns over livelihood. Unlike the aforementioned factors, strong pressures put upon the soldier by close family or job act as negative motivations—i.e. reduce the soldier's motivation for service. But it is not only direct pressure that matters. Attitudes and preferences conveyed to the soldier year-round are important in determining his/her motivation when called up for service—even when circumstances are extreme. Thus, if soldiers do not receive encouragement from their spouses, or are fearful of losing their livelihood, not only is it unlikely that they will lose these negative motivations in times of crisis, but these negative pressures will actually intensify, putting even more stress on the soldier. In contrast, social atmosphere (exemplified by patriotism and nationalism) seems to play only a minor role in the motivation of Israeli reservists.

CONCLUSIONS

The first aim of this study was to evaluate the levels of motivation of the Israeli reservists to report for duty under the threat of terrorism. A comparison between the current survey and an earlier one indicates that when the security climate worsens, motivation levels increase. However, as indicated by the literature, this finding should be taken with caution. High levels of motivation which are reported immediately following the emergence of a security threat may decline when reservists are engaged in prolonged military activity. The commitment to report for duty cannot be based solely on the high motivation levels in crisis situations. The engagement of the reservist can no longer be taken for granted. Their cooperation must be achieved by hard work on the part of the leaders of the country and the military themselves if they wish to preserve high motivation during both crisis situations and peaceful tours of duty.

The military establishment must work much harder if it wishes to maintain the loyalty of citizens serving in its forces. Evaluating the various explanations for motivation indicated that, as reported in a previous study, once again the most prominent variables found to explain motivation were the soldier's commitment to his unit and friends, and his competing commitments. The lesson to be learned from these findings is not just interesting for theorists, but has substantial implications for policy makers and military commanders. While many of the variables affecting motivation seem rooted in society and thus most resistant to change, it is precisely these variables (the military organization and its contact with the individual soldier) that are possible to improve. By improving the relationship between the individual and organization, the military itself can boost a dominant motivational factor. This seems to be the variable most likely to be changed in a given time and with a given budget.

NOTES

1. Yoram Perry, 'Is Israeli Society a Militarist Society?', *Zmanim*, Vol. 56 (1996), pp. 94–112.
2. Ruth Linn, 'Patterns of Crisis Among Israeli Reserve Soldiers', *The Jewish Journal of Sociology*, Vol. 39, No. 1 and 2 (1997), pp. 24–45.
3. Gabriel Ben-Dor, 'Civil Military Relations in Israel in the Mid 1990s', in Anita Shapira (ed.), *Independence the First 50 Years*, Jerusalem, 1998, pp. 471–486; Moshe Lissak, 'Uniqueness and Normalization in Military Government Relations in Israel', in Raphael Cohen-Almagor (ed.), *Basic Issues in Israeli Democracy*, Tel Aviv, 1999, pp. 227–245; Yoram Perry, 'Civil Military Relations in Israel in a Crisis', *Megamot*, Vol. 39, No. 4 (1999), pp. 375–399; Stuart A. Cohen, 'The Peace Process and its Impact on the Development of a "Slimmer and Smarter" Israel Defense Force', *Israel Affairs*, Vol. 1, No. 4 (1999), pp. 1–21.
4. Ben-Dor, 'Civil Military Relations in Israel in the Mid 1990s', pp. 471–486.
5. Gabriel Ben-Dor, Ami Pedahzur and Badi Hasisi, 'Israel's National Security Doctrine Under Strain: The Crisis of the Reserve Army', *Armed Forces and Society*, Vol. 28, No. 2 (Winter 2002), p. 233.
6. These figures are based on the Israeli army official plan for 2001. Amos Harel, 'Officers will serve 42 days in the reserves', *Ha'Aretz*, 8 February 2001.
7. Sara Helman, 'Militarism and the Construction of the Life-World of Israeli Males', in Edna Lomsky-Feder and Eyal Ben-Ari (eds.), *The Military and Militarism in Israeli Society*, Albany, 1999, p.196.
8. Perry, 'Civil Military Relations in Israel in Crisis', pp. 392–393.
9. Exceptions to this general trend are easily available. One noticeable exception is the case of 'conscientious objection', which is still publicly condemned, and vigorously prosecuted by military courts.
10. Anthony Smith, 'Will and Sacrifice: Images of National Identity', *Millennium*, Vol. 30, No. 3 (2001), pp. 571–582.
11. David W. Grissmer and Sheila Nataraj Kirby, *Changing Patterns of Nonprior Service Attrition in the Army National Guard and Army Reserve*, Santa Monica, 1988.
12. Shelley Perry, James Griffith, and Terry White, 'Retention of Junior Enlisted Soldiers in the All-Volunteer Army Reserve', *Armed Forces & Society 18* (Fall 1991): 111–133.
13. Sheila Nataraj Kirby and Scott Naftel, 'The Impact of Deployment of the Retention of Military Reservists', *Armed Forces & Society 26* (Winter 2000): 259–284.
14. Perry, Griffith and White, 'Retention of Junior Enlisted Soldiers', p. 113.
15. Dan Horowitz and Baruch Kimmerling, 'Some Social Implications of Military Service and the Reserves System in Israel', *European Journal of Sociology*, Vol. 15, No. 2 (1974), pp. 271–272. See also Linn, 'Patterns of Crisis among Israeli Reserve Soldiers', pp. 24–45.
16. Dan Horowitz, 'The Israel Defence Forces: A Civilianized Military in a Partially Militarized Society', in Roman Kolkowitz and Andrzej Korbonski (eds.), *Soldiers Peasants and Bureaucrats*, London, 1982, pp. 77–106. See also Linn, 'Patterns of Crisis among Israeli Reserve Soldiers', pp. 24–45.
17. Ben-Dor, Pedahzur and Hasisi, 'Israel's National Security Doctrine Under Strain', p. 233.
18. Hyder Lakhani and Stephen S. Fugita, 'Reserve Guard Retention: Moonlighting or Patriotism', *Military Psychology 5* (1993): 113–125.
19. Uri Ben-Eliezer, *The Making of Israeli Militarism*, Bloomington, 1998.
20. Dan Horowitz, *Trouble in Utopia: The Overburdened Polity of Israel*, Albany, 1989.
21. Horowitz and Kimmerling, 'Some Social Implications of Military Service and the Reserves System in Israel', pp. 271–272; Ben-Eliezer, *The Making of Israeli Militarism*; Linn, 'Patterns of Crisis among Israeli Reserve Soldiers', pp. 24–45.
22. Ben-Dor, 'Civil Military Relations in Israel in the Mid 1990s', pp. 471–486.
23. Perry, Griffith and White, 'Retention of Junior Enlisted Soldiers', p. 113.
24. Hyder Lakhani, 'Reenlistment Intentions of Citizen Soldiers in the U.S. Army', *Armed Forces & Society 22* (Fall, 1995): 117–130.
25. Ben-Dor, Pedahzur and Hasisi, 'Israel's National Security Doctrine Under Strain', p. 233.
26. Linn, 'Patterns of Crisis among Israeli Reserve Soldiers', pp. 24–45.

27. Perry, 'Civil Military Relations in a Crisis', p. 390; Cohen, '"Slimmer and Smarter" Israel Defense Force', p. 3.
28. In Israel, a sample of 500 respondents represents the country's Jewish population, numbering 4,883,300 in 1998, with a statistical error of 4 percent. In this study, which focused only on Jewish men (2,302,500), the sample error was reduced to less than 3 percent.
29. See Ben Dor, Pedahzur and Hasisi, 'Israel's National Security Doctrine Under Strain' for full details, including a full description of the research variables, composition of scales, reliabilities, and theoretical origin.

The Creation of the Israeli 'Political Bereavement Model'—Security Crises and their Influence on the Public Behaviour of Loss: A Psycho-Political Approach to the Study of History

UDI LEBEL

Since the establishment of the State of Israel in 1948 the matter of bereavement has constituted a central plank in the shaping of relations between civil society and the defence and political establishments. Bereaved parents' forgiving attitude to the establishment, and especially their faith in it, provided psycho-political legitimization of the first order to the policies shaped by the country's prime ministers. After the Yom Kippur War of 1973 bereaved parents, widows and bereaved families began for the first time to speak out against the political leadership which in their eyes bore the responsibility and guilt for their loved ones' deaths. In fact, it was at this time that one finds the beginnings of what can be termed 'bargaining' over the Israeli model of bereavement, involving the 'Hegemonic Bereavement Model' and the 'Political Bereavement Model'. This involved political behaviour on the part of bereaved parents, who became leading political and media figures, demanding reforms, taking steps so as to bring influence to bear on the shaping of policy and even bringing about a change of regime and a removal of leaders from the political stage.

The subject of this article is the fashioning of the Political Bereavement model which emerged after the Yom Kippur War, intensified after the Lebanon War of 1982 and has remained an integral part of Israeli society to this day. Since the Yom Kippur War, bereaved parents, widows and orphans have acquired a dominant public presence by virtue of which they head social movements, influence public opinion and generally express resentment over, and opposition to, consensual public policy.

This article adopts a politico-historical phenomenological methodology, exposing readers to beliefs, feelings and motives that underlie the actions and behaviour of members of the bereaved families who are the subjects of this study. This approach helps to reveal the human phenomenon through the awareness of the acting and experiencing individual.[1] The researcher's aim is to provide a 'complete'[2] and subjective description, from the point of view of the research subject, so as to be exposed to the range of that individual's interpretations regarding reality and the meaning of his, or her, forms of behaviour, which are the result of these interpretations.[3] This is a particularly important challenge for research into the behaviour of those coping with a traumatic crisis that leads to a change in outlooks and gives rise to new political behaviours.[4] In order to apply this methodological approach to the emergence of the Political Bereavement model, great stress has been laid on 'narrative discursive flooding' by providing a platform for statements and behavioural practices on the part of the initiators studied—in the present case, mainly bereaved parents.[5]

CRISES AND ANTI-HEGEMONIC BEHAVIOUR

Culture offers the public a 'toolbox' of customs, motives and strategies for action and reactions to various events, including crises.[6] However, in any given cultural area, it is possible to define a certain level of cultural hegemony, in the form of dominant behaviours and reactions that possess normative weight. Hegemonic behaviour is what happens when a single strategy from an extensive tool box penetrates all strata of society with the encouragement of those that lead it. Even-Zohar's research shows that hegemonic cultural components 'do not occur naturally', but are a political outcome of initiatives adopted by those who are capable of 'deciding what components will be preferred by the entire group'.[7]

He calls the people who have this power 'volunteer cultural initiators', meaning those who act to produce or limit the political behaviours in the cultural repertoire.[8] When hegemonic social behaviour exists, there will be a very low rate of deviation from the various actions derived from it. Even if ostensibly this is spontaneous, emotional or even private behaviour (as bereavement is largely perceived in traditional psychological research),[9] ultimately it is 'social fact' in Durkheim's terms: private behaviour which is influenced by social construction. For institutions offer set solutions to set problems,[10] and those who adopt these solutions, ostensibly on their own initiative, are actually responding to those self-same 'cultural initiators' who have in fact dictated to them what they have chosen to adopt. This generates a dominant pattern of behaviour.[11]

Relatively stable dominant patterns of behaviour are present during times of settled culture, at times not affected by crises that threaten tendencies to adopt hegemonic components of the culture in society. But during times of unsettled culture, periods of change and crisis, additional cultural systems that propose responses to people need to find ways of coping and becoming more powerful, as exclusivity to 'the truth' is opened up to competition. At this time, new strategies for action come to the fore and a new opportunity arises for penetration by subversive forms of behaviour. This combination of civil reactions to a social crisis leads to a re-examination of hegemonic ways of behaving, and this applies even more forcefully when it involves a crisis of loss and bereavement.

Two psychological strategies then translate into a cultural–political willingness to deviate from the hegemonic form of behaviour. The first is imparting significance and meaning to painful events.[12] This is a strategy which, in essence, largely involves making this crisis the last of its kind by taking action so as to prevent the recurrence in the future of the conditions that made it possible:[13] conditions whose removal sometimes involves a change in public policy, the removal of leaders from political life or the introduction of significant reforms.[14] Action which is designed to impart significance to loss enables it to be coped with more effectively on the personal level through its interconnection with broad-based social influences.[15] This is a vital resource when it comes to tackling the working through of loss.[16] Another strategy that generally leads to socio-political actions following a crisis is identification of the person who is to blame and is held responsible.

This involves a basic need on the part of the person whose entire world has been devastated. It then becomes possible to project the aggression and the anger on to the person identified as guilty of the offence. This is a functional action that makes it possible for life to go on in respect of multiple personages and institutions, with the exception of the one figure who is 'responsible' for the personal disaster.[17] Beyond this, the intellectual process that designates a specific guilty party avoids a chaotic feeling of distrust which radiates to all those surrounding the person who has experienced the loss, thereby helping to diminish the feeling of lack of control in everyday life.[18] The actions of identifying and designating somebody as blameworthy leads to a situation in which public anger is directed against that person, including the demand that he pay the price for what he has done. The individual who initiates this process is likely to acquire public status as a result of such actions.[19]

In the wake of a crisis, the individual experiences an 'interocular trauma test' as defined by Tufte: in other words, a gap between the system of beliefs in the framework of which they previously tended to adopt hegemonic cultural components and their sudden willingness to reject messages which had previously constituted an invitation to adopt hegemonic behavioural practices[20]—a dissonance that generates the motivation to undertake intense public activities designed to bring about the formulation of alternative dominant behaviours.[21] And thus, through the statement of the crisis, there arise interpretations and behaviours that challenge the 'explicitly formulated status',[22] as Even-Zohar puts it.

Many individuals then come together with an enhanced willingness to make the effort to identify the importance of undertaking a struggle against someone who has been socially designated as the person who bears the blame and the responsibility for the calamity.[23] All of this is expressed in a whole range of public behaviours and active political initiatives. In the wake of crises, individuals who have experienced trauma join together in social movements that express doubt concerning the normative order of the everyday world,[24] undertaking activities that spur some of them to no longer adopt traditional hegemonic behaviours and instead opt for new ones.[25]

THE HEGEMONIC BEREAVEMENT MODEL: NATIONALIZING ISRAELI BEREAVEMENT

The Hegemonic Bereavement model, as this author terms it, has been shaped since the very beginnings of the State of Israel. This involves paths of behaviour and public expression to be adopted by bereaved parents, paths which are dictated and curtailed in order to avoid their reactions to the death of their sons damaging the favoured status of those in charge of the country. A key element in the framework of the Hegemonic Bereavement model is known in Hebrew as 'tsidook hadin', acknowledging the rightness of divine judgment or, in a secular context, the inevitability of fate. In the modern context, this provides legitimization for the politicians' decisions which led to a son being sent to his death. In addition to the official leadership, it was the parents themselves who, in their public expressions, 'gloried' in the fact that the death of their sons in war constituted the pinnacle of the 'new Jewish' experience—something in which pride should be expressed: 'Our sons and daughters who are going off today at the command of the people to lay down their lives ... are not being sacrificed in the [concentration] camps.'[26]

Such statements indicated that they did not feel themselves to be victims and thus, if their sons fell then this was part of the collective-normative effort to build up Israel. This was a decidedly *anti-victim* discourse. The bereaved parents made it clear that they harboured no resentment or bitterness, that their sons fell in full knowledge and agreement, and that they, because of the education and the values that they had instilled in their sons, assumed full responsibility for what had happened to them. The country's leaders, themselves, when addressing the bereaved parents, made it clear to them that they were entrusted with a public role 'in maintaining that spirit [of the sons]'. Consequently, while mourning their son's death, they were at the same time to be imbued with a belief in the rightness of the

THE CREATION OF THE ISRAELI 'POLITICAL BEREAVEMENT MODEL' 79

path taken by their children, and were grateful to have had the opportunity and the honour to make such a momentous contribution to their homeland. As Prime Minister Moshe Sharett put it in the 1950s: 'These people are the bearers of fate and will bear it to the last of their days. May they be granted the strength to bear it not only in grief and sadness ... but in recognition, in recognition of the necessity of the sacrifice and out of regard for the great mission that this sacrifice has placed on all of us.'[27]

Generally, parents adopted this outlook and no anger is to be found in their public statements either on their own behalf or on behalf of their sons. A father who lost both of his sons in war wrote: 'My children's death comes suddenly upon me ... all my life I educated [them] for this, and now I am very greatly blessed by both of them together.'[28]

Moreover, the structured public behaviour of bereavement was one of restraint and de-legitimization of any public demonstration of emotions, let alone pain or anger. The bereaved parents were guided towards being 'living monuments' in their lives, through a display of public behaviour embodying a heroic fortitude. They were required to suppress and conceal their distress, their suffering and their pain.[29] The demand to demonstrate restraint—a 'stiff upper-lip' approach—was explicitly formulated by the leadership in its expectation of the bereaved parents that they not undermine the morale of those who were supposed to follow in the footsteps of their fallen sons, in order to avoid embarrassing incidents in the framework of which public doubts would be expressed by bereaved parents as to the onerous and painful Israeli reality with its many losses sustained on a daily basis.

In this reality, if there were parents who wanted to pursue paths of public action and initiative, they were channelled in the direction of activities involving approaches and institutions in which they acted in the spirit of the Hegemonic Bereavement model. These primarily involved initiatives intended to commemorate and disseminate the memory of those who fell in battle, to circulate normative messages to new recruits to follow in the footsteps of their sons, and to provide support to bereaved families in need. On the whole, these activities were coordinated by the Yad Labanim organization, whose official name is the 'Organization to Commemorate the Heroes who Fell in the War of Independence'.[30] It has acted as a key agent of memory in Israel's culture of bereavement and commemoration, with the blessing and financing of the establishment.[31]

The emphasis on the bereaved parents' activities, statements and experiences in the framework of the Hegemonic Bereavement model came about as an anti-Jewish expression in its cultural sense, part of the Zionist leadership's view of the entire Zionist undertaking, or project, in the modern era. 'I am opposed to Jewish history', proclaims the hero of popular writer Haim Hazaz' story 'The Sermon', asking, 'What does it contain? ... Edicts, libels, persecutions and acts of martyrdom, and yet again edicts, libels, persecutions and acts of martyrdom. And over and over again, and so on ad infinitum.' And so he asserts that 'Zionism begins where Judaism was destroyed, demanding the bringing about of a different people ... Please note: not a new people, not a transformed people, but a different people.'[32]

The Hegemonic Bereavement model was designed to contrast Israeli bereavement (active, defence-related, national) to Jewish bereavement from the days of the Holocaust and the pogroms. The Holocaust experience was not mentioned, nor did it have any place in the private and public books of remembrance; the memory of the Holocaust was commemorated on a separate day of remembrance from the memory of the fallen of the Israel Defence Forces (the IDF) and, as Rosental put it, these events involved 'two different planets'.[33]

THE YOM KIPPUR WAR: A CRISIS IN THE ISRAELI BEREAVEMENT CULTURE

The Yom Kippur War of 1973 was a 'fraction line', to use Carmel's term, in Israeli history.[34] A total of 2,569 soldiers were killed in the war itself, while 7,500 were injured and 301 were taken captive.[35] The war broke out in the middle of a political stalemate and as a result of a grave intelligence fiasco. Israel was taken by surprise and caught unprepared.[36] The war led to a crisis of faith in the political and military leadership, ruined public morale and set in motion a political culture of wariness and criticism of venerated leaders who were suddenly perceived as being responsible for the 'fiasco'. The loss of faith in the country's leadership and the precedent-setting feeling that the death of their sons was not necessary and happened because of something for which the country's leaders were to blame led to a whole range of new forms of behaviour.

For the first time, a link was made between Israeli bereavement and Holocaust bereavement. Since as long ago as World War I thousands had been slaughtered, fallen in battle, captured and tortured, there was no possibility of preventing the return to the most basic existential terrors over the Israeli space. As the chairman of the Yad Labanim organization acknowledged: 'Especially this year, since the Yom Kippur War. A year which marks a climax even in the history of the Jewish people, so well versed in suffering. A climax in the Jewish people's national rhetoric ... For more than six weeks on end, this people held its funerals every single day ... over one hundred funerals a day.'[37] Hadari's research shows that awareness of the Holocaust intensified in the wake of the war, with the political leadership no longer able to provide the feeling that life in a national state can provide any guarantee of being free of the existential terror that haunts the Jewish people.[38]

As shown by later studies, when it came to bereaved parents working through their loss, it was harder for those who lost sons in the Yom Kippur

War than it had been for their counterparts in earlier wars, because after this event it was no longer possible to maintain a belief in the rightness of the path, to cling to the national-patriotic meaning which saw death as a standard, accepted occurrence, and to continue to trust the country's leadership. The heroic aspect, which for years had characterized the circumstances in which sons died and helped to contrast their deaths with the bereavement involved in the Holocaust, was invalidated by the mass, anti-heroic bereavement caused by the war.

The reactions of parents whose sons were killed in the Yom Kippur War also differed from those of their predecessors, and 'the recovery process of bereaved parents from the October War was slower than in earlier wars'.[39]

Previously, bereaved parents and widows had been presented as 'superior citizens', proud of having made the supreme sacrifice of their nearest and dearest for the country and hence deserving of cultural gifts, preferential social status and the regard of the country's leaders, but following the Yom Kippur War things changed. In an interview, a war widow made the following points: 'After the Six Day War, everyone was proud of me ... I'm happy that I wasn't widowed in the Yom Kippur War. It was very different then. There was no pride in the war and I'm sure that the widows sensed this.'[40]

All of this led to a range of new, and precedent-setting, behaviours on the part of bereaved families in the Israeli space, which this paper will now discuss. All of these form part of recognizing the central component in what would become the Political Bereavement model: *recognizing that the sacrifice was not necessary—the absence of the 'justification' motif.*

BEREAVEMENT AND LEGITIMIZING THE EXPRESSION OF EMOTION

Recognition of the non-essential nature of the sacrifice led to a rapid departure from the 'restraint directive' that had been imposed on bereaved parents since the State of Israel came into being. This outlook was attested to by Yael Dayan, the daughter of Defence Minister Moshe Dayan—who symbolized the mythological sabra or native Israeli—when she wrote: 'My father and I were afraid of feelings ... We did not know how to express our emotions, and to show emotion was considered a sign of weakness.'[41] It was this attitude which characterized the behavioural strategies that were imparted to bereaved parents ever since the War of Independence in 1948. Hence during this earlier period bereaved parents and widows alike were directed to adopt a restrained form of behaviour, devoid of any externalizing of feelings of pain, 'keeping their grief',[42] accepting their fate with reverence and deference, willing to make the sacrifice.

This restrained model, which avoids exposing the public to outbursts of great pain, was shattered following the Yom Kippur War. Even in the organ of the official agent that shaped behaviour on the bereavement scene, the *Yad Labanim Journal*, large numbers of parents expressed their desire after the war to break the model's rigid rules: 'I will write my poems with a suppressed tear, choking my throat with grief—my overwhelming lament is etched within me and has no way of getting out—in grief.'[43] It was not just the families of those who had died in the war that began to depart from this undemonstrative, restrained attitude. Unlike the 'veteran' bereaved families who choked back their pain, there was formulated an overt refusal to accept the 'restraint directive'. Under the title of 'Sadness' a bereaved mother wrote that she 'keep[s] up a pretence vis-à-vis the entire world as a strong and heroic mother ... but my heart refuses to listen ... Deep down it is being torn into shreds ... I howl with a burning heart like a wounded animal in the desert, utterly alone and with no help whatsoever in the whole wide world, wasting away because of its very pain until the end of its days'.[44] For the first time, bereaved families began to speak publicly of their pain, of the difficulties of coping with their loss—the price of living in Israel.

The same also happened on the kibbutzim—the bedrock out of which was hewn the socialist culture that imposed the code of restraint on the Israeli space:

> I want to send you all an invitation to cry [Amnon Lapid wrote from Kibbutz Givat Hayim Ichud] the day and the time are irrelevant, but I give you my word that the evening programme will be a rich and varied one: crying. We will cry for hours. I will cry for my dead: Avramaleh, Ilan, Amiti, Dudu, Ozer, Ya'ir and Benny—and you will cry for yours. And together we will cry for the dreams from which we have woken up. For the gods who have disappointed ... The door is open, the invitation stands, from here onwards it is always possible to cry.[45]

Ora Spegental, a widow who lost her husband in the Six Day War of 1967, remembers the pattern of bereavement on Kibbutz Mizra prior to the Yom Kippur War: 'We did not cry, we did not yell, nothing. On Yom Kippur people cried ... Yom Kippur broke through all of this.'[46] Here she is speaking of herself as well, reporting how after the Yom Kippur War she gave her feelings full rein and began 'to lose it'.[47] She remembers very clearly that after the war, 'when we buried the soldiers here this was actually the first time that I burst into tears'. Until the Yom Kippur War, she remembers, 'Do you know what it means to cry in public? You cry in bed. Into your pillow.'[48] After the Yom Kippur War, as she describes it, 'there's no problem now to cry in public'. To her way of thinking, 'that Yom Kippur, that was one of the first times that people cried on the kibbutz'. And since then, her position has evolved in defiance of the previous custom: 'People remained quiet on the kibbutz. You don't show things. This restraint is sickening.'[49]

FROM RESTRAINED FUNERALS TO SITES OF STRIDENT SOCIAL COMMUNICATION

The breakdown of restraint has not only made its way into writing, into public expression or social behaviour, but has also erupted into cemeteries. At both funerals and war commemoration ceremonies held at military cemeteries, it is possible to observe the movement away from the former restraint, the glory and the acceptance of the justification of what had happened. For example, at Beit Hashita, a kibbutz which lost eleven of its members in the war, Israel Television filmed an angry funeral at which the collective fury was quite unmistakable, with members reviling the government and the country's leadership. This was truly a site for expressing feelings and resentment. However, these images were censured and for years were stored in the Israel Television archive. They did, however, represent a typical funeral of the Yom Kippur War period.[50]

The ceremonies marking the anniversary of the war in 1974 also demonstrated a new form of behaviour, one very different from the model of restraint and the willingness to express and accept the justification of what had happened. An example of this took place at the Kiryat Shaul military cemetery where 500 casualties of the Yom Kippur War are buried. Bereaved families interrupted the address by Shlomo Hillel, the interior and police minister, who attended the ceremony on behalf of the government. They expressed their disapproval of the political leadership, which had not been replaced following the fiasco, and were particularly scathing about Moshe Dayan. They demanded that ministers be held accountable for the death of their sons in the war. When the bereaved families left the cemeteries on that first anniversary of the war, rather than going home they went to demonstrate outside Moshe Dayan's home. Convoys of bereaved parents, headlights blazing, made their way from military cemeteries all over the country to the neighbourhood where Dayan lived. One of the parents described this as 'a demonstration to remind Dayan of his responsibility for the fiasco ... and for the death of our sons'. The parents also decided that this demonstration would be institutionalized and would take place annually on the anniversary of the war.[51] This did indeed happen for the first five years after 1974.

Apparently such behaviour resulted in the establishment backtracking from its practice of comforting bereaved families. In 1980, the bereaved families who had lost loved ones in the Yom Kippur War were furious that for a number of years no government representatives or Knesset members had attended the remembrance ceremonies for the war held at the cemeteries. It was widely remarked that the remembrance ceremonies had become orphans.[52]

BEREAVEMENT AS A PROTEST MOVEMENT

In the framework of the Hegemonic Bereavement model, public sites were brought about in space and in time where the bereaved families could be active and present. This is where society met them, looked at them and engaged in dialogue with them. These were the military cemeteries, all of the national memorials, the national memorial days and the state remembrance ceremonies for the different brigades and corps. At these sites the state conducted ceremonies, civilized behaviour and restraint were displayed, and this is how the public encountered the bereaved families.

After the Yom Kippur War, bereaved parents began to break out of these sites, instead making their way to alternative public settings which would become the central sites of action under the Political Bereavement model: civil society scene. The way they behaved there, the frameworks for interpreting their messages and the communication between them and society constituted a revolutionary change relative to society's official encounter with them at the old public sites. On 18 October, a few days after her son Yosef fell in battle, Tikva Sarid from Kibbutz Beit Hashita called for Dayan's resignation, in an article entitled 'Dayan has to go': 'The IDF was not ready and prepared on the day of judgment. The defence minister is responsible for not having made the government aware of the gravity of the situation. [He is] Responsible for the very gravest failures.'[53]

In addition, eleven institutionalized protest movements emerged in the wake of the Yom Kippur War. They asked for action to be taken in order to scrutinize the workings of the government and to remove those responsible for the fiasco from Israel's leadership.[54] As Motti Ashkenazi, one of the founders of these movements wrote, the groups included large numbers of bereaved parents.[55] Through these movements parents vented their great anger towards the country's leadership.

An example of a planned activity which set off major reverberations was the lecture at Bar-Ilan University by Defence Minister Moshe Dayan. He was due to speak on the consequences of the war. A few minutes before his speech, hundreds of bereaved parents burst into the lecture theatre in order to prevent the event from taking place. They rushed gates, repelled security guards and stormed the stage, brandishing placards bearing a message the like of which had never before been seen in Israel: 'You've come to hear a murderer.' This was the first time that such an accusation had been voiced against a defence minister in Israel. Dayan was eventually forced to deliver his address to a limited forum of professors outside the intended lecture hall.[56] This event was, however, just one of many. A precedent-setting gathering of a hundred bereaved families was held in Tel Aviv.

Many others took place throughout the country. All of them sought to make it impossible for the politicians who had been in charge of the country to escape their responsibility. This desire was further strengthened when, as a result of the pressure brought to bear by the protest movements, the government set up a commission of enquiry whose conclusions focused primarily on the military echelons' responsibility for the war rather than on that of their political counterparts. Posters, petitions and advertisements in the name of bereaved parents lamented the fact that 'the Agranat Commission had ignored the responsibility of the political echelons for the fiascos of the Yom Kippur War'.[57]

Another tactic saw bereaved mothers whose sons had fallen in the war trying to prevent Golda Meir from being awarded the Israel Prize for lifetime achievements, on the grounds of her part in the tragedy.[58] 'We were taken aback to hear that the jury intends to grant you the 1975 Israel Prize for your contribution to Israeli society and the State', they wrote to the prime minister in a petition signed by large numbers of bereaved parents.

> The feelings of many bereaved families who lost their loved ones in the Yom Kippur War lead us to implore you not to accept the prize that you are being offered. As the head of the government during the period that led up to the awful fiasco ... you cannot ignore your responsibility ... The time has come for all of those responsible to acknowledge their failures, act modestly, and vanish from the public arena. Very regrettably, these selfsame people act as if nothing had happened to the country. We see the jury's decision to award you the prize as part of a negative phenomenon, an attempt to ignore and to cover up their personal responsibility on the part of those who led the country to the Yom Kippur fiascos. Signed: Bereaved families from the Yom Kippur War.[59]

Bereaved siblings also became active in the protest movements, with the goal of furthering what they called 'ongoing civil scrutiny of government'. They wished to institutionalize openness and transparency in the government and the army, and to establish a way of opening up the IDF to public scrutiny.

THE INDIVIDUALIZATION OF BEREAVEMENT

The Political Bereavement model expresses the retreat from a commitment to collective values that had underpinned behavioural possibilities available for years. In the framework of the Hegemonic Bereavement model, the State of Israel had nationalized the bereavement experience. All of its components, from the location and practices of burying casualties to the generating of strategies for commemorating them, were handled on the state level. The Yom Kippur War substantiated Grand's predictions about those who experience trauma. Grand argues that trauma leads the affected person to act as an individual rather than as part of a social mechanism.[60] Such individuals develop a fragile identity,[61] lose their faith in others, and adopt behaviours that are not endorsed by leaders or social institutions.[62]

After the war, a family applied for permission to write something else on their son's tombstone than the standard format. In his rage, a bereaved father ripped up his son's gravestone at the Kiryat Shaul military cemetery and asked to be allowed to replace it with a different one that would give additional details that he wanted on the grave. The father went so far as to petition the High Court of Justice to impart legal validity to his application.[63] This ground-breaking step eventually led to other bereaved families clashing with the establishment over their right to design their sons' gravestones themselves. During the Lebanon War of 1982, such confrontations became more heated, as many bereaved parents refused outright to allow the standard inscription on their sons' graves that they had fallen in the 'Peace for Galilee Operation' (the war's official name). Instead, they insisted that rather than this inscription a form of words should be used indicating that their son fell in the 'Lebanon War'—the name given to the war in its early years by those who opposed it.[64]

Personal elements also began to make an appearance in the Yom Kippur War culture of commemoration and the memorial books. An example of this is to be found in Dahn Ben Amotz' best-seller *A Lovely War*. The text, by a soldier in the reserves who had served in the Southern Command, was sent at his request to Ben Amotz. 'When this letter reaches you, I will no longer be alive', the soldier wrote. Ben Amotz published the manuscript despite the family's opposition. This is a text which is utterly different from anything revealed to the public in the classic 'parchment of fire' (*Gvilei Esh*) memorial books. It is an intensely personal document that describes weaknesses, difficulties, bereavement, death, injuries and shell shock. In addition it vividly brings home to the reader the senselessness of fighting and conveys withering criticism of the state.[65]

BEREAVEMENT IN THE SERVICE OF POLITICS

Since Israel's earliest days as a state, the political leadership has sought out and identified bereaved parents who will function as 'leaders of public opinion' in the public space, publicizing pro-establishment positions, gracing political stages with their presence, and generally acting as legitimizers of political reforms and military operations. In the wake of the Yom Kippur War, bereaved parents seem to have started to act for the first time as anti-hegemonic 'leaders of public opinion' in the Israeli space,[66] taking advantage of their new status in public life in order to further ideological and particularist positions and stances that did not enjoy the endorsement of the political establishment.

The families who lost their loved ones in the Yom Kippur War began to make deliberate use of their status in order to further a variety of political initiatives, and to deprive of any public standing those politicians whom they considered to share governmental responsibility for the calamity.

An example of this is the action of eighty-four bereaved families whose sons had fallen in the Yom Kippur War, who demanded of Prime Minister Yitzhak Rabin and Foreign Minister Yigal Alon that Knesset members Moshe Dayan and Abba Eban no longer be allowed to undertake pro-Israel publicity (*hasbara*) activities in the United States. The parents argued that by allowing these two senior figures in Mapai—the party in power during the war—to undertake these activities, the authorities were going along with 'a blatant attempt to provide a character reference and rehabilitation to a group of people who had been the cause of a calamity suffered by Israel ... tantamount to a cover-up attempt designed to lead to what happened being forgotten so as to return to business as usual, as if nothing had happened'.[67]

Menahem Begin's decision to appoint Moshe Dayan as his foreign minister sparked particularly widespread fury. Great waves of anger emanated from the bereaved families who had thought that after the political revolution of the 1977 elections those responsible for the death of their sons would not make a come-back to political leadership. After Begin's decision the Tel Aviv branch of Yad Labanim House—an institution for state-level activities by bereaved parents—became, for the first time, a political protest site. Parents bereaved in the Yom Kippur War gathered there, displaying posters signed by large numbers of bereaved families in protest against Dayan's appointment. The signatories made the point that they had no potential objectives, but were simply concerned that the government should not include any of the 'fiasco ministers'. At the same time, after Dayan's proposed appointment became known, spontaneous demonstrations by bereaved parents took place opposite his home in Zahala.[68]

Posters went up on the walls of Yad Labanim centres throughout the country saying 'Begin—you've betrayed us, you've chosen the fiasco minister', or 'Dayan—the people are sick and tired of you and you are sick and tired of them, stay at home'. The families also held demonstrations outside Yad Labanim centres and military cemeteries.

Large numbers of bereaved parents participated in a tumultuous demonstration opposite 'Metsudat Ze'ev'—the headquarters of the Likud Party which had won the elections. 'We, the bereaved families, can never forget Dayan's talent for bringing down the Yom Kippur fiasco on the Israeli people. No commission can cover up his responsibility for what happened', proclaimed the chairman of the Tel Aviv branch of the Yad Labanim organization, Yosef Lotberg. After the demonstration, the bereaved families went to Menahem Begin's home.[69] 'We will not allow our children's murderer to be a minister in an Israeli government', the posters screamed. Tempers ran high and the parents refused to disperse before being allowed to meet with the prime minister elect.

Menahem Begin agreed to meet with three of the bereaved parents. Two of them occupied official positions in the bereavement hierarchy: the Tel Aviv Yad Labanim chairman and the executive director of Beit Halohem, the bereaved parents' official rehabilitation institution.[70] As they indicated to the media, 'We made clear to Mr. Begin that we will not go along with Dayan's appointment as a government minister and that we shall continue to oppose his appointment in any way possible',[71] and they began collecting the signatures of all the bereaved families from every war fought by Israel for a petition which stated that 'Dayan is not fit to hold public office... [and his appointment] will cause great suffering to many victims.'[72]

Eventually, following this pattern, bereaved parents continued to make use of their public status in order to express reservations about, or support for, various political initiatives. Until this time, bereaved parents had refrained from taking part in the national political debate. For example, a number of the Yom Kippur War's bereaved parents got together to promote a petition opposing Henry Kissinger's proposals which were supposed to lead to an Israeli withdrawal from Sinai. They presented this policy as lacking in legitimacy: 'We, the undersigned, bereaved parents and family members, hereby express our protest at the capitulation agreement and the unilateral withdrawal being carried out by the Israeli government... The real meaning of this capitulation-cum-withdrawal is that our dear ones sacrificed their lives in vain.'[73]

Similar advertisements by bereaved parents began to appear on the eve of the Camp David peace conference of 1977, this time from the Israeli political left, and specifically with the goal of furthering peace and withdrawal initiatives and to encourage the Begin government to sign a peace agreement with Egypt. A bereaved father whose son fell in the Yom Kippur War asked for bereaved parents to be included in the Begin delegation going to the peace treaty signing in Washington. Begin agreed to the request, and included bereaved parents among those going to the signing of the peace treaty as a way of helping him gain public legitimization for Israel's future withdrawal from Sinai.

THE VICTIMOLOGY OF BEREAVEMENT: MEANINGLESSNESS AND THE ASSIGNMENT OF BLAME FOR BEREAVEMENT

In the framework of the Hegemonic Bereavement model, the Israeli establishment embraced the bereaved parents and compensated them for their willingness to choose from the cultural toolbox those strategies that suit it. In return for this behaviour on their part, the country's leaders heaped praise on their fallen sons and adorned them with heroes' crowns, making them into symbols and sterling examples and explaining that in their deaths they made a contribution to the country's safety and security.

Similarly, the bereaved parents were themselves defined as noble citizens who, by virtue of the education that they gave their sons, helped endow the state with its glorious army.[74] As a result, Hegemonic Bereavement was anti-victimologic in nature. The parents did not feel themselves victims, nor did they seek to apportion blame. The Yom Kippur War changed the relationship. As Rosental wrote, 'it was, and has, remained an event that provides no significance or logic from within itself: no logic to life, and no meaning to the deaths of those who fell'.[75]

The search for meaning is illustrated by the way that the bereaved families became organized after the war. Two weeks after Motti Ashkenazi's one-man demonstration, on 17 February 1974, the protest movement's first mass rally took place outside a government meeting. Among the many placards brandished there by the demonstrators, two children held up a sign saying: 'Daddy was killed—why?'[76] The thought became widespread that this was a 'pointless sacrifice', as one bereaved father defined it: 'weren't the boys who fell stupid to give their lives for no good reason?'[77] Another bereaved father explained to Ephraim Katzir, Israel's president, 'you have to understand the special bitterness that characterizes the feelings of the parents of those who died in the Yom Kippur War ... They have this terrible nagging suspicion that the sacrifice was not inevitable. This suspicion is being blown up to tremendous proportions by all the talk of a fiasco.'[78]

In the framework of this model, the death of a son in the war was perceived as unnecessary and the blame for his death was directed at the country's leaders who had sent him to fight, rather than at the real physical enemies who killed him. On the whole, the defence minister or the prime minister was designated as being responsible for the loss.

The rhetoric which began to be disseminated by bereaved families will be defined by some behavioural scientists as a pathological bereavement: those who refuse to work through their loss completely and return to everyday life are making a point of not putting the crisis behind them, becoming public initiators who undertake intensive activities in order to identify public wrongs and remove failed leaders from office.[79] Leaders who were perceived as being to blame for the catastrophe were responsible for the sacrifices of the bereaved families. As a bereaved brother from the Yom Kippur War explained:

> I swear on this sheet of paper by the blood of my beloved brothers ... and by the blood of all the beloved IDF soldiers lying silent in their fresh graves to convey their blood-curdling cries and the heartbreak of the fathers and mothers who lost their beloved offspring ... I assume this weighty task ... The consequences of October '73 which brought a *terrible disaster* down upon us. To convey this to every single Jewish citizen in his capacity as such in order that this shall be seen and known down through the generations

The brother gave an account of how he laboured to publish a book which would describe the development of the war and would shed light on the responsibility of the politicians who had been in charge of the country.[80]

Along similar lines, dozens of bereaved parents came out with numerous public statements, expressing anger at the attempt by those responsible for the fiasco to return to public and political activities:

> We are absolutely determined to continue protesting at every opportunity and demand that those who caused our sons' deaths be held accountable. Our sons who fell commanded us by their death to enlighten the public in order to prevent them from being misled. Although some of us are sick of hearing about the fiasco, we, the bereaved families, will continue protesting against those who are responsible and those who support them.

They also stated that they would not rest and would continue to fight all attempts at a cover-up. A national convention of bereaved parents was organized.[81]

In this reality, there began what one can call a confrontation over the Israeli model of bereavement. In this clash, veteran bereaved families and their commitment to the Hegemonic Bereavement model were pitted against the newcomers to the bereavement scene, who began to adopt forms of behaviour which differed from the pattern dictated by historical conventions. 'Anyone who was brought up against the background of a century of willingness to make sacrifices for the homeland', avowed Yona Hadari, 'cannot but see himself as a traitor if he tries to disagree with it or protest against it. The terror of being labelled is greater than the power of protesting.'[82] It was in this spirit, then, that prominent public figures, and in particular large numbers of bereaved parents made their way to Jerusalem in order to ask those active in the protest movements to put an end to their actions. Motti Ashkenazi was challenged. 'You are telling the Israeli people that our sons ... died like fools. That their death in battle was uncalled for, pointless and meaningless ... You have no right ... to call them victims of a fiasco. Unwarranted victims of a fiasco. Stop your protest, please', one of the bereaved mothers demanded.[83] Other bereaved parents expressed their resentment at the meaninglessness of their sons' deaths, but chose to lay the blame not on the leadership but on the bereaved parents who defined them as such. In the advertisements that appeared in the newspapers in their name, they addressed the bearers of 'Political Bereavement' and asked them to put an end to their activities, 'if only in order to avoid calling into question the sacrifice of their sons'.[84]

Yemima Avidar-Tchernovitz—a bereaved mother and a popular children's writer of the time—asked the newcomers to put an end to their activities: 'Stop these things that a bereaved mother might interpret as meaning that when her son went off to battle and did not return, he sacrificed his life in vain'.[85] A widow indicated that the new voices were making it difficult for her to cope with the grief and the loss: 'The sky will fall in on me and on my son if they investigate what went wrong and

THE CREATION OF THE ISRAELI 'POLITICAL BEREAVEMENT MODEL' 91

it becomes clear to me that my husband's sacrifice was in vain. I know and believe that my husband fell in a just war.'[86] Shimon Peres, in his role as defence minister, wrote in his ministry's official publications as if the politics of bereavement was lacking in legitimacy. Peres spoke to the community of bereaved parents in the following words:

> That which unites those who fall in their wars must continue to unite those who remain alive. Over and above this, their memory must not be used in any shape or form in internal differences of opinion, in ideological or political arguments ... I categorically say 'no' to the use of the memory of the fallen in political arguments, 'no' in ideological arguments.[87]

'POLITICAL BEREAVEMENT': FROM YOM KIPPUR TO LEBANON

The Political Bereavement model resurfaced all the more forcefully during the Lebanon War of the 1980s, which exacted a death toll of over 650.[88] Whereas in the Yom Kippur War the leadership's shortcomings and failures were highlighted after the war, in the case of the Lebanon War these were exposed while it was still being waged. While IDF soldiers were still engaged in fighting, the war was presented by bereaved parents whose sons had fallen as an unnecessary waste of life, as a war of choice that was exacting a bloody toll for no good reason.

Large numbers of bereaved parents organized media events and became leading political opinion-setters, who garnered intense media coverage when they expressed their opposition to the IDF remaining in Lebanon. As early as the first year of the war, eight organized protest movements came into being, in addition to numerous other spontaneous demonstrations and protests against the war.

A central part in all of these was played by bereaved parents who had lost their sons in the war just weeks, or sometimes days, earlier.[89] As the fighting raged, they published advertisements in the papers and also carried placards giving up-to-date figures of the number of unnecessary deaths, as they put it, caused by the war so far. Such placards were also brandished on a permanent basis opposite the prime minister's residence in Jerusalem.[90] The government was accused of making 'cynical use of our sons' lives',[91] and again, as after the Yom Kippur War, this time public advertisements taken out by bereaved parents accused the defence minister and the prime minister of direct responsibility for their loss. 'Sharon—600 ideal casualties in your ideal war',[92] 'For what did my son die?', and 'Sharon—the murderer of our children'.[93]

Eventually, after a change of government in 1985, the IDF withdrew from Lebanon. Even before then, the defence minister was dismissed in the wake of a commission of enquiry which was also set up as a result of pressure by the protest movements, led by large numbers of bereaved parents. The commission of enquiry was originally set up in order to investigate the IDF's responsibility for the Christian forces' massacre of Palestinians in the Sabra and Shatila refugee camps. This was, however, anecdotal and many considered that this was nothing but a pretext for a response to the ever mounting waves of public protest at the time calling for the defence minister to be removed from office on the grounds of his responsibility for the overall conduct of the war and the losses caused by it.[94]

The Political Bereavement model in the Lebanese context resurfaced at the end of the 1990s when large numbers of bereaved mothers whose sons had fallen in the security zone in southern Lebanon joined together in order to influence defence policy and bring about the IDF's complete withdrawal from Lebanon.[95] In addition to bereaved parents once again taking a central role in the media and social discourse, where they presented their sons' deaths as pointless, they were also listened to by the political leaders.[96] The results of their efforts did not take long to materialize. Slightly more than two years after the 'Four Mothers' movement (named after its four founders) began its institutionalized activities, the three candidates for prime minister favoured in the 1999 elections publicly acknowledged the inevitability of a pull-out from Lebanon. On 25 May 2000, Prime Minister Ehud Barak ordered the IDF to leave Southern Lebanon immediately.

CONCLUSIONS

The impact of the number of casualties exacted by the Yom Kippur War and, in particular, the angry bereaved parents' intense anti-government activities, ultimately led Prime Minister Golda Meir to resign after admitting: 'I am incapable of bearing this burden, I have reached the end of the road.'[97] Begin had the same experience, and in the face of dozens of protest movements led by bereaved parents whose sons had fallen in Lebanon he similarly asserted: 'I can bear no more.'[98]

The bereaved parents, in both cases, were determined to become involved in anti-establishment political activity and become political initiators in the public sphere. That phenomenon comprises a number of in-depth insights.

Bereavement as a Public Parameter

Beginning with the Yom Kippur War, bereavement began to take its place on the public and media agenda. Henceforth, all military operations would be defined as 'justified' or 'effective', according to the number of victims and not according to long-term achievements.

The Defence Scene as a Hegemonic Site

In the framework of the Political Bereavement model, the political elite began to be attacked by bereaved parents, but there remained another 'hegemonic site' which was off limits to criticism—the IDF. Indeed, in the wake of the Yom Kippur and Lebanon Wars, bereaved parents were careful to stress that their anger was directed solely at politicians. This was the case, even if some of their sons died as the result of operational foul-ups: 'Our criticism is not of the IDF, but of those who sent our sons to Lebanon.'[99] It would be another ten years or so until bereaved parents would begin also confronting the defence system itself.[100]

Bereavement's New Bastions of Memory

The Yom Kippur War put an end to the era when the presence of bereaved families was limited and delineated in time and space to the military cemeteries and remembrance days. Bereavement would become a public resource for social activism in an extra-parliamentary framework, a ticket of admission to public life, present in the law courts and television studios.[101]

Constant Bargaining over Patterns of Working Through Loss

It must be emphasized that the Hegemonic Bereavement model was not replaced by its political counterpart. No paradigmatic revolutions, as Kuhn calls it,[102] occurred or coloured or changed the entire culture of the politics of bereavement, instead various individuals and communities continued to follow the Hegemonic Bereavement model, while others adopted the Political Bereavement model.

From Embrace to Confrontation: Reversal of the Establishment's Attitude to Bereaved Families

When the State of Israel came into being, in the framework of the Hegemonic Bereavement model, the establishment turned the bereaved parents into a new aristocracy. This relationship is most clearly reflected by the 1949 proposal by the head of the Adjutant General's Branch to recognize the bravery of the bereaved parents by awarding a bereaved parent's decoration to those whose sons had fallen between 30 November 1947 and 20 July 1949. A family which lost one son would be awarded a bronze decoration; a family which lost two sons would receive a silver decoration, while a family which lost three sons would receive a gold decoration, in addition to a certificate of condolence from the president, signed by the minister of defence.

The idea of the decorations was rejected but the certificate was actually issued.[103] Getting the bereaved parents to spearhead opposition to the establishment changed this relationship somewhat. In August 1998, after the 'Shayetet disaster',[104] Yoram Golan, who lost his son in the incident, wrote a stinging letter to the prime minister, Benjamin Netanyahu, inviting him to 'dance' on his son's grave and criticizing the way that the operation had been conducted, as well as the need for it.

This letter may well have been the last straw as far as official circles in the prime minister's office were concerned. In recent years they had become accustomed to bereaved parents making barbed remarks about them, but accusations that political leaders were dancing on graves of their sons had previously been unheard of. In reply to the father, Uri Elitsur, the director of the prime minister's office, wrote that from this letter: 'I learned something new and difficult: perhaps the time has come for us to have the courage to say to bereaved parents that there are also limits to what they are allowed to do.'[105] Yesterday's aristocracy was beginning to be perceived as overstepping today's acceptable boundaries of comment.

NOTES

1. Carl Rogers, 'The Phenomenological Perspective in Personality Theory', in Larry A. Hjelle and Daniel J. Ziegler, *Personality Theories*, New York, 1992.
2. For a methodology which contributed to cultural studies see C. Geertz, *Interpretation of Cultures*, New York, 1973.
3. On the adoption of this approach in research into bereaved parents, see S. Gefen-Koshilevitch, U. Lebel and N. Ronel, *Anger and Reconciliation: The Political Behaviour of Bereaved Parents—Between Rage and Forgiveness*, Tel Aviv, 2004.
4. R. Tuval-Mashiach and S. Friedman, 'Narrative and Cognitive Coping with Trauma', *Sihot*, Vol. 18, No. 2 (March 2004), p. 147.
5. On the adoption of this methodology for research into the behaviour of bereaved parents, see Gefen-Koshilevitch, Lebel and Ronel, *Anger and Reconciliation*.
6. A. Swidler, 'Culture in Action: Symbols and Strategies', *American Sociological Review*, Vol. 51 (1986), pp. 273–286.
7. I. Even-Zohar, 'Who is Afraid of the Hebrew Culture?', in A. Amir, A. Or and G. Maayan (eds.), *Differently: Essays on Matters of Past, Present and Future*, Jerusalem, 2002, p. 40.
8. Ibid.
9. On the clash of views of bereavement in which the psychological view and the political view are pitted against each other, see U. Lebel, 'Politics of Commemoration', PhD dissertation, University of London, 2003.
10. P.L. Berger and T. Luckman, *The Social Construction of Reality*, Harmondsworth, 1972, p. 87.
11. S. Hall, 'Signification, Representation, Ideology: Althusser and the Post-Structuralist Debate', *Critical Studies in Mass Communication*, Vol. 2, No. 2 (1985), pp. 91–114.
12. People who have experienced trauma view the world as less safe, have lower self-esteem and find less meaning in the world. See R. Janoff-Bolman, *Shattered Assumptions*, New York, 1992.
13. Here the author is following Frankl's logotherapist views. See Viktor Frankl, *Man's Search for Meaning*, New York, 1963.
14. Ibid.
15. Kornhauser found support for this through his findings, which indicate that political initiative only develops among classes who have suffered personally from trauma or a social crisis, such as unemployment, war, bereavement. See P. Wilkinson, *Social Movements*, London, 1971.
16. U. Lebel and N. Ronel, 'Parental Discourse and Activism as a Response to Bereavement of Fallen Sons and Civilian Terrorist Victims', *Journal of Loss and Trauma*, Vol. 11 (2005), pp. 78–109.
17. G. Tamir, 'The Adaptation over Time of Bereaved Parents who have Lost Children in Wars in Israel', in R. Melkinson, S. Robin and A. Wiztum (eds.), *Loss and Bereavement in Israeli Society*, Jerusalem, 1993, pp. 213–230.
18. A. Wallace, 'Revitalization Movements', in B. McLaughlin (ed.), *Studies in Social Movements: A Social Psychological Perspective*, New York, 1969, pp. 30–52.

19. Lebel and Ronel, 'Parental Discourse and Activism as a Response to Bereavement of Fallen Sons and Civilian Terrorist Victims'.
20. R.E. Tufte, *Political Control of the Economy*, Princeton, 1978.
21. A. Wallace, 'Revitalization Movements', in B. McLaughlin (ed.), *Studies in Social Movements: A Social Psychological Perspective*, New York, 1969, pp. 174–177.
22. Even-Zohar, 'Who is Afraid of the Hebrew Culture?', p. 39.
23. R. Janoff-Bolman, *Shattered Assumptions*, New York, 1992.
24. C. Johnson, *Revolutionary Change*, Boston, 1966.
25. P. Berger, *The Social Reality of Religion*, London, 1969, pp. 23–24.
26. 'Those Sacrificed on the Altar', in R. Avinoam (ed.), *Hearts that Talk—Fathers on Their Sons Who Fell*, Tel Aviv, 1951, pp. 10–11.
27. See Prime Minister Moshe Sharett's address to the bereaved families, Yad Labanim Conference, 15 September 1954, Jerusalem.
28. 'A Father's Lament', in Avinoam (ed.), *Hearts that Talk—Fathers about Their Sons Who Fell*, p. 26.
29. It should be borne in mind that this process can actually intensify mourning and the sense of grief, and it may encourage feelings of guilt since this behaviour involves the parent making his son into a sacrifice on the national altar. However, given the cultural climate that has been described, such feelings of guilt and complicity had to be repressed and not given public expression.
30. See correspondence by figures in the Yad Labanim organization with the Ministry of Defence, IDF Archives, 14-540/55.
31. Z. Shiff and E. Haber, *Defence Lexicon*, Tel Aviv, 1976, p. 235.
32. H. Hazaz, *The Sermon and Other Stories*, Jerusalem, 2005.
33. R. Rosental, *Is Bereavement Dead?*, Tel Aviv, 2001, p. 18.
34. A. Carmel, *Political Lexicon*, Tel Aviv, 2001, p. 676.
35. Ibid., p. 676.
36. Including: the Bar-Lev Line; the belief that Egypt would not initiate a war before rearming; that Syria would refrain from war as long as Egypt did not lead it, the belief in Israel's strategic depth following the Six Day War, and the consistent denigration of the Arab world's abilities. See Carmel, *Political Lexicon*, p. 677.
37. A. Yahel, 'From One Convention to Another', *Yad Labanim Organization Journal*, Vol. 2 (September–October 1974), p. 4.
38. Y. Hadari, *The Messiah Rides a Tank*, Ramat Gan, 2002, p. 246.
39. For a report, see N. Friedlander, 'The Recovery Process of the Bereaved Parents from the October War', *Ma'ariv*, 18 July 1974.
40. L. Hazleton, *Man's Rib: Woman in Israeli Society*, Jerusalem, 1978, p. 148.
41. Y. Dayan, *New Face in the Mirror*, Jerusalem, 1959.
42. G. Doron, and U. Lebel, 'No Longer Wrapped Up in Their Grief', *Panim*, Vol. 9 (1999), pp. 39–53.
43. H. Gil-Ad, 'To My Brother', *Yad Labanim Organization Journal*, Vol. 2 (September–October 1974), p. 83.
44. H. Anglo, 'Sorrow', *Yad Labanim Organization Journal*, Vol. 2 (September–October 1974), p. 76.
45. A. Lapid, 'Invitation to Weep', *Shdemot*, Vol. 53 (January 1974), pp. 50–51.
46. B. Zilcha, 'The Day They Learned to Say Kaddish on Mizra', *Ma'ariv*, 8 November 2003.
47. Ibid.
48. Ibid.
49. Ibid.
50. Israel Television Archives, Yom Kippur 1973 file.
51. *Ma'ariv*, 7 October 1973.
52. The same applies to the Peace in the Galilee Operation remembrance ceremonies. It also holds true in part of the first remembrance ceremonies for victims of terrorist attacks, before opposition political bodies hitched a ride on the latter during the unity government period.
53. *Ma'ariv*, 7 November 1973.
54. *Ha'aretz* Supplement, 4 October 1974.
55. M. Ashkenazi, *This Evening at Six a War Will Break Out*, Tel Aviv, 2003, p. 167.
56. *Ma'ariv*, 20 December 1974.

57. Ibid., 27 February 1975.
58. Ibid., 28 March 1975.
59. Advertisement published in *Ma'ariv*, 8 April 1975.
60. S. Grand, *The Reproduction of Evil: A Clinical and Cultural Perspective*, New Jersey, 2000.
61. R.B. Elman and D. Brothers, *The Shattered Self, A Psychoanalytic Study of Trauma*, New Jersey, 1988.
62. D. Brothers, *Falling Backwards: An Exploration of Trust and Self-Experience*, New York, 1995.
63. *Ma'ariv*, 25 March 1975.
64. I. Shamir, *Commemoration and Memory*, Tel Aviv, 1996.
65. D. Ben Amotz, *A Lovely War*, Tel Aviv, 1974, pp. 8–9.
66. U. Lebel, 'The Political Behaviour of Bereavement', MA thesis, Tel Aviv University, 1998.
67. *Ma'ariv*, 7 April 1975.
68. Ibid., 29 May 1977.
69. Ibid., 30 May 1977.
70. Ibid., 30 May 1977.
71. Ibid., 30 May 1977.
72. *Yediot Achronot*, 5 June 1977.
73. *Ma'ariv*, 22 January 1974.
74. Lebel, 'The Political Behaviour of Bereavement'.
75. Rosental, *Is Bereavement Dead?*, Tel Aviv, 2001, p. 19.
76. Ashkenazi, *This Evening at Six A War Will Break Out*, p. 177.
77. *Ma'ariv*, 14 September 1975.
78. M. Shmuel, 'Bereaved Parents: We Don't Feel the Public is Sufficiently Sensitive to Our Situation', *Ma'ariv*, 11 July 1974, p. 15.
79. K. Ginsburg, Y. Giron and Z. Salomon, 'Patterns of Mourning Reactions among Bereaved Parents', *Magamot*, Vol. 41, No. 4 (May 2002), pp. 566–583.
80. Letter by Gavriel Frein, published in Natan Donevitz' column, *Ha'aretz*, 18 December 1974.
81. *Ma'ariv*, 17 July 1975.
82. Hadari, *The Messiah Rides a Tank*, p. 173.
83. Ashkenazi, *This Evening at Six A War Will Break Out*, p. 167.
84. Hadari, *The Messiah Rides a Tank*, p. 173.
85. Ibid., p. 217.
86. Ibid., p. 217.
87. S. Peres, 'The Warrior Jew', in *Brochure for the General Memorial Day for IDF Casualties*, Tel Aviv, 1974, pp. 33–34.
88. On 5 June 1982 there began what started out as the 'Peace for the Galilee Operation', in the framework of which Prime Minister Menahem Begin and Minister of Defence Ariel Sharon ordered the IDF to go into Lebanon and clear out the bases of the terrorists who were shooting rockets into northern Israel. Despite the fact that the operation was defined as a limited one in all matters relating to the area that the IDF was to hold in Lebanon, in practice the army went all the way to the Lebanese capital. Although during the operation's first week there was political consensus in Israel about the need for the operation, as the number of losses rose, so did opposition. See A. Carmel, *It's All Politics—A Lexicon of Israeli Politics*, Tel Aviv, 2001, p. 682.
89. See *Yediot Achronot*, 3 June 1983.
90. See U. Lebel, 'The Writers of the Sons' Wills', in Y. Benziman (ed.), *Jewish Time*, Jerusalem, 2006 (in press).
91. Letter to the editor written by a bereaved mother, published in parallel in *Ha'aretz*, 26 April 1983; *Davar*, 27 April 1983; *Al Hamishmar*, 27 April 1983. The very fact that it was published in a number of competing newspapers testifies to the forum that the papers' editors decided to give this 'voice' of a soldier's mother.
92. Bereaved parents' placards described in *Koteret Rashit*, 10 August 1987.
93. On reconstituting the bereaved parents' calls, see 'Seven Days Supplement', *Yediot Achronot*, 3 April 1992. On the range of media and public behaviour on the part of the bereaved parents who lost sons in the war, see details in the book by a father whose son fell during the battle for Beaufort Castle in Lebanon, Y. Zamir, *Surviving Is Not Enough*, Tel Aviv, 1992.

94. See the book by the former cabinet secretary to the Begin government, A. Naor, *A Government at War*, Tel Aviv, 1988.
95. When the Israeli government under Shimon Peres resolved to bring the war in Lebanon to an end (1985), it was decided that the IDF would maintain a presence in a security zone—a buffer zone between Israel and Lebanon. Eventually, given the presence of the Hizbollah organization in the area, the zone concentrated the overwhelming majority of Israel's military effort, exacting a high casualty level.
96. Whereas during the Lebanon War bereaved parents had an indirect effect, this time, as a result of wide-ranging media activities, bereaved parents had frequent meetings with the defence minister and his deputy, with the president, with eight government ministers and with the representatives of all the parties in parliament. With the help of a large donation from the European Union, they extended their PR activities and became a politically influential body involved in Israeli national politics. For a summary of their influence see *Ma'ariv*, 22 June 2001.
97. *Yediot Achronot*, 11 April 1974.
98. See author interview with the cabinet secretary to the Begin government, Aryeh Naor, January 2006.
99. Bereaved parents speak out in *Al Hamishmar*, 20 May 1983.
100. U. Lebel and G. Doron, 'Penetrating the Shields of Institutional Immunity: The Political Dynamic of Bereavement in Israel', *Mediterranean Politics*, Vol. 9, No. 2 (June 2004), pp. 97–109.
101. On the bereaved parents' concentrated media presence, see S. Gefen, 'Bereavement as narrative and myth', in U. Lebel (ed.), *Defence and Media—A Relationship Dynamic*, Beer Sheba, 2005, pp. 149–163.
102. T. Kuhn, *The Structure of Scientific Revolutions*, 2nd edition, Chicago, 1970.
103. Letter from head of Adjutant General's Branch, Brigadier-General Moshe Zadok, GS/AGB to CGS, 20 August 1949.
104. Incident in which soldiers of the Shayetet, Israel's elite marine commando unit, were waylaid in a Hizbollah ambush in Southern Lebanon. Six of them were killed. This operation could have been cancelled following the identification of numerous shortcomings. The press intimated that the operation's main failures—and this was confirmed by senior army figures—were the discovery of the force that set out on the same operation the previous night, which did not prevent army heads from despatching it on this mission the next day at the same place, and, in addition, the earlier theft of personal computers from the navy intelligence division containing future operational plans, including this mission. It was hinted that because the theft was covered up, no change was made to the force's operational schedule.
105. Details and quotations from the correspondence in Y. Marcus, 'Yes, Mr. Elitsur, They Are Allowed', *Ha'aretz*, 25 August 1998.

Holocaust Survivors in the Israeli Army during the 1948 War: Documents and Memory

HANNA YABLONKA

The recruitment of tens of thousands of Holocaust survivors[1] who arrived in Israel during the War of Independence is an incomparably loaded and sensitive issue in both human and ideological-value terms. At the human level, the fact that survivors—in many cases the last remnants of their families[2]—were drafted and fell in battle is tragic. The public debate over the past twenty years has largely focused on this aspect and includes perplexity over the very need to have these men conscripted and sent to the front so soon after they made *aliya* (immigrated to Israel). Was this an act of indescribable insensitivity on the part of the Yishuv (the pre-independence Jewish community of Palestine) and its leaders?

At the level of ideological values, at that very time many leading figures in the Yishuv were heard to draw a qualitative distinction between European Jewry during World War II and Israeli youth who were being put to the test.

Here it is possible to illustrate something of the problematic nature of the subject by quoting three boldly articulate personalities. The first is Yitzhak Sadeh, the legendary commander of the Palmach, the mobile striking force of the Haganah. In one of his talks with his troops 'around the campfire' in 1947, Sadeh said:

> Some of those arriving [in the country] have abundant assets and ought to be giving *to us*, sharing with us. They are the ghetto fighters, those who fought in the forests, those who did not surrender even when they were in hell. This is heroism of the highest order, pure heroism, and they are bringing this asset with them. We shall learn from them. There's a tradition among the nations: if the flag falls into enemy hands, the battalion disbands even if most of its men remain alive, but if the flag survives, even if it's in the hands of the last man in the battalion, *the battalion exists*. And it is re-established under its flag, with new members. Diaspora Jewry has fallen but the flag survived; the flag that the fighters of the Diaspora have brought us. We shall preserve it. In their

name, with their help, and together with them, we shall ask every Jew in our country to fulfill his obligation.[3]

The second voice is that of Nathan Alterman, in his poem *The Silver Platter*, written shortly after the end of the War of Independence. Over the years, this poem has taken on a special status in the Israeli remembrance culture.[4] It captured, as a motto, an utterance by Chaim Weizmann, the first president of the State of Israel: 'Never is a state served to a nation on a silver platter'. The following lines in the poem address the establishment of Israel:

> [The nation] stands ready for the ceremony, beneath the moon
> To stand, before the dawn, wrapped in joy and awe.
> And then, a young man and young woman step forward
> And slowly, slowly march toward the nation …
> Exhausted to the limit, forgoing rest
> Dripping with the dew of Hebrew youth—
> Silently the two approach and stand, unmoving.
> No sign if they live or have been shot.
> Then the nation, full of tears and with wonder, will ask
> Who are you? And the silent pair
> Then reply: We are the silver platter
> On which the Jewish state was served to you.[5]

The third speaker, a Holocaust survivor named Benjamin Harshav (Hrushovski), penned his remarks some thirty years later. His poem is a bitter protest aimed mainly at David Ben-Gurion, Israel's first prime minister, whom he nicknames Peter the Great and accuses of callously having sent young Holocaust survivors into battle in the War of Independence:

> Peter the Great
> Paved the capital city, [St.] Petersburg
> In the northern marshes
> Atop the bones of peasants.
> David Ben-Gurion
> Paved
> The way to the Burma road, which bypasses
> The way to the way to the capital, Jerusalem
> With the bones of young men from the Holocaust.[6]

This is not a random selection of speakers. Yitzhak Sadeh was talking about a very special group of *olim* (new immigrants) who had reached the country in the late 1940s—ghetto fighters who, in his opinion, were one of the elements that nurtured the myth of Jewish heroism. Alterman asserts that the sacrifice of the young Israeli 'dripping with the dew of Hebrew youth' made the establishment of the state possible. In this context, Alterman's status as the perceived barometer of the public mood is also important.[7] The sociologist Oz Almog considers Alterman the 'poet of the Israeli nation-religion', and adds that, 'In his poems, which were very popular, he made a decisive contribution to the mythologization of the Sabra [the native Israeli]'.[8]

The words of the third speaker, a Holocaust survivor, were written—not by chance—only several decades later, in a different era, by which time Israeli society had become sectorialized, more 'privatized', and incomparably more sober. His poem tells a story of institutional and emotional alienation from the survivors who had been conscripted to fight in the War of Independence, as well as a widespread misunderstanding of the Holocaust and insensitivity to the survivors.

Sadeh, Alterman and Harshav all expressed their own personal, impressionistic truth. However, they also highlighted the complexity of the historical situation of the 1948 War of Independence as reflected after the passing of more than fifty years.

These observations have not lost their validity over the years. Indeed, they have become more relevant. One contributing factor is that the War of Independence was a formative event in Israel's history and its after-effects influence its citizens to this day. This is manifested in many ways, but one of the most striking is the crucial importance with which the defence establishment was publicly regarded, both in consciousness and in terms of material resources. Since the War of Independence, in the midst of which the Israel Defence Forces (IDF) were established, security has taken on a superior status to all other aspects of the Zionist endeavour. The focus of Zionist fulfilment and the formation of the national ethos shifted from rural settlement and the shaping of society to military service.[9] At the emotional and value levels, the War of Independence clarified for the Yishuv and the newly arrived *olim* the historical significance of the establishment of the state. In the aftermath of the war, myths such as heroism, comradeship, sacrifice, and the forging of the collective on the battlefield were internalized. The anthem of that generation was *Shir ha-re'ut* (Song of Comradeship).[10]

This impressive reinforcement of the defence ethos and the army in the Israeli public mind sheds dramatic light on the encounter with the many Holocaust survivors who had been drafted while the IDF was still in its formative stages, and at war. At the time, Holocaust survivors in Israel were a particularly weak group—immigrants, remote from the dominant political centre, who having arrived wounded were highly vulnerable after experiencing a trauma that had shattered their previous lives and left many totally alone. This article attempts to examine their military service during the War of Independence as factors in these immigrants' social and cultural integration.

It is particularly interesting to examine this issue as Holocaust survivors made up half of the Jewish fighting forces in the War of Independence.[11] If this was not enough, it should also be noted that the survivor-*olim* and the recruits from the Yishuv came from the same origins, chiefly Central and Eastern Europe. Consequently, they shared a similar heritage from the 'old country'. The *olim* were not less educated than people in the Yishuv.[12] Moreover, if one bears in mind that an army, particularly at a time of war— *a fortiori* a formative war—is a very powerful integrational mechanism, one might surmise that this would be a narrative of impressive social success. Nevertheless, the picture that emerges is more complex and one finds many signs of detachment, alienation and loneliness, accompanied by desperate attempts to overcome them.

The first part of the article looks into social and cultural aspects of the matter as described in official documentation of the time. The second part examines the reflection of these aspects in the survivors' memoir literature.

Scholars who wish to investigate the IDF as a mechanism of integration for the survivor-recruits will have no trouble finding an abundance of contemporary official sources. Furthermore, recruits from the Yishuv produced copious cultural source material about the experience of military service. The picture is completely and utterly different when it comes to the feelings of Holocaust survivors who had become *olim*. Only decades later did survivors like Harshav begin to confront the experience of having been drafted to fight in the War of Independence. Hence, information concerning survivors' feelings about the army as an apparatus for social integration must be sought mainly in memoirs, despite the shortcomings of this genre as a historical source.

The main weakness of memoirs, of course, is that it is susceptible to the tricks and failings of memory, particularly as the writers age. Moreover, the contexts of society and consciousness in which the literature was written change, and may affect, what is written. Furthermore, it is difficult for readers of this literature to distinguish between what the writers actually knew as the events took place and what they learned about the period in question later. However, a memoir has some advantages, the most obvious being their ability to record the most important events from the standpoint of the writer, those that made the most lasting impression on him or her. Due to this propensity, memoir literature can tell us much about the mood of the time. Likewise, cross-checking among several sources in memoirs may elicit recurrent facts and descriptions that can legitimately be considered reliable sources.

SOCIAL DETACHMENT

Detachment and alienation are not exclusive to survivor-*olim*. Indeed, they are characteristic of immigrants at large. However, the survivors, as immigrants, had one particularly conspicuous distinguishing feature—they had no family, nuclear or extended, in Israel or abroad. This was one of the tragic results of the Holocaust, which had left them scarred and alone. Thus, they experienced a very special kind of total detachment, utter loneliness, accompanied by a desperate need for some kind of personal contact with people in the Yishuv. The poet Nathan Alterman, mentioned above as a barometer of the period, captured the crux of the matter in his poem 'A Guy in the *Gahal*'.[13]

> And we will see him crawl or cringe
> Or queue with a plate
> And we will know: Homeless and friendless [and feeling bad]
> It is cold to fight the war of the generation.
> This country has not yet given him
> Its hand, or a shelter of his own,
> Nor was he given any joy of the joys that were part
> Of our lives.
> No, because it was only *his life*, refugees from the sword
> He received from it on the beach
> But his life too, somewhere in the evening
> He gave back when he fell on its behalf.[14]

Alterman's poem emphasizes two of the most heartbreaking motifs of the conscription of Holocaust survivors: the detachment of the *olim* from the homeland for which they fought and falling in battle so soon after their arrival, after having escaped from the Holocaust alive.

Most accessible contemporary sources of documentation point to a failure in integrating the survivor-*olim* socially but do not suggest that the subject was ignored or swept under the rug. With regard to orders, the Haganah and its successor, the IDF, made preparations for an intake of the survivor-recruits. Notably, however, most of the orders are dated 1949. Therefore, a letter to the intake control officer from the chief intake officer in July 1948 is exceptional. The letter gives the following instruction:

> Arrangements should be made immediately to muster the intake police and explain to them the special attitude to new olim who have come from the Nazi inferno after having spent long years in the quarantine camps. They should know that they have to treat them courteously, be pleasant toward them, *and make them feel that they are coming home.*[15]

At the official level, attention was focused on three key areas.

1. Family Matters and a Solution to the Problem of Loneliness

Survivor-recruits were given assistance in looking for relatives or acquaintances. This was done through the daily and weekly papers published specially for members of Gahal.[16] An attempt was made to start up a family hospitality project for members of Gahal; this was done by contacting families. The idea of opening hostels was also considered. There was an emphasis on hospitality at festivals, particularly on the night of the Passover seder.[17]

2. Education and Instruction

Attention was paid mainly to the quality of the instructors who would be in contact with the survivor-recruits. 'The platoon commander at such a base has to be an officer with proven combat ability ... exceptional pedagogical skills, and first-class personal qualities'.[18] The need to keep soldiers abreast of events in their own languages and to conduct public information activities was also stressed.[19]

3. Social Activities

Social activities such as field trips and parties were organized for Gahal recruits and finally, in consideration of the poor mental and physical condition of many of the survivor-recruits, it was recommended that a budget be created to send them to resorts.

> The meetings with olim from Cyprus are painful. Their physical and mental frailty is palpable ... We will never be able to feel the pain and everything they went through before they came here and joined the army ... Sending them to a recreation camp after the four days of regular leave would provide some small solution to the problem.[20]

That year, the IDF cultural service issued a booklet titled *How to Welcome Our Brethren*,[21] which, in the main, instructed non-immigrant soldiers about numerous problems that survivor-recruits faced. The *olim* were described with a measure of patronization:

> They are very different from those who arrived in earlier waves of aliya. ... During their years in the camps and the countries of the Holocaust, some of them developed peculiar characteristics that may sometimes be alien to us, *excessive concern* [emphasis in the original] about a morsel of bread ... mistrust of others.

The most important part of the booklet is the analysis of the difficult situation these recruits faced in Israel. The sources of the hardship are objective: the gruelling war, the army organization, the lack of time to arrange adequate housing, the intake camps, and working conditions. Moreover, some *olim* had been inducted directly, without being able to make basic arrangements for life in Israel. 'Army life is tough', the author of the booklet cautioned, 'but it is infinitely tougher when you have no home and no quiet spot away from the front.'

There were also subjective reasons for this:

> We have not taken special pains to ease the conditions ... This refers to the way we encounter the olim in daily life. On the one hand, we examine each of them to see how suitable he is for a position in the army; on the other, we do not have the time and patience to care much about others' woes. Thus, an attitude of indifference and apathy toward members of Gahal has developed.

The essence of the booklet is a confession of the institutional and human failure of the army to absorb the survivor-recruits.

At this stage it is possible to gauge the feelings of the *olim* at that time from the perspective of the establishment only. Importantly, these reports do not speak in moderate tones. A report titled *Problems of Overseas Recruitment* stated that 'since most of the Gahal men do not know Hebrew ... they are unsuited for service postings ... They are concentrated in combat units. To boost their morale, it is essential to eliminate the feeling that they are simply cannon fodder'.[22] Another source—the cultural officer of the Eighth Brigade, who had many survivor-recruits in his ranks—reports:

> The new immigrants, who come mostly from Poland—that's where the main difficulty lies ... There is no sense of the joy of [being in] the Land of Israel, they are unforgiving of the hardships, they are not impressed by the might of the Israeli army. ... The new olim speak Yiddish, have a second-class-citizen complex, and sense that the command echelon and non-immigrant soldiers treat them with disregard ... You can detect a note of disgruntlement.[23]

Even from the perspective of time, the reports about the survivors' feelings speak in a similar vein. Over thirty years would pass before Avraham Adan would write:

> It was my first encounter with the Gahal soldiers. They spoke Yiddish ... I presented them with the plan for the coming week ... Their reaction was surprising: They had been in the country for two weeks and I was the first one who had gathered them together for a talk and gave them a lengthy explanation of what was happening and what we had in mind for them. Until that day, they had not been given a chance to speak and no one had asked about their feelings, their opinions about the training maneuvers, and the attitude toward them. ... They said that the junior commanders who trained them had treated them humiliatingly. The young squad commanders shouted at them and even threw stones at them. Some noted heatedly that the way the commanders treated them reminded them of how the Germans had treated them.[24]

Several problems are raised in these sources—the language problem; the separation of survivor-recruits into special units;[25] the strong sense that the army viewed them in a very instrumental way; and the fact that they were all junior soldiers while the command echelon was filled with Israelis only. But does the memoir literature corroborate these claims?

There is an interesting echo of this sorry situation in the summary of psychological research conducted by the IDF between March 1948 and April 1949.[26] The main finding in the study was a perceptible decline in soldier morale. The reasons cited were a lull in the fighting, a decrease in tension and fervour, and the induction of new *olim*. Duration of residence in the country was a key factor in a soldier's mood. Low morale was found among 29 percent of non-immigrants as against 43 percent of *olim* who had been in the country for less than a year. In other findings, 81 percent of all Gahal soldiers felt that they had not been given a chance to get to know the country; 88 percent claimed they had not been given adequate information about available options in Israel; and 69 percent believed that they had not been given a chance to learn Hebrew.

Most important in regard to integration, when asked if they had acquired friends in the country, 14 percent responded that they had acquired 'many', 52 percent 'a few', 18 percent 'almost none', and 13 percent 'none'. By comparison, 81 percent of the Israel-born respondents reported having 'many friends'. The survivor-soldiers' attitude toward Israel corresponded to these findings. In a survey by the Institute for the Study of Public Opinion among Gahal soldiers, 71 percent of interviewees expressed a negative opinion about Israel and its residents.[27]

The army's psychological studies provide additional indicators of the lack of integration. With a large degree of consensus, the *olim* expressed negative opinions about Israel in this order: *protekzia* (the 'old-boy network'); disinterest in *olim* and negative attitudes toward them ('only a few are willing to make friends with us', 'We get lost in Tel Aviv'); egoism, political-party discord; and neglect of the poorer classes.[28] Finally, perhaps the most blatant indicator of the problematic nature of social integration through army service was the way those wounded in battle felt about their relations with their units. Sixty-three percent of survivor-recruits, as against 55 percent of the Israel-born, expressed dissatisfaction with the level and quality of relations.[29]

Ben-Gurion defined the situation well in his speech at the seventeenth convention of the Teachers' Union: 'Our volunteers in the Jewish units of the British army went out to the survivors of the camps ... Dozens, hundreds went to the camps in Germany, Austria, and Italy ... For some reason, people did not open their hearts when these remnants came to the country.'[30]

By interpreting the official documentation from the time, one may outline the reasons for the failure to integrate the survivor-recruits with young people from the Yishuv into the defence forces. First, the two groups had different and, at times, conflicting expectations of one another.

The survivors, alone and bereft, had expected—albeit idealistically—to find a warm home in Israel. They expected compensation for their suffering, a sense of family, and a warm reception. These hopes were dashed. When they arrived in the midst of a war for survival, they were drafted immediately.

Moreover, young Israelis were used to seeing themselves as the central, dynamic element in the national revival movement;[31] this marginalized the survivor-recruits in the national-revival narrative. Another reason for the social failure in the army was the difference in socialization between a youth from the Yishuv and a survivor. The survivors, accustomed to a daily struggle for survival, reached Israel with rich experience in life, as described by Haim Gury: 'They carried such deep chasms that they may have been unfathomable ... In retrospect, I understand that we were little kids beside them, with their experience of life.' The survivors were also recruited at a slightly older age than the young Israelis. Even so, most command positions went to non-immigrants.[32] This problem was particularly severe for survivors who had held command positions before *aliya* and served as privates in Israel. The army explained this on the grounds that these recruits were professionally unsuited to local conditions, especially in regard to command of the language. Even so, the documentation shows that the survivor-recruits were deeply embittered about this.[33]

The lack of a common language was a serious obstacle indeed. This made things difficult not only at the professional military level but also, and most importantly, in the context of this article, at the interpersonal level. Naturally, one may assume that this was of greater concern to the Gahal recruits, who were seeking a path to the hearts of their brethren in Israel, who carried heavier emotional baggage, and who were looking for relief, than it was for the non-immigrants. In his contemporary book *In the Fields of the Philistines*, Uri Avneri tells the story of Issachar, a refugee who had come to Israel, 'and here, among us, he became closemouthed because he had no command of Hebrew. But when he met Polish and Yiddish speakers, the dam burst and his poor interlocutor would be drowned in a flood of musings, experiences, and any old thing that had accumulated in his fertile mind since the last outpouring'.[34]

Finally, two other factors that encumbered the process of social assimilation deserve mention. The first was the psychological effect of applying the label Gahal (overseas recruitment) to the survivor-recruits. This excused non-immigrants from having to treat them as individuals and allowed them to get by with the most superficial of generalizations. More importantly, it made it easier to accept the stigmas, i.e., the idea of attributing any behavioural deviation to Gahal, at face value.[35] Secondly, the young Israelis, weary of the burden of fighting, did not take the trouble to contemplate others' misfortune or muster the strength to listen.[36] This fatigue undermined the encounter and affected its outcome.

CULTURAL ALIENATION

The detachment of the *olim* and the fact that they remained 'like in the forest there ... alone and foreign', as Abba Kovner described them in his book *Face to Face*,[37] were reflected in many ways. One example is the marginality of the Holocaust in the heroism myth of the War of Independence and the almost total absence of survivor-recruits in the historiography of that conflict—except in recent years—and from creative works about it. Particularly conspicuous is their marginality in the culture of commemoration of the 1948 war, which was the toughest, the most important, and the most formative war that Israel has fought.

The multi-volume *History of the Haganah*, edited by the historian Yehuda Slutzky, makes astoundingly laconic and brief mention of Gahal as a fighting force: 'Members of Gahal brought with them the desperate heroism of the war of the ghettos and the atmosphere of partisan fighting ... They made their mark as brave fighters.'[38] The same applies to the other historiography about the War of Independence in Israel's first four decades.[39] The contribution of survivor-recruits who were not in Gahal but had immigrated between 1945 and 1947 is not mentioned at all. By the time the War of Independence began, they were already considered part of the units to which they had been assigned, even if not all of them were socially assimilated.[40] Thus, from the moment that survivor-recruits were assimilated into a fighting unit, they were a part of it and the glory of victory went to the brigade and its reputation. Since the brigade had long since been considered part of the Yishuv, this again strengthened the credit given to the centrality of soldiers from the Yishuv in the 1948 victory.

The only part of the army identified with the survivor-*olim* was Gahal, which by its very name distinguished it from the other units. The name Gahal—an acronym for the Hebrew *giyyus huts la-arets* (overseas recruitment)—had no meaning in the conceptual sense of heroic values, in contrast to the names of the Yishuv units, such as Samson's Foxes, Negev Beasts, and Palmach (an acronym for 'strike forces'). Only in the 1990s did historiography begin to address itself to the subject of Gahal and its contribution to the War of Independence.[41]

There is no monument to Gahal anywhere in the country. Not until December 1997 did the Philatelic Service issue a commemorative stamp honouring Gahal. These matters are all the more important in light of the tragic fact that as many Holocaust survivors fell in the War of Independence as men from the Yishuv.

Literature and stage plays by the '1948 generation' extol the persona of commanders from the Yishuv—Yoram in Yigal Mosenson's *In the Negev Prairies* and Uri in Moshe Shamir's *He Walked in the Fields*. The survivors were marginalized. In *The Generation of '48*, historian Emmanuel Sivan notes that 80 percent of the memorial booklets for the fallen of 1948 were for Sabras or quasi-Sabras.[42] His explanations for this are simple. Few *olim* were fluent in Hebrew or left manuscripts in Hebrew that could be published at the end of the war as part of what the IDF calls its combat heritage. Many had been recruited shortly after they arrived in the country, before they had time to write anything. Memorial projects are by nature created by relatives who seek to preserve the memory of their loved ones. Few survivor-*olim* had relationships of this type, i.e., they had no one to commemorate them. If all this were not enough, their painful past in the Holocaust was in more ways than one an antithesis, in terms of values, to the myth of heroism that was cultivated in the War of Independence.

The only bearing the Holocaust had in shaping the heroism myth of the 1948 war was in connection with the ghetto uprisings. This statement is backed by much evidence—perhaps most obviously the order to report for a national service census. The announcement contains the following words: 'From Modi'in and Yodfat, from the walls of the Warsaw ghetto, and from the camps we have been cast out; from the decks of the *Hannah Senesh* and the *Exodus* and from the land of the Patriarchs, a single cry can be heard: "Join up for National Service!"'[43] All the historical precedents in the order refer to instances when Jews rebelled against their fate and resisted the enemy, in most cases by force.

The military authorities did not, at the time, understand the Holocaust as a whole as a personal catastrophe—a fact that also made the encounter with the survivors more difficult. A key issue that elucidates this point concerns the matter of drafting only sons, i.e., their parents' only offspring, for service in combat units. The survivor-recruits were a special case as only sons, since many of them were the sole remnants of their families.

Early in 1948, Yisrael Galili, head of the Haganah National Command, introduced a directive to the effect that 'Comrades aged 18–35 who are their parents' only sons will be exempt from the draft'.[44] The issues and difficulties that arose from the Only Sons order were summarized at a meeting of the executive committee for the National Service Census. Several remarks made in the debate follow:

> Dr. Avniel (chair): 'Some people believe that the sons of parents who are not in the country or *who are no longer alive* may also be classified as only sons'.
> Yossef Yizra'eli: 'It turns out that half of those who have to enlist belong in the category of only sons. When the decision about only sons was made, it was intended for only sons of parents in this country. Then, only a few people would have been involved. Now they've started including the last remnant of a family, a son whose brother is serving, etc. All of this means half the army. I therefore propose making a basic amendment, as follows: An only son of parents living in the country who has no sisters'.[45]

Clearly, then, the Holocaust was not perceived at the level of personal catastrophe at the time. In other words, it was not construed as the existential personal experience of an individual and his/her immediate family. Some of the survivors were bitter about this. One of the heroes of the Warsaw ghetto uprising, Simcha Rotem (Kazik), wrote to the Haganah High Command:

> In the light of the High Command's order to exempt only sons ... I wish to call your attention to the Partisans Platoon, whose men are not merely only sons but are also the only members of entire families that were exterminated by the Nazis ... It is a national necessity and obligation to protect these people and keep them alive.[46]

Kazik's letter went unanswered.

This set of facts suggests, ostensibly, that the army and service in it did not serve as instruments in the social integration of the survivor-*olim*, who indisputably made a substantial contribution to the War of Independence. The term 'ostensibly' is used because analysis of the memoirs of survivor-recruits and the patterns that they followed in settling into Israeli society after the war finds a somewhat surprisingly different picture.

THE ARMY AS AN INSTRUMENT OF INTEGRATION AS VIEWED BY SURVIVORS

Survivor memoirs do not always include an 'Israeli' chapter; the authors frequently focus solely on their Holocaust experience. This is the case in the early wave of memoir writing, born from the sense that anyone who survived had a duty to remember those who had perished. During the later wave of memoir writing, chiefly in the 1980s and 1990s, the last sections of various works focused on *aliya* and the authors' accounts of their lives in Israel. This literature was written largely from a sense that time was running out and the ancient need to 'tell thy children' had to be met. Thus, these works also accorded importance to the author's role in the national rebirth. This part of the article is based on twenty-four memoirs of this kind.[47] As a collective characteristic, it should be noted that all but two of the authors are men. All but one of the authors were born in the 1920s and all but one have published their books within the last twenty years (1986–2006). The publishers' names recur again and again.

A significant proportion of the works were published by the Ghetto Fighters' House, largely because of a personal connection with this institute and its staff. Some were published by the Ministry of Defence, frequently due to a connection with the army or with military activity. Many authors published their books by themselves. The surprising thing is the absence of publishing houses that are strongly associated with Holocaust literature, such as Yad Vashem or the Moreshet publishing house at Givat Haviva. One of the reasons for this is that these publishing houses prefer to concentrate on the Holocaust period and give much less attention, if any, to the periods preceding or following it. Another fact worth mentioning is that the memoir is not ordinary literary writing for artistic purposes; instead, as mentioned above, it has a clearly defined goal.

This article probes survivors' memoir literature about their military service for indicators of trends of integration into Israeli society and evidence of a sense of alienation that formed during military service. From the standpoint of methodology, of course, it is problematic to base ones study on memoirs that, for the most part, were written more than forty years after the events. However, the limitations of this literature actually make it advantageous in a way. Since army service constituted the first encounter with the country for many survivors, it was deeply etched into their memories. One may assume with a fair measure of confidence that it is the very experiences of alienation that remained in the survivors' minds for years—and these are the feelings that lie at the core of concern in this article. Memoirs were examined as an indicator of integration on the basis of several parameters: how the survivors viewed their recruitment; officers' and soldiers' attitudes to their past; recreational leave; the language problem; the question of Hebraizing their names; visiting the wounded; and the drafting of last remnants of families. These parameters were selected from those expressed above in the documentary material from the War of Independence period. There will be an attempt to compare the feelings reported by *olim* who made *aliya* in 1945–1947 with the feelings of those who arrived in 1948, or later.

Much significance has been attributed to the fact that the survivor-recruits were all in combat units. Some served in the legendary Palmach or other combat units of the Haganah and the IDF. At any rate, all were tested in battle to a greater or a lesser extent. Military service and, especially, shared combat duty are powerful instruments of integration.

SURVIVOR VIEWS OF THEIR CONSCRIPTION

One cannot find a single memoirist who complained, even in retrospect, about having been enlisted to fight in the War of Independence, even though they knew they might fall in battle and even though they were Holocaust survivors, sometimes the last remnant of their entire family. Some authors considered their induction a natural sequel to their *aliya*. Others viewed it as an exciting and meaningful experience in their new post-Holocaust lives. Chandeli furnishes an example of the first type in the chapter titled 'In the Homeland', in which he states simply, 'From Haifa [the port] we were taken to the Binyamina training camp' (p. 114). Examples of memoirs attributing deep emotional meaning to their induction are more plentiful. Wircberg writes:

> One by one we walked through the door.... We walked over to the table and, with the right hand on the butt of a pistol and a Bible and the left arm raised skywards, we repeated after him the few words spoken in a deep, confident voice: 'I swear allegiance to the Haganah and to the weapon and am ready to sacrifice my life for Eretz Yisrael. I am ready to receive orders.' During the few seconds that I stood at attention ... with my hand on the butt of the pistol, a wave of memories flooded me—moments of great fear, as I stood before the Nazi commanders who thought nothing of my life. They were armed; I was empty-handed at the time.... Therefore, I felt that I was not just swearing allegiance to the Haganah but that I was swearing several additional oaths: an oath to avenge the blood of my murdered parents and my poisoned relatives, an oath to avenge the honour of my downtrodden and humiliated people, an oath to avenge the blood of Jews who forfeited their souls in the crematoria ... and then, for the first time, I felt that I had not been wrong to struggle and stay alive. (p. 158)

Sad expresses a similar theme: 'We were proud to be part of the same entity and to take part in the [Jewish national] rebirth' (p. 78). The last example is from Aviel:

> When he took up his rucksack, he felt for a moment that he had reclaimed the bag he had taken with him on his wanderings ... Coming to his senses, he reflected about the difference between this rucksack and its predecessor. Back then he had left his home, which was going up in flames, never to return, to save his life—to survive. Now he was heading out to keep the fire from his home ... so that he would have somewhere to return to. Back then, not a living soul remained in his blazing home; now he was leaving behind a life that embraced hopes of generations. (p. 293)[48]

The texts paint an unvarying picture of the survivor-recruits' strong motivation to participate in the War of Independence. There are two obvious reasons for this: recognition of the difference between their helplessness during the Holocaust and being armed and facing the enemy in a battle for their new home; and the sense that this fighting would somehow avenge the death of their families because fighting for the homeland would invest their death with meaning and expunge their humiliation.

This positive point of departure in regard to recruitment is overtaken by bitterness regarding social contact with soldiers from the Yishuv. However, the date when the survivors made *aliya* impacted on the extent of his bitterness. Authors who arrived in the country immediately after World War II (between 1945 and 1947), express their disgruntlement somewhat more gently or forgivingly than *olim* who arrived between the end of 1947 and 1949, the years of the War of Independence.

In the indicators that describe the social encounter in memoirs, one may find an overlap between the memoir texts and the official documentation of the time.

The Attitude toward the Olim's Past

Observers of survivor memoirs will be surprised to discover that almost none of the authors adopted a Hebrew surname. Sad, Kleinberger, Kolpenicki, Blaustein, and Wircberg had been the authors' names since childhood. For the survivors changing one's surname was no mere technical matter. It signified disengagement from the memory of one's family, most of which had not survived. It is also very likely that the authors were particularly sensitive to the preservation of memory and for this reason few changed their names. For many survivors, personal remembrance of the Holocaust was a two-sided coin: memorialization of families and also, in the first years of statehood, the experience of a reception in Israel that was sometimes decidedly cold.[49] The memoirs of several survivors describe a profound feeling, which did not diminish with time, of being hurt by the attitude toward their past. Ron notes, 'The thing that aggrieved me and has left a bad taste to this day was our commanders'[50] contemptuous attitude and unfathomable scorn toward "soap" and "human dust" such as us' (p. 123). Blaustein goes further in Shlain's book:

> As we stood to attention and shouldered arms, the squad commander turned to me and said something in Hebrew that I did not understand. The young soldiers around me burst into laughter. While I was still wondering what to do, one of the soldiers standing beside me, a young sabra, erupted scornfully: 'Leave him alone! You can see there's something up with one of the "sheep" that survived'[51] ... I could not sleep all night. Those contemptuous words 'one of the sheep' pierced my heart and pounded in my head without respite. (p. 175)

These two authors are typical of the group of *olim* who arrived in 1948 and were drafted into the IDF. This type of account is rarely found in the writings of those who immigrated before statehood and before the War of Independence, were taken to Zionist youth villages and kibbutzim, and enlisted in the Palmach and the Haganah. There are several reasons for these differences. Many of those who arrived between 1945 and 1947 were young people who had come in organized groups to agricultural settlements and got an opportunity to adopt the outward components of Israeliness forcefully and quickly. They considered it a great achievement to succeed at this. When it was time for them to join the army, they were often recruited along with their own group, usually to the Palmach, where they became 'Palmachniks' for all intents and purposes. Most *olim* who arrived in 1948–1949 were drafted very shortly after their arrival and still retained all their foreignness. Moreover, they were identified not with a prestigious Israeli unit but rather with Gahal, which carried a stigma relative to the Israeli military formations, or to one of the new brigades formed after the Declaration of Independence, such as the Seventh Brigade, whose first battle ended with one of the IDF's most stinging and painful defeats—the battle of Latrun.

This state of affairs, even several decades on, aptly captures the mood among 1948 *olim* as they did their army service, as cited in the part of this article that discusses the attitude of the establishment.

Indicators of Social Integration

It is reasonable to assume that the language problem made life more difficult for recent arrivals than for young people who had already been in the country for at least a year and who were young enough to become fluent more easily. Several memoirists address themselves to this issue. Ron writes:

> Most unfortunately, they could not issue every recruit with a ready-made command of Hebrew and we sorely lacked this piece of equipment. Most people spoke Slavic languages and there were small groups of Hungarian speakers like me, Romanian speakers, and French speakers. When we were put into units, the commanders sometimes spoke a little Yiddish, but in general they spoke nothing but Hebrew. Today, I have the impression that they actually did know our language but refrained from letting it be known in order to set themselves apart from the rabble—us, the new olim—'Holocaust refugees', 'human dust', 'soap' … Throughout my service in the IDF, my friends and I were troubled by the language problem. In our unit, all the privates were olim and only a few spoke Hebrew, and even those who did, spoke it poorly. In contrast, the commanders … were old-timers in the country … Even if they did know other languages, most of the commanders hid the fact. (pp. 123–124)

Sad also describes the difficulties that befell the survivor-recruits in communicating with commanders. 'In the evenings, after showering, members of the platoon would sit in a semicircle with the commander facing them … "Lads", he would say, and his words would be translated, "I know you've had a hard day"' (p. 155). Although Sad, unlike Ron, expresses no bitterness, he does deeply regret the language problem he faced.

The command echelon, a matter mentioned in several historical sources, appears only once in the memoir literature and is described matter-of-factly there. 'Their company, Company B in the revived Sixth Battalion, was manned mostly by immigrant kids from the training farms along with a few Israeli Sabra youth from the Yishuv. The platoon commanders and the higher command were veterans of the Sixth Battalion' (Aviel, p. 297). All the memoirs make it clear that the senior command was held by soldiers from the Yishuv. The official documentation of the time completes the picture and makes it clear to scholars that this issue, like other matters, did not always sit well with the survivor-recruits.[52]

The issue of command also sheds light on the differences between *olim* who arrived between 1944 and 1947 and those who came during, or after, 1948. Some of the former became squad commanders and sergeants, indicating some degree of integration, at least in regard to the Yishuv establishment's trust in these recruits' ability to function. The memoirs clearly show that it was indeed a functional integration in the main.

The indicators discussed thus far make it very clear that, insofar as the memoir literature is concerned, the survivors were strongly motivated to be in the army. What is more, all such *olim* served in combat units and considered their enlistment a great privilege. This was the case, however, at the national symbolic level only. At the social level, the reality was very different and contained a great deal of loneliness.

When one discusses the social integration of Yishuv soldiers and survivor-recruits as depicted in the memoir literature, one should work from the general to the specific—from the survivors' feelings about the collective they have just joined to the feelings of their companions in the unit, their comrades-in-arms, and their fellow Holocaust survivors.

At the broad national level, Sad expresses with amazing precision a feeling that features in all the memoirs:

> We absorbed the atmosphere without knowing it. The events of the days were reflected in our consciousness like a continuum and no longer appeared to be separate events, each existing in its own right.... We were mentally prepared to accept the reality in which we were living without protest as part of the overall experience that we had been undergoing ever since we had disembarked from the *Teti Panama*. (p. 185)[53]

Sad later adds, 'We shared the general pathos and were moved together with everyone'. There is a similar depiction in Schuv about the night of 29 November 1947, when the United Nations voted in favour of partitioning Palestine into two states. 'Anyone who did not see the spontaneous joy has never seen joy in his life. The fact was that this time the "new olim" were "on the inside". We were drawn into the crowd and became an integral part of it. Old-timers kissed olim and Holocaust refugees embraced old-timers. *For one moment* we were one united people' (p. 197). None of these writers deny the sense of the greatness of the occasion and of national cohesion. Naturally, however, they were non-recurrent sensations, dependent upon dramatic circumstances that lacked enduring, meaningful social significance. In response to the question, 'How did you join up with a cohesive fighting squad?' Hella Kleinberger responded, 'That was the secret of those days. We all volunteered for the war and there was one focused bond—the bond of comrades-in-arms ... [Was there] another bond, a social one? I really don't remember that we had the privilege of getting to know them, talking, or sharing joyful occasions' (p. 67). Shermann notes, 'It was in the days before statehood. The atmosphere in the Yishuv was of a small community. Some people were insiders and some were outsiders. I was an outsider, an oleh, alone, with no brother or family, with friends but no spiritual bond; the connection was circumstantial, the friends were friends in need' (p. 94).[54] The use of the concepts 'insider' and 'outsider' is not exceptional; Schub also used it in the above excerpt. The sense of utterly superficial social relations with non-immigrants runs through the memoir literature. It is a narrative of great loneliness and a powerful, frustrated yearning for a sense of belonging. The loneliness is expressed both in the unit and—perhaps even more so—when the survivor-recruits went on leave.

> As *aliya bet* [clandestine immigration] escalated and many former fighters arrived, the partisans' platoon in the armoured corps grew larger. But the strange thing is that, despite our physical integration into life in the country, building it and defending it, as well as the Zionist fervour that burned within us, we did not find the 'right formula' to integrate into Yishuv society. (p. 196)

All the memoirs express this simple idea in different ways. For Freiberg: 'Soldiers in our group who came to visit us on the kibbutz during their short periods of leave told us about their unhappy social life. Despite their wish to integrate into non-immigrant society, despite their military service and the fact they fight together, they are not accepted and quite a few people actually make fun of them' (p. 57). Sherman writes: 'We had no social life beyond our own small group, the four of us. Surrounded by strangers, we had to find our own way' (p. 95). Sad remarks, 'I felt the lack of personal contact with non-immigrants in the Yishuv. Relations were matter-of-fact, formal, dry, and there was no dialogue' (p. 153).

The survivor-recruits' sense of isolation while on leave from the army is heartrending. Brandt writes about it in his memoirs:

> Since I had no family and nowhere to go on Shabbat and festivals, on more than one occasion I replaced comrades on duty so that they could go on leave. ... There were several times when I felt a distressing loneliness. I particularly remember one especially sad Seder night when I stayed on my own in the camp because none of my acquaintances could be bothered to invite me to the Seder ... The army was the only home I had. (pp. 160–161)

The official documentation seems to indicate that the military authorities had become aware of this sense of loneliness and even sought a way to alleviate it.

With one exception—Moshe Ron—none of the memoirists was wounded in the War of Independence. Ron describes another dimension of his loneliness, the one he experienced in the hospital. His solitude was interrupted only by visits from his friend Yossi, a survivor who would later become the well-known artist Yossi Stern. His account of having been wounded and hospitalized makes no mention of any visit by comrades from his unit. His story is definitely consistent with the official account from the time.

Finally, there remains the particularly painful issue of conscription of only sons and last remnants of families. Two memoirs take up the matter. Aviel writes about his *hakhshara* (agricultural training) group, whose members were presented with two choices at the height of the War of Independence: either to volunteer immediately for the Palmach and put plans for settlement on hold or to settle in a border area and thus combine defence and rural settlement. Most decided to enlist immediately in the Palmach. Aviel belonged to the minority. 'My soul was torn in two', he wrote:

> His loved ones rose before his eyes, forsaken.... They remained scattered on foreign soil.... Their silent will still rang in his ears: A survivor should remain in order to describe what was done to us, so that the family's memory not be extirpated under God's heavens. If I come to harm, it will all be obliterated, both the memory and the continuity. I am the only son left, but unlike only sons who leave their parents after they've gone, there will be no one left after me to lament and mourn the loss of an 'only son'. There will be no grieving after I die; the grief will die with me. (p. 291)

Shub addresses himself to the issue in a bittersweet fashion:

> I remember an episode when they passed the law exempting only sons from combat duty and allowing them to serve in the rear. There was someone who, as an only son, asked for the letter of the law to be applied in his case. The response of the High Command was a slap in the face. They said that only the parents of a soldier were entitled to submit the request for a transfer.... Since we had no parents, the law did not apply to us. (p. 198)

From the perspective of time and considering the fact that both of Shub's sons became pilots in the Israel Air Force—the pinnacle of military service in Israel—these words were apparently not intended as an attack on the establishment.

CONCLUSIONS

The power of the emotional experience of establishing the state and participating in the War of Independence swept most of the survivors along with the general passion of 'national revival as an act of revenge'. The official sources and memoir literature, however, clearly show that the army as an integrative setting for the survivors failed. The survivors were excluded from the War of Independence myth of heroism and self-sacrifice.

However, from the standpoint of general integration—cultural, economic and social—the story of the memoirists is primarily a narrative of particularly impressive success. Military service and combat duty in the War of Independence, the most formative of Israel's wars, gave most of the survivor-recruits, who were also very recently-arrived immigrants, a sense of belonging and a love of their new home. They created the environment that gave the immigrants a place in Israel's formative society. This fact is highly significant in Holocaust remembrance in Israel and in inculcating the Holocaust as a component of national identity. These were exceptional developments—things that normally develop among immigrants but slowly, sometimes over an entire generation. The survivors' memoir literature, as opposed to official documents of the time, is graced with a perspective of foreknowledge. It extols the narrative of this great social victory. Despite the authors' unconcealed criticism of the army and the people in it regarding social and cultural integration, most of them considered their military service as an essential first step down a path that quickly led them to the status of ordinary Israelis, shapers of culture and of society itself.

NOTES

1. For the definition of a Holocaust survivor, see Hanna Yablonka, *Survivors of the Holocaust: Israel after the War*, New York, 1999, pp. 1–2. The article refers to them as *olim* and not as immigrants to identify with how they viewed the significance of their coming to Israel.
2. Statistics provided by the Soldiers' Commemoration Division show that 275 IDF soldiers who fell in the War of Independence were the last surviving members of their families.
3. Yitzhak Sadeh, *Around the Campfire*, Tel Aviv, 1989, p. 14 (emphasis original).
4. See, for example, Maoz Azaryahu, *State Cults*, Be'er-Sheva, 1995, p. 125.
5. Nathan Alterman, *The Seventh Column I*, Tel Aviv, 1977, pp. 154–155.
6. The poem appeared under Harshav's *nom de plume*, Gabi Daniel, 'Peter the Great', *Igra 2*, Tel Aviv, 1986, pp. 199–200.
7. Dan Miron, *Four Facets in Contemporary Hebrew Literature*, Jerusalem and Tel Aviv, 1962.
8. Oz Almog, *The Sabra: The Creation of the New Jew*, Berkeley, CA, 2000, pp. 13, 60, 82.
9. For an expanded discussion, see M. Lissak and D. Horowitz, *Origins of the Israeli Polity: Palestine Under the Mandate*, Chicago, 1978.
10. Lyrics by Haim Gury, a War of Independence poet, and composer Sasha Argov. Comradeship is described as 'love sanctified by blood' and as something 'great and burning'.
11. Yablonka, *Survivors of the Holocaust*, pp. 81–83; See also Emmanuel Sivan, *The '48 Generation: Myths, Portrait, and Remembrance*, Tel Aviv, 1991, pp. 73–101.
12. See Yablonka, *Survivors of the Holocaust*, pp. 9–17, for a demographic profile of the survivor-*olim*.
13. Gahal—acronym for *giyyus huts la-arets* (overseas recruitment). Most such recruitment took place in displaced persons camps in Europe and the recruits were mainly Holocaust survivors.

14. Alterman, *The Seventh Column I*, p. 144 (emphasis original).
15. Letter from Chief Intake Officer to Intake Control Officer, 3 July 1948, IDF Archives (hereafter, IDFA), 1042/49/1440 (emphasis added).
16. A collection of news items for immigrant solders, Circular 1/3/4 (undated), Welfare Service, IDFA.
17. Report on Gahal Welfare Activities, 2–9 March 1949, IDFA, 853/51/1453. See also Report on Gahal Welfare Activities, 6–13 April 1949, IDFA, 852/51/1453. Importantly, all of this activity took place in 1949.
18. Appendix to the Standards for a Central Training Base from the Head of the Manpower Division at the General Staff, nd, IDFA, 852/51/1453.
19. Correspondence about foreign-language newspapers to members of Gahal, 1042/49/277.
20. To the General Staff Manpower Division 3 from the Gahal Officer, 10 September 1948, IDF Arch. 852/51/1451.
21. IDFA, 355.34/IDF.
22. *Problems of Overseas Recruitment*, 21 Oct. 1948, IDFA, 1042/49/277.
23. To the Inspection Officer from Haim Ben-Asher, Cultural Officer of the Eighth Brigade, 3 November 1948, IDFA, 292/27.
24. Avraham Adan, *The Ink Flag*, Tel Aviv, 1984, pp. 211–212.
25. This problem did not exist for survivors who were recruited for the Palmach.
26. General Staff, Manpower Division, Psychological Research Unit, IDFA. The sample comprised 2,333 soldiers, 600 of whom were members of Gahal.
27. Institute for the Study of Public Opinion, October 1949, IDFA.
28. Responses to the question 'What is good about the country?' included devotion to homeland, kibbutzim, a sense of homeland, a well-developed sense of nationhood, valiant warriors. Notably, opinions were divided about the positive aspects whereas there was a strong consensus about the negative opinions.
29. Survey conducted in hospitals, July 1949, Institute for Applied Social Research, December 1949, IDFA.
30. David Ben-Gurion, 21 September 1949, files of speeches, Ben-Gurion Archives (hereafter, Ben-Gurion Arch.).
31. Lissak and Horowitz, *Origins of the Israeli Polity*, p. 210. The discussion here also includes the notion of *olim* as objects for induction rather than objects with expectations, wishes and desires of their own.
32. For figures, see Sivan, *The '48 Generation*, pp. 63, 82.
33. For correspondence on the subject, see IDFA, 852/51/243 and IDFA, 5205/49/60.
34. Uri Avneri, *In the Field of the Philistines*, Tel Aviv, 1949, p. 238.
35. Nathan Shacham, 'The Ink Flag', *Al Hamishmar*, 17 April 1949.
36. *How to Welcome our Brethren*, Israeli Defence Forces Archive, see n. 21.
37. Abba Kovner, *Face to Face: Zero Hour I*, Merhavia, 1955, p. 214.
38. Yehuda Slutzky (ed.), *The History of the Haganah*, Vol. 3, No. 2, Tel Aviv, 1972, p. 1468.
39. For example, Meir Pa'il, *The Emergence of Zahal (IDF)*, Tel Aviv, 1979, p. 100; Netanel Lorch, *The History of the War of Independence*, Tel Aviv, 1958, p. 379.
40. This was crudely expressed, for example, in *Yiftah Brigade Bulletin*, January 1949, IDFA, brigade files: 'As if we were longing for the good old days, when our camp was pure and we could be comrades and friends, sit together round the camp fire, sing, and tell stories ... and today, what do we have in common with them.'
41. Yaakov Markovietzki, *Whispering Ember*, personal diary (unpublished); also Sivan, *The '48 Generation*, and Yablonka, *Survivors of the Holocaust*.
42. Sivan, *The '48 Generation*, p. 134.
43. Jewish Agency, National Committee, Centre for the National Service Census to Hebrew Youth (nd), IDFA 679/56/21.
44. Letter from Galili to Amitai (Ben-Gurion), United Kibbutz Movement archive, Galili section.
45. Minutes of executive committee of the National Service Census Centre, 28 March 1948, IDFA, 679/56/21. Ten requests from survivors for exemption from service on the basis of this law are in our possession; none was answered.
46. Simcha Rotem (Ratheujzer) to High Command, United Kibbutz Movement archive, Galili Section.

47. The authors and titles of the books (all of which are in Hebrew) are as follows: Avraham Aviel, *The Freedom and the Loneliness*, Tel Aviv, 2000; Yosef Govrin, *In the Shadow of Perdition*, Tel Aviv, 1999; Mark Hermann, *From the Alps to the Dead Sea*, Tel Aviv, 1985; Mordechai Goldhecht, *That I Should Live and Tell*, Tel Aviv, 2001; Beni Wircberg, *From the Vale of Killing to the Vale of the Gateway to Jerusalem*, Ramat-Gan, 1967; Ya'akov Chandeli, *From the White Tower to the Gates of Auschwitz, The Story of a Holocaust Survivor from Saloniki, Greece*, published by author, 1992; Eliezer Lidowski, *And the Flicker of the Flame Did Not Ebb*, Tel Aviv, 1986; Simha Meir, *I'm Not Stacek*, Jerusalem, 1989; Ya'akov Sad, *Those Who Walk the Paths*, Tel Aviv, 1994; Dov Freiberg, *Like One of the People*, Ramle, 1996; Shlomo Perl, *They Call Me Shlomo Perl*, Tel Aviv, 1991; Haim Kozinski, *Adolescence in the Inferno*, published by author, 1999; Hella Kleinberger, *It Comes Back to Me*, Tel Aviv, 1989; Koppel Kaplinski, *Fated to Live—The Lachwa Ghetto Uprising*, Tel Aviv, 1999; Tirza Kaspicki, *On a Thin Wire*, Tel Aviv: published by author, 1988; Moshe Ron, *A Modern Odyssey*, published by author, 1999; Amit Reicher, *Jacob's Ladder or the True Story of Citizen Ya'akov Sheptinski*, published by author, Tel Aviv, 1991; Baruch Schuv, *Beyond the Skies of the Cloud*, Tel Aviv, 1995; Aliza Vitis Shomron, *Adolescence in the Fire*, Tel Aviv, 2002; Avigdor Shahan, *In the Sizzling Frost*, Tel Aviv: Ghetto Fighters' House, 1988 (hereafter, Shahan); Yitzhak Sternberg, *Under a Different Identity*, Tel Aviv: Ghetto Fighters' House and Hakibbutz Hameuhad, 1984 (hereafter, Sternberg); Margalit Shlain, *One of the 'Sheep'*, Benzion Blaustein, *Partisan and Fighter*, published by author, 1996; Menahem Shermann, *From My Parents' Home to My Country*, Tel Aviv, 1989.
48. Also Shlain, *One of the 'Sheep'*, p. 174, and Kaplinski, *Fated to Live*, p. 255.
49. Yablonka, *Survivors of the Holocaust*, pp. 44–61.
50. Adopting a Hebrew surname was a Zionist fashion at the time.
51. After World War II the murdered Jews were described as sheep that went to the slaughter house, referring to their alleged lack of resistance.
52. Yablonka, *Survivors of the Holocaust*, p. 134.
53. The *Teti Panama* was the first ship to arrive in Israel after the Declaration of Independence. Sad was aboard.
54. See also Schuv, *Beyond the Skies of the Cloud*, p. 196. 'We, the *ma'pilim* [clandestine immigrants], the partisans, the *katzetnikim* [former concentration-camp inmates], and whatever other nicknames they gave us, wanted with all our hearts and souls to be partners, to be "insiders", but only a few managed it. The vast majority of the survivors remained on the outside.'

The Military and the Media in the Twenty-First Century: Towards a New Model of Relations

YEHIEL LIMOR and HILLEL NOSSEK

During the 2003 war in Iraq, the manner in which the United States conducted relations with the media, proved surprising to many, but an examination of the Gulf War of 1991, as well as the war in Afghanistan, provides early evidence of the contemporary relationship between the military, the government and the media. These two wars essentially gave rise to a new pattern of military–media relations whose foundations were laid a decade or two earlier. The essence of the new model is one of warfare managed, and waged, far from the eyes of the media, essentially deactivating the latter's ability to act freely.[1]

From a historical point of view, one can define the Deactivation Model as the third stage in military–media relations in the modern era. The first stage, defined as the Self-Mobilization Model, reached its peak in World War II and was characterized by an identity of interests, wherein the media voluntarily rallied to the aid of the military. The second stage, the Parallel Model that developed in the wake of the Vietnam War, embodied rivalry between the media and the military, similar to the media's relations with political institutions or other organizations in society. Recognition of the growing power of the media and the related structural processes on global and local media maps made politicians and military personnel aware that media interests—especially those of international media conglomerates—are not necessarily identical to those of the state and society in which these entities operate.

The present study examines key global changes in military–media relations during the twentieth century, focusing on the inapplicability of known models to the realities of military–media relations and wars in the twenty-first century. It maintains that these one-dimensional models, that were never entirely consistent or perfect, are no longer capable of theoretical or practical conceptualization of the reciprocal relations between the military and the media. Consequently, the Multidimensional

Model is offered. This includes several components of known existing models yet maintains a dynamic pattern that adapts itself to structural and technological developments and changes on the media map, as well as to changing political and social realities.

As clarified below, the *Multidimensional Model* may also manifest various practical implications. Its application by security and military authorities in Israel, as in other democratic countries, demands a reformulation of the basic concepts of relations between the military and society, on the one hand, and between the military and the media on the other, entailing the formulation of compatible policies and organizational deployments accordingly.

THEORETICAL BACKGROUND

Any discussion of military–media relations must proceed from at least two theoretical points of departure—one addressing relations between the state/government and the mass media and the other those between society, including the media and the military.

Classic mass media literature identifies four basic types of relations between the state and media: Authoritarian, Libertarian, Totalitarian and Social Responsibility.[2] The Authoritarian Model, applying rigid supervision and censorship of the media, characterized European regimes of the seventeenth to nineteenth centuries. The Libertarian Model was, and remains, a purely theoretical model that was never fully realized. The Totalitarian Model, according to which the media are part of the state, or the ruling party, and are therefore subject to strict supervision, was common in communist regimes, most of which disappeared in the last decade of the twentieth century, although some of its components are still applied in theocracies and some other countries.

The fourth model, Social Responsibility, perceived to be a characteristic of democratic states, is effectively an unwritten compact between the state, society and the ruling authorities, on the one hand, and the media on the other.[3] At the heart of this compact is a kind of agreement according to which the authorities and society forgo external supervision of the media in exchange for the media's commitment to a sense of mission and social responsibility and their imposition of self-supervision and restraint. Effectively, the government does not entirely abandon its supervisory authority, but rather only forgoes supervision *before* publication, wherein the state and the government maintain effective means of *post*-publication control should the media violate the terms of the friendly agreement.

The fifth model, the Developmental Model,[4] seeks to explain relations between the state/government and the media in developing countries. According to this model, perceived by some as transitional, the media are charged with fostering social, cultural and economic progress and is a partner in efforts towards the achievement of national objectives determined by the ruling authorities.

All these models were subject to criticism from the outset and none were applicable to the late twentieth century[5] and, *a fortiori*, the twenty-first. On the other hand, they cannot be discounted entirely, as they still constitute the theoretical basis for any discussion of relations between state/society and the mass media.

Insofar as the matter at hand is concerned, the most outstanding weakness of these models, especially Social Responsibility, is that they assume the existence of a nation-state and *ipso facto* relations between it and its media. Globalization, the formation of supranational political and economic entities, structural changes in global and local media maps and technological innovations have all given rise to new realities for the media from both a structural and functional point of view, as well as in a cultural–social context for which an appropriate theoretical framework is still lacking.

As explained below, these new realities may have direct implications for state–media relations in general, and military–media relations in particular. In the practical sphere, the state and the military will have to develop patterns of thinking and behaviour in their relations with the mass media, addressing them not only as a mediating factor between the ruling elites and the general public but also as an institution that seeks to consolidate its status and reinforce its autonomy.

Reciprocal relations between the military and society in democratic countries may be situated along a continuum between two extreme and perhaps even theoretical models, the separatist army[6] and the nation in arms.[7] The differences between the two models are described by Horowitz and Lissak as follows:

> The separatist army model exhibits a clear dividing line between the civilian sector and the army accountable to it, whereas the nation in arms model has rules of the game that delineate well-differentiated areas of activity in which—and only in which—co-operation between the civilian and military sectors is expressed.[8]

The location of these relations along the proposed continuum is not static and may shift in times of war and crisis.

MILITARY–MEDIA RELATIONS: MUTUAL INTERESTS

Reciprocal relations between the military and the media must be assessed in practical, as well as theoretical, terms delineating the interests of the respective parties that shape these relations.

Bar-Haim[9] claims that reciprocal relations between the military and the mass media are effectively based on a triangle of interests: Access to information, censorship and options for real-time reporting from the battlefield. These interests essentially conflict with, and oppose, one another. While the media seek full access to information, the military insists on retaining at least partial control over its accessibility. Moreover, while the media advocate the elimination of all censorship, the military controls media content to prevent publication of information liable to adversely affect and disrupt its activity. Finally, the media desire maximum freedom for direct, real-time reporting from battle areas, while the military attempts to limit this freedom.

An examination of relations between the military and the media through the proposed prism substantially reduces the scope of interests of both sides, especially when some are common to both or not necessarily opposed to one another. From the military's point of view, at least six interests are identified that not only mandate relations with the media but also prescribe the manner in which they are to be conducted.

Legitimization of Armed Forces and Conscription

In democratic countries with mandatory conscription and those whose armed forces consist of volunteers or hired personnel, the military requires extensive social recognition and legitimization of its existence and conscription/recruitment to prevent a decline in motivation among professional army volunteers and conscripts. As such, the media may be of assistance, not only in intensifying legitimization but also in empowering the military ethos in society. In the Israeli case, the media may act as agents of socialization, consolidating social support for recruitment to both compulsory and permanent service, as well as reserve duty and volunteering for elite combat units.

Securing Public Support for Security Policy and Military Action

In non-democratic countries, the regime and the military determine security policy or activate the armed forces without taking public opinion into account. In democratic states, however, public opinion is of considerable, and sometimes even decisive, significance in shaping policy and military activity. The media are likely to serve as highly influential agents of change by fostering public opinion that is either supportive of, or hostile to, the policies and activities of the regime and the military. In the Israeli case, one may point to the Lebanon War as an example of the media's influence on public opinion regarding security and the armed forces. Another example of the possible effect of the media on public opinion concerns issues such as the 'targeted killing' of terrorists, debated during the early years of the al-Aqsa Intifada.

Rallying Public Support for Maintenance and Empowerment of the Military System's Status

In the modern democratic state, various institutions and sectors are involved in a constant struggle over allocation of national resources. Each of the interested parties strives constantly to preserve, and even increase, its relative share of resources to ensure the effective realization of its objectives and maintenance of its status in society. Furthermore, the media may have a significant role in shaping public opinion and consolidating the views of decision-makers. Public discussions in the media about the development of weapons systems in the United States or the debate over the Lavi fighter plane project in Israel are tangible examples of the media's importance in the battle for public opinion.

Use as Strategic and Tactical Weapons

Skilful exploitation of the mass media, whether through manipulation or mutual cooperation, is likely to have strategic and even tactical significance. The intentional publication of information about new weapons, reports on military readiness and home front morale, or, alternatively, the blocking of publication of information liable to aid the enemy, essentially compound military empowerment in the strategic and tactical spheres alike.

Reinforcing Home Front Morale, Especially in Times of War and Emergency

In such situations, the media are likely to play a key role in strengthening home front morale. Even though civilian authorities are generally responsible for home front affairs, such issues are of considerable importance to the military, as positive reports about morale and the home front situation affect the fighting forces and their determination, particularly by diminishing conscripts' motivation to desert and help their families.

Public Relations for the Military as a System and Development of the Military Ethos

Like any public or private organization, the armed forces also seek to develop a public relations system that bolsters *esprit de corps*. For armies, public relations, and the media as a key instrument thereof, are of additional importance. The armed forces, as a professional guild, use public relations for instrumental purposes that have nothing to do with their formal objectives. A positive public image reflects on all uniformed personnel. Military careers are only of limited duration, following which soldiers resign and enter civilian life. Hence a positive image can help discharged veterans find employment in the civilian market more easily. Many officers opt for politics after retirement, thus encouraging the development of close relations with the media.

From the media's point of view, one may discern at least three interests furthered by maintaining permanent two-way relations with the military and security agencies.

Information

The military system and armed forces are an important source of information in any society. Regular flows of information to the media cannot be maintained without a solid infrastructure of reciprocal relations between the two parties. From the media's point of view, these reciprocal relations are of particular significance, at least when compared to relations with other institutions and organizations in society, as the military is a closed and compartmentalized body that may be deployed in remote areas to which physical access is nearly impossible. Without its cooperation, the media cannot obtain the desired information.

Supervision

One function of the media in a democratic society is to serve as a 'watchdog of democracy', to supervise activities of the government and its agencies, including the military. This demands reciprocal ties with the military to obtain not only information *per se* but also evaluations and commentary by its experts and pundits, without which this supervisory function, assumed as part of the media's social responsibility, could not be fulfilled adequately.

Commercial and Professional Considerations

Fierce professional and financial competition among the media demands attention to military affairs because of their significance to the public. General interest media that avoid covering security and military topics are liable to find themselves in a professional position inferior to that of their competitors and consequently also lagging behind them commercially.

MILITARY–MEDIA RELATIONS THROUGHOUT THE WORLD

Military–media relations are as old as the press itself. For hundreds of years, the press operated under authoritarian regimes whose close supervision, manifested in various ways, prevented publication of any undesirable information. On the other hand, the military had no independent status in determining media policy or shaping relations with the press. Such roles were assumed by the central authorities, of which the military was only one branch.

The development of democratic regimes in Europe and the United States and the growth of the popular press since the nineteenth century effectively created new patterns of relations between the military, the state and its citizens and between the military and the media. There were at least two attempts at identifying and defining these patterns or models, each addressing modern communications of the twentieth century and ignoring military–media relations in earlier periods.

Moskos's typology distinguished three distinct chronological periods:[10] Modern (pre-Cold War: 1900–1945), Late Modern (Cold War: 1945–1990), and Postmodern (since 1990). The transition from one period to another and the differences among the periods are a result of international political changes and the internal structure of democratic societies. Each is characterized by different kinds of relations with the media. In the Modern period, relations were incorporated, in the Late Modern manipulated and in the Postmodern courted.

Incorporated relations are essentially a kind of continuation of the Authoritarian Model, wherein the media accept the rules of the game determined by the ruling authorities, including the military, although without the governmental coercion entailed in authoritarianism. According to this model, the media consider themselves to be recruited to the war effort and perceive their role as assisting the armed forces and the state in vanquishing the enemy. Such behaviour was most evident during the two World Wars, when journalists were drafted into the fighting forces and the media acceded to strict, official and unofficial, censorship.[11]

In the manipulated relations of the Late Modern period, the military largely maintained control over the media, but the latter were no longer embedded in the fighting forces as they were in previous wars. Control of the media and their content was accomplished primarily by the tendentious selection of media teams that were accredited and thus had access to the troops. In fact, according to Moskos, the media realized that they were manipulated by the army, even though no formal censorship was imposed. Other salient reflections of manipulated relations were perceived during the Gulf War,[12] the Falklands War,[13] and the Grenada War.[14] Although the Vietnam War was considered open to free coverage, the media were subject to manipulation by the military nonetheless, which effectively imposed censorship on reports from the field.[15]

Courted relations, characterizing the Postmodern Model, reflect conditions under which the media enjoy autonomy and no longer exhibit any organizational or logistic dependence on the military, which must now court the media like all other organizations. Courted relations during the 1990s occurred in Somalia, Haiti and Bosnia, among other places.

Moskos's typology has one overt shortcoming. Relations between the military and the media are assessed through the prism of the US Armed Forces and the wars they fought until the late twentieth century, but essentially ignores wars and conflicts in which the American military was not involved, such as those of the Middle East, India–Pakistan, Iran–Iraq or Chechnya. Moreover, it does not differentiate between democratic and non-democratic states.

Although Moskos does not ignore the effects of social changes or new communications technologies, he does overlook changes in the status of the nation-state, its reciprocal relations with the media and in the media's function and structure, as explained below. Moreover, Moskos's point of departure in characterizing the Postmodern stage, according to which the military's contemporary missions and functions differ from those it fulfilled traditionally, especially the use of force to impose peace or carry out global policing, has already proved to be inapplicable to the first two wars of the twenty-first century. American military forces (along with those of other countries) were dispatched to Afghanistan, as well as to Iraq—not to make peace between two distant countries but, at least as formally declared—to defend their own interests.

Another taxonomy, proposed by Thrall,[16] is based on two key patterns assumed to reflect modern post-World War II realities and is based primarily on the American experience, although he claims that the US is an appropriate and desirable role model for other democratic regimes and that its patterns of military–media relations are emulated by them accordingly.

One such pattern, suggested by Thrall, accorded total freedom to the media, as typified in the Vietnam War. The result of this policy, according to the military and the government, was manifestly deleterious, contributing to the withdrawal of troops from Vietnam and defeat in war. Based on this conception and perhaps on the myth regarding free and open coverage, the White House orchestrated a new pattern, based on a more restrictive policy towards the media, as implemented in the wars in Grenada, Panama, the Persian Gulf and Afghanistan. The constraints imposed were assumed to enable the administration to control the flow of information to the public and thus also to shape public opinion. The media, for their part, still adhere to the Vietnam model and attempt to apply it wherever possible.

The two pattern systems are linear and are presented as a historical-chronological development, wherein each new pattern invalidates or replaces its predecessor. As none of these systems responds to the complexity and dynamics of modern wars, we require a new kind of model capable of portraying an up-to-date picture of military–media relations, as demonstrated below.

MILITARY–MEDIA RELATIONS IN ISRAEL

Military–media relations in Israel may be divided roughly into five periods:

- The establishment of Israel in 1948 until the 1973 Yom Kippur War;
- The Yom Kippur War to the 1982 war in Lebanon;
- 1982 to the 1993 Oslo Accords;
- The Oslo Accords to the outbreak of the second al-Aqsa Intifada in late 2000;
- Thereafter (see Table 1).

Each of these periods has its own features regarding the military's relations with the media and vice versa.

TABLE 1
A RETROSPECTIVE VIEW OF MEDIA–MILITARY RELATIONS IN ISRAEL

Period	Military–Media Relations	Media–Military Relations
1948–1973	Closure	Committed
1974–1982	Partial Openness	Critical
1983–1993	Increasing Openness	Complex: Cooperative and Critical
1994–2000	Increasing Openness	Complex: Critical and Cooperative
2000–	Increasing Openness and Renewed Closure	Complex: Committed and Critical

During the first period (1948–1973), the military manifested a restrictive attitude towards the media. Effectively, publication of practically anything concerning military affairs was prohibited unless permitted by the military censor. This situation is reminiscent of McQuail's Prohibition phase that characterized authoritarian regimes in Europe in the seventeenth to nineteenth centuries. The military censor blocked publication of any item deemed by the military to be undesirable, including those that could adversely affect morale, even if state security was not compromised. The media, for their part, usually did not contest this policy, largely because it was held in thrall by the myth of an 'invincible and omniscient army', intensified by victories in the Sinai Campaign of 1956 and the Six Day War of 1967. The 'committed press', recruited by the authorities to assist in the achievement of national objectives,[17] was gradually replaced. The Israel Broadcasting Authority (IBA), despite having gained independence in 1965, perceives itself to this day as a national media institution charged with reflecting the authorities' views and nurturing social consensus rather than criticizing it, while the printed press considered the military sacrosanct and unassailable at the time. The independent views expressed in the weekly *Ha'olam Hazeh*, for example, were untypical of the Israeli media.

The Yom Kippur War caused a deep social–political crisis in Israeli society, which did not leave the media untouched. Journalists acknowledged their willingness to cooperate with the political and military establishments, admitting that their silence also contributed to the catastrophe.[18] In subsequent years, partly as a result of the Agranat Commission's investigation of failings during the earliest days of the 1973 war, the press gradually began developing an increasingly critical attitude towards the military. Issues previously deemed taboo were now accorded coverage. The military could not remain indifferent to social changes—of which the press's new stance was only one manifestation—and now found it necessary to adapt its media policies accordingly and to display some degree of openness and transparency.

In the third period, following the Lebanon War (1982), the military became more open to the media as part of a broader and gradual process that obscured the previously inflexible boundaries between it and society as a whole. The public debate regarding the Israeli military presence in Lebanon that intensified over the years and often blurred dividing lines between political and military issues contributed its share as well. Furthermore, widespread involvement in national and local politics also led military personnel to develop closer relations with the media as preparation for their civilian careers in which, they realized, reciprocal relations with the press would constitute an integral part of their political and public activity.

Increased openness was also due to the military's interest in using the media as a means of increasing the defence budget and/or preventing cutbacks therein, demanding more cooperation on the military's part and even more extensive disclosure of information. The first Intifada that broke out in December 1987 engendered receptivity towards the media as well, although not necessarily as a matter of policy. The events of that struggle demonstrated that the country was now facing a new situation. Up to that time, the military had become accustomed to complete, or nearly complete, control of battle zones and *ipso facto* of the information flow, including the banning of reporters from military zones (or, alternatively, by admitting them with a military escort and strict control over content reported).

Now, international television networks and news agencies distributed personal camcorders to residents of the Occupied Territories, enabling information on military activity to flow freely from the Occupied Territories even when *bona fide* journalists were kept out. As a result, the Israel Defence Forces (IDF) adopted a practical and generally unofficial policy of relative openness, often because there was simply no other choice.

The press, for its part, cooperated with the military, at least at the beginning of this period and especially as long as the battles in Lebanon lasted. This situation was epitomized by an article published in Israel's most popular daily, *Yedioth Ahronoth*, whose headline read 'Quiet! [We're] Shooting!' which implied that during wartime the media should stand by quietly and lend a hand of support. Cooperation, or voluntarily rallying to the cause, eventually began to attenuate and the press resumed its criticism of government policy in general, including IDF operations, reflecting and perhaps even widening gaps in the national consensus regarding Lebanon. In subsequent years, the media continued to display ambivalence towards the military, manifesting both voluntary cooperation and criticism.

The first Intifada also helped reinforce the trend towards cooperation and voluntary commitment, as did the Gulf War of 1990–1991. In both cases, there was no existential threat to Israel, but the press, perhaps in keeping with its 'social responsibility' approach, felt it should help close national ranks, consolidate consensus, raise morale and obviously avoid appearing overly critical. In one instance, the prestigious daily *Ha'aretz* sought to prevent public panic by suppressing publication of information about defective gas masks.

On the other hand, the press began expressing more and more criticism of the army, not only because it was on the front lines of the ideological rift concerning the Occupied Territories, but also because many political officials, journalists and rank and file citizens had started to question the need to allocate large parts of the defence budget at the expense of other social needs, especially when Israel was not facing the risk of imminent war.

The third period effectively gave rise to the infrastructure for the relations obtaining in the fourth (1993–2000), i.e. an increasingly critical approach and a steady decline in the military's willingness to cooperate with the media. Two key factors intensified the media's critical attitude towards the army. The Oslo Accords, signed in 1993, sharpened issues concerning the IDF's presence in the Occupied Territories and especially its handling of the Palestinian population. Euphoria about a 'New Middle East' was accompanied by waves of disapproval regarding the behaviour of soldiers and officers towards Palestinians.

People felt that there was no longer a need to behave as a conquering army towards a civilian population with whom a peace agreement had been signed. The second factor, rooted in the period of the first Intifada or even earlier, was the loss of preferred status by military correspondents of the printed and electronic press, who had once constituted the principal channel through which relations between the military and the media were conducted. Ongoing coverage of events in the Occupied Territories was provided by numerous reporters in the respective geographic areas who did not feel bound by the same system of give and take that military correspondents accepted in their relations with the armed forces. Nevertheless, relations between the media and the ruling authorities did not assume the adversarial character believed to prevail in modern democratic states.

The fifth period began in September 2000. It was characterized, at least at its inception, by extended openness on the military's part. Issues previously considered absolutely taboo could now be published, such as the names and numbers of IDF units (including those formerly classified as top secret[19]) or the names of unit commanders. One noteworthy manifestation of this new openness was the granting of permission to IDF officers, including junior officers, to be interviewed by the media, including the disclosure of their names, positions, ranks and responsibilities.

For the first time since the establishment of Israel, the IDF effectively adopted a declared policy of decentralization, wherein information was provided not only by the IDF spokesman or General Staff officers, but also, and sometimes primarily, by field officers. The longer the Intifada continued, the greater the openness towards the media. Civilian correspondents were allowed (controlled) visits to combat units, including those in Palestinian Authority areas. On the other hand, the policy adopted during Operation Defensive Shield, especially during IDF activity in the Jenin refugee camp in mid-2002, may be characterized as an attempt by the military to institute a local version of the Deactivation Model applied successfully by US forces in the Afghan war several months earlier, thereby reversing the overall trend of increasing military receptivity towards the media that was typical of previous years.

The press's attitude towards the military during this period is complex: critical on the one hand, and committed and cooperative on the other. Chronologically, the latter attitude apparently preceded the former. Dor, for example, claims that during the first three weeks of the second Intifada, the press (primarily the three major leading Israeli dailies) supplied its readers with 'a one-sided, partially censored, often harsh and in any event overtly unbalanced, news-oriented world view ... in stark opposition not only to the facts *per se* but also to the factual reports that the field reporters of those very newspapers sent to their news editors'.[20] In other words, the newspaper editorial boards—and, as such, the press as a whole—voluntarily rallied to the cause of cooperation with the authorities.

Dor essentially portrays only one dimension of the situation. First, he assesses the press's handling of the Intifada only during its first three weeks; second, he does not address the electronic press and, third, he only examines the news sections of the three dailies and not the other sections, especially the editorials. From a broader perspective, the press's attitude does not appear one-sided or one-dimensional at all. Notwithstanding their cooperation and voluntary commitment to the support of the military (or the government), the papers, especially *Ha'aretz* and local papers belonging to the same chain (Schocken), are replete with critical articles about the military, censuring military operations themselves and questioning the government policies that the military carries out (Table 1).

The media's importance became evident to military and state authorities as a whole during the early days of the 1973 Yom Kippur War. The gap between official information directed towards the public and rumours engendered a severe credibility gap. The political and military establishments attempted to cope with the problem by appointing a senior IDF reserve general (Aharon Yariv), who had previously served as head of the Intelligence Corps and the prime minister's advisor on terror, to be responsible for the military and national information services.[21] After the war, there were various attempts at institutionalizing the IDF information and spokesman's system and the consideration of media issues in the decision-making process, including systematic staff work and position papers.

One practical reflection of such institutionalization was the appointment of IDF Spokesman's Office representatives at the geographical command level and subsequently at lower echelons as well. Another stage in this institutionalization, at least from a professional point of view, was the recruitment of trained media personnel as IDF spokesmen, a function previously filled by military officers. At the same time, media issues began assuming a permanent place in the syllabi of all IDF command courses from company commander level up.

Despite increasing awareness of the importance of the media to the achievement of military goals, a substantive gap emerged over the years between such awareness and its practical application, as evidenced by the status and professional training of IDF Spokesman's Office representatives at various command levels. Although, *prima facie*, such representatives are supposed to serve as staff officers of rank and status equal to others, in practice they rank lower and have less professional training and experience than other staff officers.

STRUCTURAL AND FUNCTIONAL CHANGES IN THE INTERNATIONAL AND NATIONAL MEDIA MAPS

The basic assumption of this study is that the development of relations between the military and the media, in the international arena as well as in Israel, is not necessarily of a linear nature. This assumption is anchored in developments that took place over the past few decades and may be assessed on three levels. The first two, structural and functional, concern developments and changes in the international and national media maps, while the third relates to changes in the society in which the media operate.

THE STRUCTURAL LEVEL

At least eight structural processes taking place on the media map are likely to have implications for military–media relations in the modern era. It should be indicated that they are not necessarily unique to the mass media and effectively reflect global macroeconomic processes.

Mass Media Concentration

The concentration process (whereby fewer and fewer hands are controlling more and more media outlets) that typifies the contemporary mass media industry takes place simultaneously in two spheres—international and national. From a global point of view there may be a growth of international and supranational media conglomerates that encompass a variety of electronic and printed media channels in numerous countries. A similar process takes place in the national sphere, as more and more of the media are held by fewer and fewer owners. This is evident not only in the US, where the number of corporations holding most of the media market declined from fifty to only about a dozen within two decades,[22] but also in Israel, where a very small group of media barons own most of the major media outlets.[23] The practical significance of concentration is that governments and other organizations find it difficult to cope with major international or national conglomerates that have amassed not only media power and economic status power but political clout as well.

Decentralization and the Multi-channel Media Environment

Parallel to the centralization taking place on international and national media maps, one may also discern an inverse process of decentralization and channel multiplicity. Modern technology now enables just about everyone to produce a newspaper with a home computer and printer, to burn CDs with a simple device or to produce video and audio cassettes using rather simple and cheap means. The Internet also opens new horizons for those who would like to operate mass media channels of the printed or broadcast variety. Many of these new and smaller media outlets are created and operated by people or organizations that, intentionally or otherwise, do not perceive themselves as bound by the professional and ethical codes that govern the operation of the major media. Practically speaking, this means that all official organizations, including the military establishment, now have to cope with an increasing number of media channels whose operators are sometimes unknown and/or free of professional and ethical constraints.

The Weakening of National Identification among the Mass Media

The old and familiar examples of state–media relations, like models of military–media relations, perceived the media as an integral part of the state and society in which they operate, engendering partnership in the national interest. Centralization and the emergence of international media conglomerates governing the media in different countries effectively sever the link between the media and national identity and interests. The chief interest of the media controlled by international conglomerates is economic in nature.

Their success is not measured according to their social responsibility but rather their ability to compete with other national and international conglomerates, especially regarding profits. One practical implication of this situation is the possible development of dual loyalty on the part of the media—to the state/society and to their respective owners. As such, the state or society, including the military, can no longer rely on the degree of cooperation it previously enjoyed.

Decline in the Status of Public Broadcasting and the Rise of the Commercial Media

In most democratic countries apart from the US, state/public broadcasting was perceived as the chief bearer of national messages and thus a loyal ally of the government. By the 1970s, the status of the public media began to erode gradually as a result of deregulation measures allowing private entrepreneurs to enter the media market and operate commercial broadcasts on television and radio. The new channels not only eroded public stations but also raised some serious retroactive questions regarding the justification of their continuation, especially because such channels are financed primarily by licensing fees that have become a kind of obligatory tax, even if many of the taxpayers did not watch or listen to them at all. The proliferation of commercial channels ousted public television from its premier status, or at least weakened it.

Online News Around the Clock

Until a couple of decades ago, the media provided information to the public via predetermined channels at rigidly fixed intervals (except for extraordinary cases), such as daily papers or regular television and radio news broadcasts. The development of specific news media organizations such as CNN and Sky and Internet news channels has rendered news a product manufactured online 24 hours a day.

Increased Economic and Professional Competition Among Media

Information is one of the most important outputs of media organizations. Competition among the media, although based on professional norms and achievements, is economic in nature. Hence financial considerations largely determine the spheres and scope of coverage for many media channels.[24]

The Decline in the Significance of Old and Well-Established Media Channels in Favour of New Ones

Ongoing surveys about media consumption in the western world reflect a slow but consistent decline in readership of daily newspapers or viewing of television news broadcasts, representing a decline in 'hard news' consumption and a concomitant increase in time devoted to the consumption of other media channels, such as the Internet or cable television (primarily entertainment programmes). The practical significance of this process is that every establishment, including the military, is finding it more and more difficult to direct information towards the general public through the major, established hard news channels and is therefore developing new ways of getting its message across.

High Personnel Turnover Rate

Centralization and decentralization processes, as well as the rise in power of the private commercial profit-oriented media, have led to a high turnover of journalistic personnel. The multiplicity of new channels intensifies professional mobility, while efforts towards maximizing profits engender a preference for young and cheap personnel over veteran employees who entail higher salary costs. The inevitable result is a downturn in professionalism, as reflected in the journalistic quality of reports and perhaps even in their credibility.

THE FUNCTIONAL LEVEL

At least eight functional changes are relevant to relations between the authorities—including the military—and the media and their personnel:

Speed Counts—Not Accuracy

Fierce competition among the media, especially the electronic and online media, may lead to the publication of information before it has been verified.

Shorter Life Span for Information

Cut-throat competition and technological innovations enable not only rapid dissemination of information over media channels but also the equally rapid removal of it. Such deletions may occur not only to make room for new information but also in cases in which material is found to be erroneous or imprecise. Information that is published and deleted rapidly—especially on the radio and the Internet—is difficult to locate and reconstruct, as it leaves no trace or residue except among those directly exposed to it.

The Future of Traditional Journalism

The Gulf War created new journalistic realities in which the role of the reporter as information gatherer was assumed by the television camera transmitting unedited live broadcasts.[25] The situation repeated itself during the early days of the US attack on Afghanistan in 2001 and the fighter helicopter attacks on Gaza and Ramallah during the Intifada in the same year. Modern technology shattered old and accepted boundaries in the media—and especially between the printed and broadcast media—and also had direct implications for the functions of journalists and editors.[26] Moreover, the Internet now allows anyone to disseminate information freely, thereby obscuring the boundaries between the supply of information by professional, responsible journalists and by untrained partisan elements.

Increasing the Importance of the Media in Inter-Media Agenda Setting

The media themselves provide one of the chief sources of information for the media and thus contribute to inter-media agenda setting. The multiplicity of new broadcast and online media channels and the massive quantities of information flowing through them thus increase the media's importance in setting the inter-media agenda.

Cutbacks in Text and Increased Significance of Visuals and Headlines

The modern printed press relate to information as a product, packaging and marketing it in a light and easily digestible manner using brief texts, extensive photography, graphic aids and large, eye-catching headlines. A systematic examination of the printed press over the years reveals a steady decline in space allotted to text and an increase in the relative share of headlines and photographs.[27] The same is true for the electronic media: shorter news broadcasts (more bulletins and fewer in-depth programmes) and rapid, brief and fast-paced sound bites. The result is that readers, viewers and listeners receive less information than they did previously.

More Entertainment and Less Hard News

The boundaries between news—especially hard news—and entertainment are becoming increasingly blurred. Information is entertainment and entertainment is information and the combined result—infotainment—is gradually taking the place of classic news.

More (Fast-paced) Commentary without Facts

Another important function of the media, besides the supply of information, is the provision of commentary. Indeed, all the media make extensive use of commentators to explain and interpret the information for their readers, viewers and listeners. Pressures of competition demand a constant increase in the quantity of information supplied to the public. The more information released, the more likely it is to be brief, partial and unverified. Commentary is adversely affected as well.

Intentionally or otherwise, instead of interpreting information, it becomes a substitute or complement for whatever is lacking. This is particularly evident in live wartime broadcasts, such as those of the wars in Afghanistan and Iraq. Air time had to be filled and in the absence of authentic information about events on the front lines, commentary, often uncorroborated by facts, takes the place of reporting.

Erosion of Journalistic Ethics

Intense competition among the media and the immediate nature of reporting engender the erosion of journalistic ethics. The Internet, in which information may be promulgated with virtually no supervision, also erodes professional and ethnical norms. Ethical regulations are becoming a dead issue even in countries that purport to adhere to them. The media, which always found it difficult to maintain effective internal supervision systems to ensure the application of ethical norms, are now virtually helpless as professional standards deteriorate.

SOCIAL–CULTURAL PROCESSES AND THEIR EFFECT ON MILITARY–MEDIA RELATIONS

In the last two decades of the twentieth century, the status of civil society, operating parallel to governmental authorities and comprising non-governmental organizations, interest groups and various volunteer bodies, gained strength in the western world. One characteristic of civil society is its challenge to the state's role as the supreme authority[28] and some even claim that its growth was made possible largely thanks to developments in communication.[29]

At the same time, many western democracies experienced an increased awareness of the existence of multicultural society that recognizes the social and cultural status of fringe groups and sectors in addition to, and at times instead of, a given society's unifying and consolidating components. In several such countries, individualistic values such as self-fulfilment, self-expression and legitimization of the 'other' now head the list of personal and social values. The common denominator, based on shared national identity, has effectively become an amalgam of groups that do not necessarily share ethnic, cultural or even moral features. Within such a society, the military is perceived primarily as a means of defending the nation-state and its citizens against an internal attack and existential threats to its sovereignty.

All the above applies to the Israeli case as well, wherein a decline in the military's status and significance, as perceived by the public, was engendered by geopolitical changes in the Middle East (especially after the collapse of the Soviet Union and the death of veteran Arab leaders, notably Hafez Al-Assad in Syria and King Hussein of Jordan); the attenuation of existential threats to Israel and subsequent optimistic assumptions (following the Oslo Accords) that the entire Middle East would be peaceful.

This situation was also reflected in a steady reduction of the defence budget and increased criticism of the military in the press. Another reflection of the military's weakening position, relevant to the case at hand, is the attenuation of military censorship[30] that was forced to limit its activity to banning publication of material embodying 'almost certain tangible damage to [state] security', as defined by the Israeli Supreme Court of Justice.[31]

The military, realizing that the boundaries between it and civil society had become less rigid, now attempted to adopt a more civil and humane image. This may explain the gradual rise in the frequency of officers' meetings with their soldiers' parents, intensified concern for the soldiers' needs (for example, special arrangements for viewing of major sporting events, even at remote emplacements) and the retraction of the cellular telephone ban at military bases.

From a broader perspective, some perceive the military at the end of the twentieth century in terms of its reciprocal relations with society, declaring it to be a postmodern military that no longer functions according to the long-prevailing 'people's army' format. This view was reinforced by the statements of various high-ranking commanders (particularly Chief of Staff Ehud Barak, who was elected prime minister in 1999), indicating that the battlefield of the future is no longer the place for a large army based on mass conscription but rather for a small and smart army based on professional, skilled personnel aided by advanced, sophisticated technologies.

Criticism of this postmodern conception may be summarized as follows: the military has become an interest group that seeks to maintain its status in society. Ben-Eliezer even defines this pattern of relations as 'military versus society',[32] claiming that the development of society–military relations in Israel differs from that taking place in western countries according to Moskos's conception of a postmodern army whose objectives are not necessarily of a military nature. The army whose chief objectives were to defeat the enemy now seeks to institute peace or separate forces with potential for conflagration or severe friction.

A second characteristic, closely related to the first, is the reciprocal penetration of civilian and military spheres of activity. This is reflected both in the introduction of civilian elements and considerations in areas previously of a military nature alone, as well as in integration of military personnel in civilian activity (such as involvement and mediation in civil agreements between countries). A third feature addresses the army's involvement in multinational forces whose authority and legitimization originates in organizations other than its own nation-state.

THE SCHOLARLY DEBATE

Many scholars believe that the development of military–society relations in the western world is linear in nature, obscuring the rigid boundaries between the military and society (including the media) and as such also redefining these reciprocal relations. Their basic assumption is that international and national developments have assigned new functions to the modern army, contradicting all expectations that familiar models of military–society relations—and *ipso facto* also military–media relations—will apply in the new era as well. This is primarily because the new trends in military structure and purpose are not entirely derived from the nation-state and the objectives it sets for its army, necessitating attention to the global environment in which these states and their armed forces operate.

In contrast, this paper's authors maintain that the linear conception no longer applies to the realities of the twenty-first century. Consequently, any attempt to separate military–society/media relations from the national setting and base them chiefly on an international one would be premature and possibly also fundamentally erroneous. The great wars of the twentieth century—and especially the international geopolitical developments that followed them—constituted the background for the linear conception. Events taking place at the beginning of the twenty-first century—the terror attacks in the United States on 11 September 2001 and the wars in Afghanistan and Iraq—may buttress the argument that the linear conception is premature.

Developments in military–media relations are reflected in two spatial patterns: Closed Space, long characteristic of military–media relations in Western countries and still applicable in many cases, and Open Space,

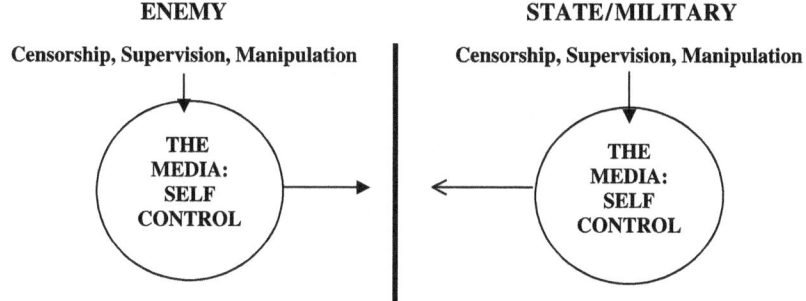

FIGURE 1
MILITARY–MEDIA RELATIONS IN CLOSED SPACE

typical of contemporary realities and anchored in social and media-related processes, as well as technological developments.

The two patterns reflect military–media relations in a state at war with one or more states. Closed Space (Figure 1) is based on three basic components that each of the fighting states attempts to maximize:

- Control and supervision of information through a variety of techniques, including formal censorship, manipulation and other restrictive mechanisms, such as barring journalists from battle zones, requiring prior clearance of reports and so on.
- Imposing obstacles to the two-way flow of undesirable information across borders, such as strict censorship, sophisticated jamming of enemy broadcasts and the like.
- Securing cooperation on the part of the media, which perceive themselves as committed to the national war effort and therefore voluntarily avoid publishing information that the government and military deem deleterious not only to physical security but also to public morale.

The 1991 Gulf War, the 2001 war in Afghanistan and especially the 2003 war in Iraq are outstanding examples of Closed Space military–media relations in which the Deactivation Model was fully, or almost fully, applied. In the Gulf War, allied forces manipulated the media to guarantee the coverage they desired and excluded unfavourable reporting. For example, only a limited number of reporters were allowed to enter the battle zone and visit facilities and military units under the close supervision of military officers.

To prevent the flow of alternative information from enemy territory, Iraqi television and radio stations were bombed early in the war. Similar manipulation on an even broader scale was applied in the war in Iraq:

The embedding system, with which the media cooperated from lack of choice, enabled the military to control media personnel, who even agreed to adhere to their military escorts' instructions. Reporters not included among the embedded personnel were stopped by allied forces and expelled from Iraq.[33]

On the other hand, the media rallied to the national effort and avoided independent information gathering or critical handling of material received through official channels. Although such behaviour aroused considerable *post facto* criticism, the pattern repeated itself—even without the application of official censorship—during the war in Afghanistan and to an even greater extent during the war in Iraq. Enemy broadcasting stations were silenced at the outbreak of war, journalists were denied access to battle zones, the media were fed a near-exclusive diet of official information and avoided criticizing the authorities or the military as part of an overall, across-the-board trend of voluntary commitment.

The British army behaved similarly during the Falklands War of 1982. The conditions imposed on reporters who asked to join the British troops was that material had to be approved in advance and reported exclusively through army and navy communications channels. Thus, even if no formal censorship was applied, it was imposed in practice with the consent and cooperation of the media, which reported each military success to their readers out of a sense of partnership and national pride.[34]

In contrast to the prevailing view, this paper argues that the Closed Space pattern has not disappeared but rather perseveres to this day, given the appropriate conditions and circumstances, not only in totalitarian states but also in democracies. Nevertheless, in the face of twenty-first century realities, especially developments in military–society relations, structural changes in the international media map and technological innovations, there are few cases in which democratic countries can operate under Closed Space conditions. In practice, one may consider Closed Space and the Deactivation Model it embodies to be a special instance of *Open Space*, as explained below.

The Open Space pattern (Figure 2) is based on the assumption that wars in the present era are not merely local conflicts between two rival nations but rather constitute part of a global and supranational system in which various factors besides the direct players may manifest a variety of political, economic and other interests. Moreover, contemporary wars will continue to take place in a media environment of unprecedented character, influenced by the presence of non-national and supranational actors, headed by television networks and international news agencies that are motivated by economic and professional interests and display no attachment or loyalty to any specific nation-state.

Even when Closed Spaces are attempted, the result is far from impermeable. Modern technologies render it easy for any of the warring parties to overcome technical and other obstacles that had previously

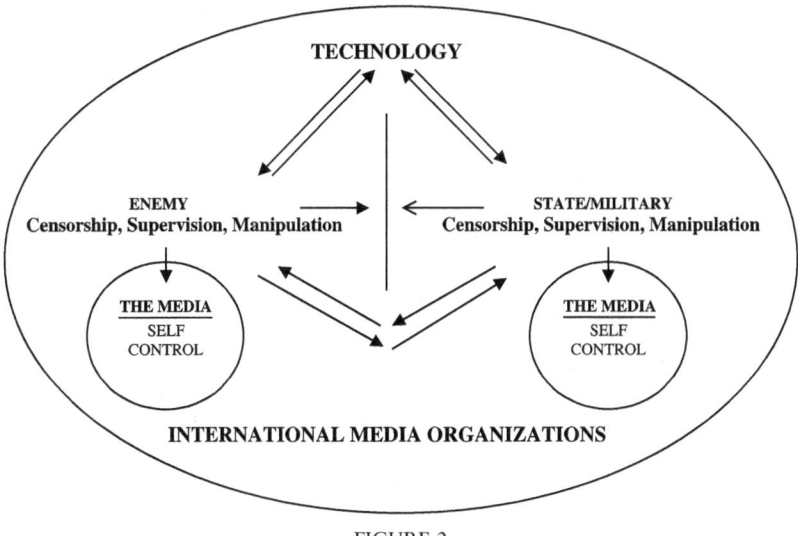

FIGURE 2
MILITARY-MEDIA RELATIONS IN OPEN SPACE

prevented the free and copious flow of information. Television networks and news agencies exploit technological innovations to provide worldwide media consumers with up-to-date and varied information direct from the battlefield. Salient examples include the CNN camera placed in Baghdad during the Gulf War, the fax machine that transmitted reports from Moscow during the attempted military coup in the late 1980s; and the television camera placed at Yasser Arafat's headquarters in Ramallah, transmitting live reports of the Palestinian leader's status when he was confined to his office, surrounded by Israeli tanks. The Internet also enables transmission of alternative live reports, differing from those provided by the state and the military.

In Open Space, the effect of the speed and scope of reporting increases and becomes relevant to all warring parties. In the Vietnam War, that took place mostly in Closed Space, the American public was not provided with up-to-date information about the war and its horrors, resulting in poor public involvement in war-related issues. It took a long time for Americans to begin protesting against the war and demanding the withdrawal of US troops from Vietnam. The war against Palestinian terror took place in Open Space, with reports of the second Intifada reaching the Israeli public by live broadcast from the Palestinian Authority areas. Demonstrations soon followed in Arab countries and European capitals, their participants furnished with ample television and press reports.

Open Space creates the infrastructure for development of a Multi-dimensional Model of military–media relations. Two variables or 'principal actors' are involved in this model—the military and the media, with reciprocal relations between them partly resulting from the influence of two mediating or intervening factors, namely Warfare Type and Battle Theatre (Figure 3).

Each of these four variables—the military, the media, warfare type and battle theatre—is effectively a super-variable that comprises sub-variables classifiable in various categories. For example, 'the military' can be a professional, volunteer or mercenary army or a people's army, each of which may have differential needs regarding the media. 'The media' includes three sub-variables—national, international and enemy media—each of which embodies several subcategories, such as news agencies, photo agencies, daily newspapers, radio and television stations, periodicals, the Internet, local media, community media, press photographers and even freelancers or rank and file citizens who supply information voluntarily.

The 'warfare type' variable may incorporate categories such as total war; limited war; war of attrition; low-key war; and the war on terror. It also possesses related sub-variables ranging from conventional to non-conventional warfare. Both the military and the media are likely to have differential objectives and needs regarding each type of war, affecting the pattern of practical relations between them. The 'battle theatre' variable includes categories such as fighting on enemy territory (near or distant), the border or the home front, urban or rural fighting and more.

Interaction among the four variables shapes the operative model of military–media relations. Practically speaking, there may be situations in which one state will simultaneously apply various patterns of relations with the media, in accordance with its particular type of military, media, warfare and battle theatre. Moreover, the media too may seek parallel or simultaneous application of several patterns, depending on battle theatres and warfare types. The variety of models resulting from interaction among the four variables may include some that are already familiar from the past (e.g. Self-Mobilization, Deactivation, Parallelism, Courting or Openness),

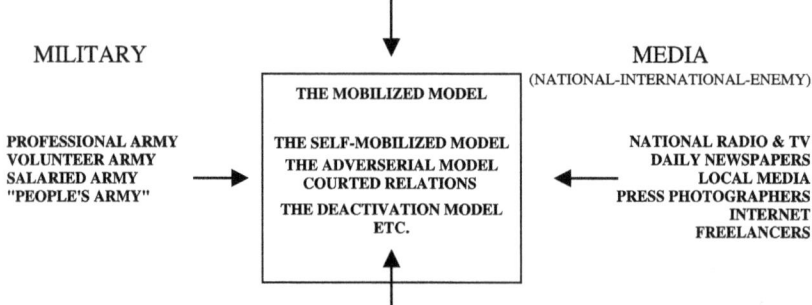

FIGURE 3
MULTIDIMENSIONAL MODEL OF MILITARY–MEDIA RELATIONS

along with new ones that emerge as a consequence of local interaction and technological innovations applied by the media.

For example, one may explain the relations applied by US troops in the 2002 war in Afghanistan and later also in Iraq as a consequence of interaction among the following variables: limited war conducted by a professional army in enemy territory far from home, wherein the enemy media was deactivated at the start of the battles, the international media had virtually no prior presence in the battle area and the national media are totally dependent on the military's willingness to allow it access to battle areas. As far as the US military was concerned, these practical relations followed a pattern that combined two previously-discerned models: Deactivation, applied in the Gulf War, Grenada and Panama, and Self-Mobilization, familiar from the World War II era. In the case of Britain, the Deactivation Model was applied in the Falklands War. From the point of view of the US and British media, the Self-Mobilization Model was applied to the exclusion of all others, especially Parallelism (i.e, Rivalry).

The above description of relations obtaining in the wars in Afghanistan and Iraq is only partial and not exhaustive, as it focuses solely on the battle theatre. Effectively, relations between the military and the media (and in this case the American media) were not limited exclusively to remote battlefields. At the same time, the US military exhibited other patterns of relations with the media at home, such as Courted Relations. These patterns changed once the fighting died down in Afghanistan and Iraq: The American media gradually resumed the Rivalry Model behaviour, criticizing the administration and the military, while the military not only applied Courted Relations to achieve a sympathetic media but also adopted the Openness Model that entails greater voluntary cooperation with the media.

A retrospective glance at limited time periods, such as the war in Afghanistan or the 2003 war in Iraq, may indeed demonstrate that one is not dealing with rigid one-dimensional models of reciprocal relations between the military and the media but rather a multidimensional and dynamic one. Hence assumptions by scholars such as Moskos regarding the linear development of relations between the military and the media do not necessarily pass empirical tests. On the contrary, the situation prevailing at the advent of the twenty-first century indicates that previous patterns need not disappear entirely and may in fact recur and take root as a direct consequence of circumstances and local combinations of the four variables: Type of military, media, warfare and battle theatre.

CONCLUSIONS

What are the likely practical implications of the development of Open Space and consolidation of the Multidimensional Model of military–media relations?

Firstly, the military and the media will have to prepare themselves, both conceptually and practically, for a twenty-first century characterized by Open Space patterns. The military might do well to consider establishing a new professional Media Corps whose commanders and soldiers will function as staff officers at all command levels from the General Staff down to the lower echelons, like their colleagues in intelligence, logistics, personnel, communications, and will be included in all decision-making processes.

The difference between the projected situation and the one now prevailing in the IDF and other armies that already possess military spokespersons and/or special officers responsible for contact with the media is not one of semantics alone. By crude analogy, a media officer may be said to fulfil a dual role as an intelligence officer charged with gathering information about the enemy, analyzing the battlefield and the forces operating therein and estimating the enemy's moves, while also functioning as an operations officer who proposes courses of action to be taken. The spokesperson, according to the proposed conception, is only one of the tools that media officers may apply in the course of their work.

The wars of the future will not resemble those of the past at all. They may be of different types and waged in different places simultaneously. Far from home and also on the home front; high-intensity and low-intensity; conventional and non-conventional; targeting regular troops, as well as terror organizations or guerrilla forces.

Each type of war, or warfare, in each of the areas will demand a suitable pattern of relations with the media as a whole or with particular types of media. At times, one of the familiar models may suit a given situation, whereas in other instances it will be necessary to apply a different pattern or develop a new one.

The new realities of Open Space and the Multidimensional Models demand a new conceptual approach on the media's part as well. The senior status long accorded to the media establishment or to owners and chief editors of media organizations is liable to attenuate and erode. In an era of multiple channels and actors on the media map, in which military–media relations are not conducted only by the upper echelons (cabinet ministers, generals, owners or editors) but also at field level in battle areas, the media must prepare themselves both conceptually and organizationally. The Multidimensional Model and Open Space effectively wrest the coverage monopoly from military correspondents, with actual reporting carried out by other professional reporters or even rank and file citizens reporting incidents in print, audio or video.

NOTES

1. Yehiel Limor and Hillel Nossek, 'Military and Media in the Twenty-First Century: Towards a New Model of Relations', Lecture at the Annual Conference of the Israel Political Science Association, Tel Aviv University, June 2002.

2. Fred Siebert, Theodore Peterson and Wilbur Schramm, *Four Theories of the Press*, Urbana, 1956.
3. Yehiel Limor, 'The Mass Media in Israel', in Ephraim Yaar and Zeev Shavit (eds.), *Issues in Israeli Society*, Tel Aviv, 2003, pp. 1017–1103.
4. William Hachten, *The World News Prism: Changing Media, Changing Ideologies*, Ames, IA, 1981.
5. See John Nerone (ed.), *Last Rights: Revisiting Four Theories of the Press*, Urbana, 1995; Denis McQuail, *McQuail's Mass Communication Theory*, London, 2000.
6. David Horowitz and Moshe Lissak, *Troubles in Utopia: The Overburdened Polity of Israel*, Tel Aviv, 1990.
7. D.C. Rapoport, 'A Comparative Theory of Military and Political Types', in Samuel Huntington (ed.), *Changing Patterns of Military Politics*, New York, 1962, pp. 71–101.
8. Horowitz and Lissak, *Troubles in Utopia*, p. 249.
9. Aviad Bar-Haim, 'Interaction Between the Israeli Defence Forces and the Media: A Content Analysis of the Press'. Paper presented at the 5th biennial conference of European Research Group on Military and Society, Zurich, 3–6 October 1996.
10. Charles Moskos, 'Towards a Postmodern Army?', *Democratic Culture*, Vol. 4–5 (2001), pp. 213–232.
11. George Thompson, *Blue Pencil Admiral*, London, 1947; Jeffery Smith, *War and Press Freedom*, New York, 1999.
12. See Robert Fisk, 'Free to Report What We're Told', in Micha Sifry and Christopher Serf (eds.), *The Gulf War Reader*, New York, 1991, pp. 376–380.
13. David Morrison and Howard Tumber, *Journalists at War*, London, 1988.
14. Geoff Mungham, 'Grenada: News Blackout in the Caribbean', in David Mercer *et al.* (eds.), *The Fog of War: The Media on the Battlefield*, London, 1988, pp. 291–310.
15. Daniel Hallin, *The 'Uncensored War'*, Berkeley, 1989.
16. Trevor Thrall, *War in the Media Age*, Cresskill, NJ, 2000.
17. One phenomenon worthy of mention and even separate discussion is the recruitment of journalists during various periods, especially wartime, to serve as military correspondents in the IDF Spokesman's Unit.
18. Dan Caspi and Yehiel Limor, *The In/Outsiders: Mass Media in Israel*, Cresskill, NJ, 1999; Uri Avnery, 'Information that Put the Public to Sleep', in Tali Zelinger (ed.), *By Our Military Correspondent*, Tel Aviv, 1990, p. 39; Yeshayau Ben-Porat *et al.*, *Failure*, Tel Aviv, 1975.
19. Examples include the *Shaldag* commando unit, the Israel Air Force rescue unit (No. 669), the Intelligence sigint unit No. 8200, and agents assigned to enemy territory (unit No. 504).
20. Daniel Dor, *Journalism under the Influence*, Tel Aviv, 2001, p. 11.
21. Although during the Six Day War as well, a reserve general (Chaim Herzog) was appointed as National Spokesman, he held that job as an individual and not as the official responsible for the entire information system.
22. Ben Bagdikian, *Media Monopoly*, Boston, 2000.
23. Yehiel Limor, 'The Little Prince and Big Brother, or: The Media Industry in Israel in an Era of Change', in D. Caspi (ed.), *The Media and Democracy in Israel*, Tel Aviv, 1997, pp. 29–46; Limor, 'The Mass Media in Israel'; Caspi and Limor, *The In/Outsiders*.
24. Doug Underwood, *When MBAs Rule the Newsroom*, New York, 1993; John McManus, *Market Driven Journalism*, Thousand Oaks, CA, 1994; Yehiel Limor and H. Nossek, 'Economic Censorship: The "Invisible Hand"'. Paper presented at the conference on Capitalism and Communication in the 21st Century, London: The Centre for Communication and Information Studies of the University of Westminster, 13–14 June 2002.
25. Elihu Katz, 'The End of Journalism: Notes of Watching the War', *Journal of Communication*, Vol. 42, No. 3 (1992), pp. 5–13.
26. Michael Bromley, 'The End of Journalism?', in Michael Bromley and Tom O'Malley (eds.), *A Journalism Reader*, London, 1997, pp. 330–350.
27. Yehiel Limor and Ziva Kantor, 'To Hell with Text! What's Important Are Headlines and Pictures: Changes in Front Page Style in the Israeli Press—1948–1998', paper presented at the Annual Conference of the Israel Communication Association, Haifa, December 1999.
28. Peri, 'Changes in Security Discourse in the Media and in the Perception of Citizenship in Israel'.

29. John Hall, 'In Search of Civil Society', in John Hall (ed.), *Civil Society: Theory, History, Comparison*, Cambridge, 1995, pp. 1–31.
30. Hillel Nossek and Yehiel Limor, '50 Years in a "Marriage of Convenience": News Media and Military Censorship in Israel', *Communication Law and Policy*, Vol. 6, No. 1 (2001), pp. 1–36.
31. Israel High Court of Justice, file 680/88.
32. Uri Ben-Eliezer, 'From Nation in Uniform to Postmodern Army: Military Politics in Israel in the "New Era"', *Democratic Culture*, Vol. 4–5 (2001), pp. 55–97.
33. Among the reporters arrested and expelled from southern Iraq was Israel Television correspondent Dan Semama.
34. Glasgow University Media Group, *War and Peace News*, Milton Keynes, 1985.

Three 'Travelling' Models of Politics and the Mass Media in the Context of Israeli National Security

GIDEON DORON

Consider the following situation. A reporter who has joined a fighting unit on a combat mission, as so many did during the 2003–2004 war in Iraq, learns from informants that her unit is about to fall into a deadly ambush. What should she do? Tell the unit's commander about the ambush and save lives? Or be professional: Keep the information to herself and thus protect her sources for a first-hand news item, a 'scoop' to be published the next morning that will gain her fame and glory? Most rational people would no doubt opt for the first possibility. For the majority, the value of saving human lives surpasses the value of maintaining professional integrity, at least in such extreme cases. This personal dilemma captures in a nutshell the essence of political relations with the media in the context of national security.

To simplify conceptualization of the argument presented in this paper, politics and the mass media are treated here as two distinct entities despite their entanglement in everyday life. Starting with this premise, three conceptual models or archetypes, each based on a specific type of relation maintained between the two entities, are presented here. The first model, the *political control model*, entails political control of the media. The messages transmitted reflect the preferences of specific politicians or political actors and are frequently authored by them. Within this model, the mass media represent an instrument to be utilized by the political sphere, but especially by leading decision-makers, to disseminate their platforms and reinforce their positions.

The second model, the *market* or *regulatory model*, is diametric in its disposition. According to this model, political and policy preferences are formed and influenced by shifts in public attitudes as they find expression in the written and electronic media. The media operate according to market principles; the political system responds in due course. Direct relations between the systems are, in principle, minimal, with political organs resembling traffic controllers whose role is essentially confined to maintaining order (i.e., the preservation of manageable communication networks by administrative means, such as the licences that assign broadcast frequencies). The United States mass communication system embodies the epitome of this structure of relations.

The third model, the *mixed model*, represents an intermediate case: The political system does not control the media but does determine the scope of their content and the general rules guiding their operation. Stated differently, the mixed model depicts a situation of regulation not only of the substance of messages—the main attribute of the control model—but also the means of their transmission—the core of the regulation model. Hence, due to the absence of comprehensive political control over content, regulation remains minor in scope and depth. Societies choosing to function according to this model select the proportions or mix of oversight and enforcement best attuned to their culture.

Over the years, relations between the media and Israel's political system have travelled along this conceptual continuum. Beginning with the control model adopted following independence, a shift to the regulatory model was observed in the 1980s but especially the 1990s; in recent years, major elements of the mixed model have been incorporated. This article describes the practical implications of the three models as observed within the Israeli context.

The main argument presented here is that although the three archetypes represent stages in the unidirectional development of interactions between the media and the political system within the broad framework of the Israeli reality, the models fluctuate within the national security context because they display keen sensitivity to security-related events. This article shows that the logic guiding these interactions in the arena of national security differs, as a rule, from the logic guiding relations between the two institutions in non-security contexts. Therefore, despite the persistent trend in policy toward an open approach to the mass media, changes in the perception of national security occasionally, and often voluntarily, resurrect the controlled access to information associated with the first, closed model. As a result, fundamental questions pertaining to journalistic freedom, freedom of information, or the place of military censorship in an open society, to name just three, create tensions whenever gaps surface between the interpretations of a security event's seriousness offered by various 'media entrepreneurs'.

The first part of this article presents the conceptual framework underlying the movement between the three models and the attendant variations in transmission of security-related information by the mass media. In the second part, analysis of the control mechanisms applied by the state to the media, this framework is employed to portray the gradual evolution of the relationship existing in Israel between the media and the political system since the 1950s.[1] The concluding part of the article demonstrates the postulated 'travelling' of trends in information transmission with several examples.

GOVERNANCE AND COMMUNICATION: A CONCEPTUAL FRAMEWORK

It is possible to treat communication—those messages comprised of words, pictures and voices transmitted by a certain producer to a consumer along a variety of transmission technologies—as either a public or a private consumption good. National security is, however, uniformly considered to be a public consumption good. The 'public' or 'private' aspects of communication are unrelated to the character of the transmission medium, its type of ownership, or the identity of its producer. Similarly irrelevant is the consumer's identity. Producers, like consumers of communication, or of security, may be private persons or public bodies. The good itself will be public when it exhibits specific attributes and private in the absence of those attributes.

Two basic features determine a good's public status. The first is jointness of supply; the second, externalities. Jointness defines a situation where a good appears on the utility functions of all a society's members irrespective of any part they may play in its production.[2] Stated differently, because it is impossible to divide or ration a public good, it is also impossible to exclude anyone from its consumption. In contrast, a private good is characterized by a direct relationship between the good and its consumer. Little effort is required to prevent an individual who did not pay for a private good from enjoying it. For instance, if a person does not pay for the pair of shoes she wishes to wear, she will not receive the item. Alternatively, when individuals cannot be prevented from consuming a good even if they contributed nothing to its production (as in the case of security), the circumstances invite free riding, a form of economic behaviour that characterizes rational actors (and, in principle, all members of society) who aspire to benefit from a good without contributing to the cost of its production.[3] In order to reduce free riding, society delegates enforcement powers to the state, which acts in its name and obliges citizens to join the army or pay the taxes that enable the joint supply of security.

A public good's second attribute is known as externalities or spill-over effects, that is, a good's production may entail the transfer of costs (or benefits) to individuals having no direct connection (or any intention of establishing such a connection) to the good's consumption. For instance, negative benefits accrue to person A if person B, during production of some consumption good, pollutes the air that person A breathes irrespective of whether person A is directly involved in obtaining or using the good produced. In such circumstances, the injured party can, in principle, demand compensation from the polluters for the damages incurred; in practice, however, it is more convenient to delegate such authority to the state, which then acts against the polluters on behalf of all the injured parties. Allocation of third party functions to the state is essential when precise delineation of the private property rights transgressed becomes problematic. For example, the difficulties involved in assigning property rights to the polluted air floating above our heads has encouraged the categorization of air as a public good and, as such, subject to collective responsibility.

It follows that security is unequivocally a public good, primarily due to the jointness of its supply, whereas land-based channels of communication (i.e., television and radio) are public goods primarily due to their externalities. Therefore, the 'public' quality of these two goods, the subjects of the present article, do not vary with their producers, be they public or private. For instance, security can be provided by an army of mercenaries or by professional soldiers, and the weapons used can be produced by private or public sector firms. Analogously, private firms can provide communication over public channels. The issue of privatization obviously impinges upon this structure.[4] Privatization does not imply that the government is no longer obligated to produce public goods. On the contrary, a government can transfer this function to private firms without losing its theoretical or practical responsibility (exercised, for example, through the regulation of quantity and quality) for the good's production and distribution on behalf of society.

Furthermore, situations can arise where goods having public attributes may yet be traded like any other private good.[5] Sporting events readily illustrate this pattern because they exhibit both attributes that define public goods. So, in principle, it makes no difference whether the number of spectators at a specific event are few or many. It has already been noted that a public good is characterized by universal supply and the spill-over of costs/benefits onto those uninterested in the good's consumption. However, if one were to build a fence around the venue, the event's public quality would not be nullified although it would now be possible to demand payment (the price of admission) for the pleasure of viewing the game.

Charging admission makes it possible to exclude all those unwilling to help finance the event through its consumption. A technical constraint—the stadium's enclosure—thus allows us to create a good that, irrespective of its obvious public attributes, can be treated as a private good and distributed according to a market mechanism that sets prices at the equilibrium between demand (to view the event) and supply (the number of seats within the enclosure).

Viewed from this perspective, declarations of national sovereignty and international recognition of its borders are earmarks of a good's public character. To continue the analogy, a country's borders, like a stadium's walls, transform a public good into a 'national' good. All those found outside the designated borders are, by definition, excluded from the consumption of national goods. Immigration laws prevent entry into the country and thereby confine access to national goods to established residents, the nation's citizens. That is, all those 'inside' are eligible, in principle, to partake in the benefits produced by national goods although, as Kook has demonstrated, the effective conduct of affairs may differ dramatically.[6] What this means is that in practice policies often limit enjoyment of a gamut of the public goods (e.g., political and civil rights, the benefits flowing from identification with symbols) produced within national borders to selected groups of citizens or control individual access to those goods.

One can nonetheless assume that the exclusion of citizens from the consumption of national security is more problematic than their exclusion from the consumption of goods unrelated to their survival. Furthermore, although one may be aware that security is not consumed equitably—for instance, citizens living close to the border are more susceptible to injury and are thus required to consume greater quantities of this good—one tends to ignore such distinctions. These behaviours do not, however, apply to communication. To understand why, it is necessary to define the concept.

Communication is a multi-dimensional phenomenon concept encompassing a broad range of mechanisms and messages. Therefore, if one does not restrict its scope or delimit its components, the construction of causal links between communication and its outcomes becomes rather complicated. For present purposes, this article confines the concept to the mass media—the information transmitted along electronic channels—whose unregulated consumption may influence the capacity to produce a public good—national security—under the direct responsibility of national decision-makers. In other words, just as advertised items differ from unadvertised items, national security within the context of the mass media differs from national security outside this context.

To be specific, whether the messages transmitted contain substantive data or specific images, and irrespective of the type of transmission (written or broadcast), the mass media per se represent salient components in a nation's endeavours to produce security. This insight, if only intuitively, has already affected military deployment and operations on the micro level: communication officers, spokespersons, information officers and other performers of similar tasks have been routinely attached to combat units for some time.

However, the impact of the media is even greater on the macro level, where national security policy is made: Outcomes may vary with the manner in which policy is presented by the media. Consider deterrence, a major component of military strategy; if portrayed effectively, deterrence is likely to reduce the costs of producing security. Security itself is often media-dependent because it is defined in part by the images its producers wish to arouse among adversaries. To illustrate, transmitting a message that an aggressive act committed by one side will initiate retaliatory measures by the other side may constitute an effective deterrence. Similarly, the media and the images broadcast are vital for inspiring contributions to the security effort, a factor instrumental in reducing free riding. Moreover, because the media influence public opinion especially, but not only, in democratic regimes, and because public opinion affects the substance and direction of policy, control over the media has a strategic value in the production of security.

Continuing this line of argument, it soon becomes evident that the defence leadership will naturally aspire to maximize control of information so as to minimize interference in the production of security. This tendency to control information is observed in every organization interested in undermining its competitor's advantages.[7] In the area of national security, control of information is meant to thwart any political or military gains an enemy or rival hopes to achieve. This control has even been used on occasion to forestall an ally's exploitation of the benefits to be gained from third-party relations, as evidenced by the eruption of the Pollard affair (involving an American navy officer spying for the Israelis) on the US–Israel agenda in the mid-1980s. This tendency generally grows with the perceived intensity of the threat.

As has been seen, externalities represent the primary justification for treating communication as a public good. It is in this sense that the messages carried by telephone and the Internet, but especially by satellite communications, respect no political boundaries. The national sovereignty that defines security's orbit is therefore extraneous to the issues intrinsic to communication; unlike security, it is technically difficult to confine the reach of messages. With respect to substance, complexities balloon in response to the social features of communication, which are unrelated to any pre-planned correspondence between electronic messages and security interests. In open, democratic societies, a broad range of normative and other messages indirectly or negatively related to security are produced, transmitted and received. Nevertheless, such messages can collectively impact on security. For instance, a message depicting a humane and sensitive enemy or one stressing the economic and psychological stress suffered may eventually undermine the motivation to combat that enemy. It is thus incumbent upon every democracy to decide on the measure of such messages it can afford to receive.

An argument can readily be made that the competition between values—and the attendant messages—is influenced by perceptions of a concrete threat to survival. The more confident a society, the less its existence is in question, the more it will tend to produce and receive a range of messages, including those containing subversive information regarding its regime and social structure. Alternatively, the more tangible a threat, the greater the tendency of systems responsible for security to control the menu of messages communicated. Under conditions of threat, concern for the national interest is transformed into an existential imperative, a call to arms. Research has indicated that even under conditions of what is sometimes labelled a democratic peace, when the likelihood that the interests of one democratic state will pose a threat to a neighbouring democracy is marginal, the policy apparatus prepares itself—through laws, regulations and procedures—to respond to a potential deterioration in the status quo.[8]

Attitudes toward the miscellaneous information transmitted by the media are usually distinguished from attitudes toward security-related information. As previously stated, security is considered to be a 'pure' public good; alternatively, communication, when viewed from the perspective of security, is an 'optional' public good.[9] Thus, like the privately operated railways and national airlines that conduct their business with persistent losses covered by state subsidies and which can be recruited to transport masses of individuals or arms during crises, attitudes toward the media are subject to current exigencies. Open societies will permit the free provision of information only so long as they remain immune from an existential threat. Yet, reality is rarely dichotomous in the sense that people infrequently find themselves in a state of either war or of 'perpetual peace', in the words of Immanuel Kant;[10] life more closely resembles a fluid continuum of intermediate circumstances. Correspondingly, attitudes toward media-transmitted messages also fluctuate with assessments of the state of national security. Decision-makers consequently opt to exercise influence over the media as needed.

It is therefore possible to identify three types of relationships that are maintained between the media and the national security arena, each structured in response to the intensity of the perceived threat to national existence. At one end of the security spectrum, representing periods of crisis, there is an interest-oriented policy of control over the information produced and communicated. At the other end, representing an absence of threat, whether real or perceived, the media tend to operate in an open, unencumbered fashion. The degree of control brought to bear will depend on how the threat to survival is perceived by the nation's leadership.

However, because control over information (whether in the name of security or some other goal) also endows decision-makers with advantages in non-security areas, disagreements frequently arise in democratic countries over questions such as the public's 'right to know' and transparency. In the next part of this article, it will be shown how the political system in Israel maintained control over the media for decades, a policy shielded by the umbrella of 'security needs'. It will also be shown how, after Israel's survival appeared assured, other values came to direct and structure relations between the two entities.

THE POLITICAL-CONTROL MODEL

The dynamics and challenges of nation building, in addition to the influence exerted by socialist ideology on the project's realization, produced an interventionist political system that has dominated Israeli society from its beginnings. The state's involvement in the private life of its citizens, including the material read or heard, led to Sharkansky's labelling

Israel as 'the most socialist [state] outside the Eastern Bloc'.[11] The Zionist politics that induced a surfeit of parties active within its pre-state institutional framework and the lack of meaningful steps taken to alter this political polygamy prior to the establishment of Israel in 1948, resulted in what Akzin calls a 'party-state'.[12]

In addition, the majority of Zionist parties, especially those joining governing coalitions, maintained party machines. In return for party loyalty and electoral support, this mechanism provided party members with benefits ranging from housing, jobs and medical insurance to recreational facilities and, of course, a constant flow of information invested with the appropriate commentary about the party as well as national affairs. Within this framework, party-affiliated Hebrew newspapers—such as the Histadrut's *Davar*, Mapam's *Al HaMishmar*, the General Zionists' *HaBoker*, the Herut Movement's *Herut*, the Communist *Kol HaAm*—as well as papers published in English, Yiddish, Hungarian, Romanian, Russian, Polish and German were commonly read. Funding for this project came from party coffers, particularly Mapai's. Several parties have retained this practice; for example, the Mafdal continues to publish *HaTzofe*, and Agudat Yisrael *HaModia* as well as *Yated Ne'eman*.

Like the ideology and world view held by Israel's founding fathers, but especially by its first prime minister, David Ben-Gurion, intervention and regulation of the media were rationalized by perceptions of the country's fluctuating, yet enduring, security needs. A classic example of the system and its implications is provided by the informal editors' committee, established shortly after independence. The committee's members included the editors-in-chief of all the Hebrew newspapers and the English-language *Jerusalem Post* but excluded *Kol HaAm*, the Communist Party organ.[13]

Originally, the group was invited to attend security briefings delivered by the prime minister (who usually filled the position of minister of defence as well); over the years, invitations to similar sessions were extended by other ministers and senior officials. The information communicated to this coterie was kept from the Israeli public even when details appeared in the foreign press. These meetings thus set the stage for the type of self-censorship that buried information sensitive to security or embarrassing to policy-makers. For instance, the public was denied timely knowledge of arms deals made with foreign powers; Israel's involvement in the Kurdish rebellion and the agreements signed with the Romanian and Ethiopian governments that paved the way for immigration to Israel from these countries.

Regulation and oversight, rooted in what Feldman calls voluntary 'social responsibility' in the Japanese context, was reinforced by formal mechanisms.[14] To illustrate, the media were forbidden to report information related to the capture of spies or Israel's nuclear programme. These strictures were supported by Israel's censorship law, the *Emergency (Defence) Regulations* (1945), a revision of the *Press Ordinance* issued by the British Mandate that prohibited publication of either general or detailed information that might endanger Israel's security, its citizen's well-being or public safety. Responsibility for deciding whether the information obtained fell under these broad and somewhat vague restrictions was shifted to the editors themselves. In two cases, the first in 1953, the second in 1988, the Supreme Court voted to restrict the jurisdiction of the military censor.[15] Nevertheless, whenever the country felt besieged, public and official attitudes toward censorship on the one hand, and the media's attitudes, on the other, swayed in favour of the censor.

It was David Ben-Gurion who established the margins of control over security-related information. As prime minister and minister of defence almost continuously between 1948 and the early 1960s, Ben-Gurion received daily reports from the Mossad, the General Security Services and military intelligence. During this same period, the office of the IDF spokesperson belonged to the intelligence services. Hence, in principle if not in practice, no security-related information could reach the public without it first being reviewed by Ben-Gurion.[16] This strategic location, coupled with Ben-Gurion's personal predilections, clearly influenced the character of the information transmitted to the public by the electronic media. As television reached Israel only in 1968, radio was the sole outlet available for state control. Ben-Gurion rationalized his refusal to permit the entry of television by quoting 'equality'—television would introduce the 'uneven' consumption of information—a principle ostensibly adopted by all educational, cultural and social institutions. This 'system' reinforced regime management of items issuing from the IDF spokesperson's office and forestalled any serious criticism of their content.

Returning to radio, Kol Yisrael (the Voice of Israel) staff members were, in effect, state employees who received directives dealing with everything from programming mix to proper Hebrew spelling and pronunciation. Creation of a uniform broadcasting language for an audience made up mainly of immigrants with varying levels of education was certainly a primary policy objective, and one shared with other networks, including the BBC. Yet, these directives were also designed to cultivate a defined national identity through the inculcation of the Hebrew language and an unambiguous political orientation. For example, Israel's major enemy during those years, Egypt's President Gamal Abd al Nasser, was labelled the 'Egyptian tyrant'; immigrants to Israel were dubbed 'olim' (those who ascended) whereas emigrants from Israel were termed 'yordim' (those who descended), both derived directly from Zionist ideology.

With the exception of Galei Tzahal, the IDF radio station established in 1950 (although its mandated target audience was the standing army, it in fact operated as a reservoir of talent for the civilian station, Kol Yisrael), the broadcast media market was bereft of competition; such competition, had it existed, might have improved the station's performance. Whatever competition emerged was waged between the station's three main units: the Hebrew Department, Kol Tziyyon LeGola (broadcasts aimed at the Jewish Diaspora) and the Arabic Department. As a rule, neighbouring countries considered Kol Yisrael's news broadcasts in Arabic to be more reliable than the broadcasts produced by Arab governments and transmitted in Hebrew to Israel's Arabic-speaking population. This competition with Arab stations over the listening audience—a rivalry crucial when public opinion among the enemy is perceived to be a strategic factor in national security—apparently influenced the decision to open Israel's first television station in 1968.

Several meaningful steps preceded the inauguration of television. The first involved launching the Israel Educational Television Network in 1965, a step partially financed by the Rothschild family. The second involved the transformation of the government-run Kol Yisrael into a public network, the Israel Broadcasting Authority (IBA), also in 1965. The third was the construction of an alternate regulatory mechanism, the IBA's Plenum and Public Council, which replaced direct government control with indirect public regulation.[17]

However, council members were (and remain) appointed according to party affiliation; appointees tended to be second-rank party members who, at least during the IBA's early years, promoted the interests of their political backers. IBA dependence on the government likewise remained in force as a result of Ministry of Finance funding and approval of its operating budget. Hence, when elected representatives, whether as members of the government or the Knesset Finance Committee, were displeased with the media's presentation of policy (or officeholders), they could respond by reducing the budget. This financial yoke effectively removed the need for explicit threats.

Television viewing rates, which quickly transformed *Madurat Shabbat* (the *Saturday Edition*) into Israel's main news broadcast, were impressive. A decade after its introduction, 80 percent of the Jewish population regularly watched the programme. The rates in the Arab sector, whose experience with television had begun with Arab-produced programmes received in Israel, were even greater.[18] Programming during the early evening hours (17:30–19:00) was dedicated to the Arab community, with subtitles in Arabic added to programmes broadcast in Hebrew.

THE MARKET OR REGULATORY MODEL

Israel's mass media began to free itself of the state's stranglehold in the mid-1970s. Viewed in terms of the three models posited at the beginning of this article, this period exhibited a gradual transition from the first, political control model, to the second, the market or regulatory model. When searching for the source of this movement, a plausible explanation lies in Israel's military victory over the Egyptian and Syrian armies in the 1973

Yom Kippur War. Despite the dreadful early losses, the ultimate victory may have convinced Israel's policy-makers that the threat to the country's survival had waned. Believing that this was truly the case, the time was optimal to relax control and permit the entry of other media. Other, more blatant yet essentially political factors certainly contributed to this about-face, such as the proposals raised by the liberal members of Israel's new political party, Dash (the Democratic Movement for Change).

Originating in the post-Yom Kippur War protest movement, Dash later demanded that the media be opened to competition as one condition for its entry into the 1977 government coalition. Also deserving mention were the anti-monopoly, liberal attitudes held by Menachem Begin, the Likud's leader,[19] and the Labour Party's official commitment to liberalization, which had been part of its platform prior to the 1977 elections. Yet political leaders found it easier to promise change than to implement their promises. Preparations for opening the media, realized in the form of a second television channel, took a further fifteen years to complete. In the interim, a 1986 amendment to the *Bezek Communications Company Ltd. Law (1937)* supported the introduction of cable television, a step that helped solve the problem of the by then blossoming illegal private ('pirate') television stations.

With respect to radio, its very low infrastructure costs allowed pirate stations to start broadcasting programmes targeted especially at the religious, ultra-nationalist and Arab sectors. The continuity of these transmissions, like television programmes in the past, indicates a demand for special types of messages otherwise ignored by the mainstream stations. A partial response to this demand became available recently with the development of new telecommunication technologies. However, beyond the problem of the content, which often embodies gross infringements of the law, and the formal issues posed by the operation of unlicensed stations, a situation that makes a farce of legislation, pirate radio stations in the Israeli context display two features that influence national politics and security.

First, like Abie Nathan's Peace Ship, which transmitted political messages in the 1970s, pirate stations in the 1990s, particularly the right wing Station 7 and the religious and Arab stations, freely broadcast political messages that are often inflammatory in nature and clearly violate the laws regulating propaganda broadcasts. Moreover, several political leaders who see nothing untoward in the operation of these pirate stations frequently utilize them to further their careers. Second, the unregulated broadcasts often interfere with the frequencies used to guide commercial air traffic, as well as military communications; hence, they directly jeopardize public safety.

Despite the clearly commercial goals of cable television, the channels have been placed under the purview of the minister of communications. The eleven-member Council for Cable and Satellite TV includes five members directly appointed by the minister; the government appoints the rest. Additional control of the channels is exercised through the prohibition to broadcast national news in Hebrew: only local news is permitted. This damper was not imposed on the two currently operating commercial channels: Channel Two, inaugurated in 1993 and Channel 10, inaugurated eight years later. Like the IBA and the Council for Cable Television, the public council overseeing Channel Two (and since 2001 also Channel 10) also includes fifteen members appointed by the government.[20]

With respect to its conditions, the law establishing the Second Authority for Television and Regional Radio closely resembles that formulated for the IBA, but with one glaring exception: the income accruing to the concessionaires operating Channels Two and 10 rests on commercial advertising whereas the income accruing to Channel One rests on government allocations. It follows that although Channel Two, like Channel One, is a public good—both carry messages along land-based channels—Channel Two has been privatized whereas Channel One is awaiting privatization. Moreover, Channel 10, the new supposedly public channel, is not a privatized good but a private good: Its messages are carried along the private cable system. The fact that the government tends to treat Channel 10 as if it is a privatized good is normatively unjustifiable in terms of the conceptual principles delineated earlier.

The further opening of the Israeli media occurred subsequent to the Peled Commission's report, released in 1997. The report recommended the introduction of additional technologies such as satellite transmissions as well as a third commercial channel, and the approval of five targeted channels, four aimed at unique audiences—Russians, Arabs, Sephardim (Jews of Middle East extraction) and observant Jews—and one dedicated solely to broadcasting news. Although the idea of targeted channels was formulated in the language of media pluralism, a concept that Israel's liberals found difficult to dispute, the model chosen was, surprisingly, the multicultural model, a format that apparently aroused considerable opposition. However, because the project's initiators were able to anchor both models in normative arguments based on liberal premises, it apparently became simple to 'sell' the public one model disguised as the other. The Commission's report likewise proposed replacing the concession system with licensing, a move that would significantly open the media's structure. Support for this proposal came from an unexpected direction: in its 1988 report, the Zuckerman Commission, convened to review operations at the IBA's Channel One, recommended that the channel be privatized while strictly protecting its public character.

Thus, satellite television became available in 2000; a year later, the operators of Channel 10 were chosen, as were the operators of the all-news channel and of the Russian-language channel. After this programme for opening the airwaves is consummated, Israel will thus have adopted, in practice, the open market model that represents the mirror image of the political control model that characterized the mass media since the nation's infancy.

THE MIXED MODEL: POLITICS, THE MEDIA AND NATIONAL SECURITY IN ISRAEL

Throughout Israel's history, changes in relations between the media and the political system have been functions of decision-makers' perceptions of national security. It can be argued that the shift toward adoption of the open model of these relations has been policy-oriented, that is, decision-makers and media entrepreneurs have responded in a conscious and orderly fashion to several of the changes experienced by Israeli society since the early 1960s. These changes included assurance of the nation's existence in the face of external threats and, especially since the 1990s, the transition to more liberal patterns of political behaviour.[21] Within the framework of this argument, the structural transformation of the mass media has proven to be a significant factor in the process.

An analysis of the development of the mass media in Israel only in terms of a progression from closure to openness does not, however, contribute much explanatory power to the *travelling model* concept advanced here. That is, the model of mass communication adopted within the context of national security cannot be viewed as either open or closed—it is mixed. Put differently, it would be expected that the decision to 'travel' from openness to closure occurred in the presence of real or perceived security threats; hence, when such threats are removed or no longer exist, we would expect a unidirectional yet reverse movement from a controlled to an open model of communication.

Yet policy decisions rarely conform to the latter format because policy-makers, depending on their innate inclinations, tend to exploit actual or create bogus security threats in order to extend their domination over the media due to their role in forming public opinion. One need only recall Machiavelli, who taught us in *The Prince* that no better device exists for gaining control over public opinion than to start a small war.[22] More specifically, it has often been publicly noted that in order to advance party interests and personal goals, Israeli politicians had readily taken advantage of the (security) 'situation' (as it is popularly called) and released classified information.[23] How, then, can one ascertain whether a decision to turn from the open (or market) to the closed (or political control) model issues from real security needs? Conversely, how can one ascertain whether national security merely rationalizes a politician's fundamental aspiration to control information en route to realizing his or her own ends?

Observation of the play of market forces in situations marked by perceived existential threats offers one effective approach to clarifying the issue. In other words, if one can identify any voluntary movement of media entities from the open to the closed model in cases where the option of non-movement is available, our basic argument will be supported. Stated differently, it is possible that when a situation is perceived as a security crisis, the media tend to respond in varying degrees of what has been called 'social responsibility'. This means that in such circumstances, media people tend to behave like stock investors in a market characterized by uncertainty. They reduce risk. Hence, the media will provide only that information that supports, or at least does not interfere with the security endeavours.

Confrontation with issues such as democratic norms, transparency and sensitivity to civil and human rights will be postponed to more tranquil times. This tendency may materialize in the voluntary self-regulation of communication networks conducted as if the act had been prescribed by an official order. From a different perspective, this tendency toward voluntary closure during crises may be considered a breed of patriotic mobilization for defence. That is, when under threat, everyone—including the media—become soldiers, or at least IDF spokespeople.

Still another dimension of this volitional silence pertains to the professional interests of media people. The role of the media is to report on events as they occur. If reports fall below the expected quantity or quality, one's livelihood, status and reputation may be at stake. To protect their own interests, reporters and commentators must develop exclusive sources of information or at least ensure continued access to insiders. This group bears no resemblance to an editors' council of the type that characterized the first model. Instead, its members are favourites, and are considered reliable by defence personnel because of their 'responsible' attitude, they will know what information to reveal, how to word it and when to deliver it.

Imposition of any legal form of censorship is superfluous for the majority of this circle's members. The most effective deterrence against those few who would act 'irresponsibly' is a severance of ties to their sources. During peace, these journalists are major constituents in the external coalition supporting the defence system. During crises, when the public's hunger for information escalates media support for the defence system intensifies with the naturally increasing dependence on a limited number of official sources or spokespersons.

It is difficult to explain the media's silence and their fealty to Washington during the 1990–1991 Gulf War and the 2003 US war in Iraq without linking that behaviour to these interests. American media journalists, who are rarely suspected of unprofessional behaviour or of lending blind support to their government, cooperated with the coalition forces and even lent a hand in the deception and communication blackout accompanying the 1990–1991 attack on Iraq. Only after the conclusion of that war were critical positions and commentaries voiced in the national and international media. It follows that the distinction between what is perceived as a 'security objective' versus a 'political' one can assist in deciphering the behaviour exhibited by the media during different security contexts.

It appears that the more a situation is defined as threatening national security (i.e., posing a direct danger to survival, with war being an extreme case), the stronger the tendency for the media to support government policies. This proposition, although not revolutionary, is sustained by the early empirical study conducted by Reuven Kahane and Shlomit Canaan in 1973 on the 'behaviour of the press during periods of tension and its influence on public support of the government', and by Dina Goren in 1977 in her analysis of Israeli press treatment of terrorist attacks prior to, and following, the Yom Kippur War.[24]

Nevertheless, there is still a need to explain the criticism voiced by the local media against security-related military operations initiated by the Israeli government. The explanation rests on our understanding of the media's function as a mediator.[25] This function is time-dependent and responsive to consumer demand. If, at the first stage of a security crisis the common interest of the government, the media and consumers—survival of the political system in which all these three participate—appears to be identical, the practical expression of that correspondence will be unanimity.

The public will want to know what is happening (although it frequently abstains from such demands even if that knowledge ensures the effective conduct of military operations), and the media will comply by transmitting the 'facts' in appropriate measure. At later stages of the crisis (at least in democratic societies), the public may also wish to understand what happened and why, if it were possible to act differently and whether the time has come to search for lower-cost solutions to future crises.

To meet these demands, the political commentary broadcast by the mass media will acquire a distributive function, meaning that it will provide alternative 'interpretive packages', as suggested by Gamson and Modigliani, to compete with the official interpretive packages (i.e., policies) already available.[26] In effect, this role will be realized and normatively sanctioned only after the concrete security threat has subsided. Our argument implies that this scenario conforms to the government's 'natural' tendency to control media-distributed information so as to delay the appearance of critical interpretive packages as long as feasible.

An illustration from the field of collective behaviour can help to clarify the character of these fluctuations. Large coalitions tend to rule and survive during what are considered grave security crises but shrink or even disappear when the threat is removed.[27] When faced with an existential threat, everything, including political rivalries, is deferred for the sake of solidarity. Once the situation returns to 'normal', rivalries are resumed. Doron characterizes this process as a retreat from a *super game* to that of a *zero sum game*.[28] During a super game, every participant plays a cooperative game against the common source of the threat; during a zero sum game, every player plays independently, even when the game is against a former member of the 'team', meaning the government.

If this account is accurate, confirmation should be found in the changes in behavioural patterns exhibited by the media subsequent to their autonomous decisions. For this exercise to be fruitful, the relevant decisions must have been made under conditions free of government influence and oversight. What came to be called the 'Helicopter Disaster' and how it was treated by Israel's Channel Two, a channel relatively unfettered by government intervention in its editorial policy and coverage, adequately meets the analytic requirements.[29]

At 19.00 hours on 4 February 1997, while the IDF was still present in southern Lebanon, two Yassur helicopters collided with each one another on their way to a mission in the region. Seventy-three soldiers were killed in the collision, one of the most serious peacetime accidents in IDF history. Because the event was witnessed by several members of Moshav Sha'ar Yeshuv in northern Israel, over whose land the collision occurred, it was impossible to impose a communication blackout. Due to the magnitude of the disaster, without any formal government guidance, Channel Two executives decided to apply the programming mix usually adopted during periods of national mourning. Advertising was thus cancelled and the channel's schedule, including nightly entertainment, was revised. The channel's underlying premise was that given the bleak national mood, demand for advertising and light entertainment would be non-existent; the will of the audience would be honoured. Voluntary mourning lasted three days.

To place this decision in perspective, it should be compared to other instances of high demand for information, such as the 2001 lynching of two Israeli soldiers by a Palestinian mob in Ramallah. During that event, an editorial decision was made to provide extensive news coverage immediately following the event. While very little new information was transmitted during the many hours of broadcasting, the repetitive showing of the same footage presumably met public demands for information.

Regarding the Helicopter Disaster, a review of the decision reveals the economic criteria that motivated the decision to adopt the mourning formula in this as in other cases of national tragedy; such considerations, in fact, are not unusual for commercial television. Given that, the response of Channel Two's Public Council promises to be more interesting in light of its responsibility for authorizing programming changes. It was therefore found that the Council's members, apparently succumbing to the tragedy of the disaster like the rest of the population, had approved the mourning formula almost reflexively. However, within a few days, when the public began to recover from the shock, a series of discussions were held in the Council that supported a return to the regular programming mix. Stringent criticism of the operational aspects of the affair erupted, as could be expected, only much later.

CONCLUSION

Open and free communication is a salient characteristic of democratic regimes. However, scholars and critics tend to treat the media as if they were self-managed autonomous and isolated entities; they tend to forget that these institutions are run by rational actors whose interests overlap with those of other social actors. Extreme situations that promote this interest-oriented congruence are provided by national security-related events, especially during wartime. Assuming this to be the case, it is difficult to expect media people to behave much differently than other members of society, especially politicians.

In normal circumstances, when group survival is not in doubt, so-called 'professional' considerations influence decision-making. In effect, these considerations tend to rationalize interest-promoting behaviour. Thus, governments almost instinctively avoid revealing information that might invite public censure. Bureaucracies, as suggested by Max Weber similarly protect themselves behind smokescreens of secrecy erected to prevent a reasonable measure of transparency.[30] Politicians, too, attempt to control information and tailor it to results that will at least not undermine the likelihood of their political survival and re-election.

These observations encourage us to interpret the Israeli government's early attempts to control media-transmitted information and regulate independent channels of transmission as a combination of the leadership' desire to steer the country toward what they consider an exalted mission while safeguarding their political status. After Israel's security was ensured, accompanied by multiple channels of communication, government capacity to exert control receded. Changes in the nation's media map expressed these together with other trends. In the foreseeable future, this map will be altered (if it has not already been breached) by a media captained by individuals and groups interested in producing subversive messages. Viewed less pessimistically, this situation can potentially sustain a lively discourse that may very well fortify the democratic streams in Israeli society.

NOTES

1. See Gideon Doron, 'The Politics of Mass Communication in Israel', *The Annals*, Vol. 555 (January 1998), pp. 163–179.
2. See Paul Samuelson, 'The Pure Theory of Public Expenditures', *Review of Economics and Statistics* (November 1954), pp. 387–389. See also Gideon Doron, *To Decide and to Implement: Chapters in Public Policy*, Tel Aviv, 1986.
3. See Mancur Olson, *The Logic of Collective Action*, Cambridge, MA, 1965.
4. See Itzhak Katz, *Privatization: In Israel and Abroad*, Tel Aviv, 1997.
5. See Peter Steiner, 'The Public Sector and the Public Interest', in Robert Haveman and Julius Margolis (eds.), *Public Expenditures and Policy Analysis*, New York, 1977, pp. 27–66.
6. See Rebecca Kook, *The Logic of Democratic Exclusion; African-Americans in the United States and Palestinian Citizens in Israel*, Lanham, MD, 2002.
7. See Gideon Doron and Udi Lebel, *The Politics of Bereavement*, Tel Aviv, 2003.

8. See Martin Sherman and Gideon Doron, 'War and Peace as Rational Choice in the Middle East', in Zeev Maoz (ed.), *Regional Security in the Middle East*, London, 1997, pp. 72–102.
9. Doron, *To Decide and to Implement*.
10. See Immanuel Kant, 'Perpetual Peace', in Lewis Beck (ed. and trans.), *On History*, Indianapolis, 1963.
11. See Ira Sharkansky, *The Political Economy of Israel*, New Brunswick, NJ, 1987.
12. See Benjamin Akzin, 'The Role of Parties in Israeli Democracy', *Journal of Politics*, Vol. 4 (1955), pp. 507–545.
13. See Doron, 'The Politics of Mass Communication in Israel'.
14. See Offer Feldman, *Politics and the News Media in Japan*, Ann Arbor, 1993.
15. See Amnon Rubenstein, *The Constitutional Law of the State of Israel*, Tel Aviv, 1980.
16. See Gideon Doron, 'Israeli Intelligence: Tactics, Strategy, and Prediction', *International Journal of Intelligence and Counterintelligence*, Vol. 2, No. 3 (1988), pp. 305–319.
17. See Dan Caspi and Yechiel Limor, *The Mediators*, Tel Aviv, 1992.
18. See Doron, 'The Politics of Mass Communication in Israel'.
19. See Moshe Maor, *The Right Way for Society*, Tel Aviv, 2004.
20. See Caspi and Limor, *The Mediators*.
21. See Doron and Lebel, *The Politics of Bereavement*.
22. See Niccolo Machiavelli, *The Prince*, Tel Aviv, 1988.
23. See Doron and Lebel, *The Politics of Bereavement*.
24. See discussion of the findings of these two studies in Gideon Doron, 'The Politics and Logic of Transmitting to the Public Military Images', in Udi Lebel (ed.), *Communicating Security*, Beer Sheeva, 2005.
25. See Caspi and Limor, *The Mediators*.
26. See William Gamson and A. Modigiliani, 'Media Discourse Public Opinion on Nuclear Power: A Constructionist Approach', *American Journal of Sociology* (1989), 95, pp. 1–37.
27. See William Riker, *The Theory of Political Coalitions*, New Haven, 1992, for a general theoretical statement on coalitions. See also Dan Korn and Boaz Shapira, *Coalitions: Israeli Politics, 50 years, 100 Cases*, Tel Aviv, 1997.
28. See Gideon Doron, *Games in Israeli Politics*, Tel Aviv, 1988.
29. The economic rational that underlies the operation of 'privatized' television channels is discussed in Gideon Doron, 'The Economic Impact of Mass Communication: The Case of Channel II', *Kesher* (May 2001), pp. 111–117.
30. See Max Weber, *From Max Weber: Essays in Sociology*, New York, 1960.

Nuclear Ambiguity and the Media: The Israeli Case

YOEL COHEN

Media coverage of Israel's nuclear policy is heavily censored. This contrasts with coverage of other aspects of defence policy and military-related developments. Major news organizations have more than one full-time military correspondent (one of the most coveted posts in Israeli journalism), as well as a military reporter covering day-to-day events, a defence reporter covering the defence ministry and the military industry and a staff military commentator. Despite the considerable media content on military–defence matters, most Israelis do not think it excessive. In a 1986 poll of 1,172 Israeli Jewish respondents, 68 percent replied that the media placed the correct amount of emphasis on the Arab–Israeli security issue, 26 percent too much, and 6 percent too little.[1]

Israeli nuclear policy is based on non-disclosure of the country's nuclear capability. Israel's formal position—as enunciated by politicians and diplomats since the 1960s—is that it will not be the first to introduce nuclear weaponry into the Middle East region, which is tantamount to Israel not confirming whether it possesses the Bomb. This phrase may be interpreted in any number of ways. What is the Middle East? Could Israel become the second nation to introduce such weaponry?

The policy of ambiguity or non-confirmation has two primary origins. First, Israeli officials have long believed that confirmation of any nuclear capability would generate widespread public pressure within the Arab world to develop nuclear parity with Israel. Given that Iraq and Iran developed nuclear programmes irrespective of the ambiguity policy the validity of this reasoning may be questioned. Secondly, under the 1976 Congressional Symington Law, a US government is forbidden to provide economic assistance to any country developing a nuclear programme unless it is placed under international supervision. A third reason concerns France, which cooperated with Israel in the 1950s to build the nuclear research centre at Dimona. France conditioned cooperation on complete secrecy over its role.[2] French customs officials, for example, were reportedly told that the largest of the reactor components, such as the reactor tank, were part of a desalination plant bound for Latin America. Some sections of the project were even kept simply as oral understandings between the two countries. Shimon Peres, one of the architects of the nuclear project and of the ambiguity stance surrounding it, remarked that 'it is forbidden to print any details about the project—whether right or wrong. One among other factors is the [Arab] embargo on the State of Israel. There are those which supply us with parts, and with regard to the embargo we have undertaken not to disclose the source of the purchase, and therefore the government is obligated to classify the source'.[3]

'Ambiguity' should not be confused with nuclear secrecy. Suspicions that Israel possesses the Bomb are part of the country's defence strategy. The value of the nuclear ambiguity posture lies as much in the enemy suspecting that a country possesses the nuclear weapon as in secrecy. A nuclear capability so secret that its potential enemies do not suspect its existence loses its value as a deterrent. Some see the nuclear alert at the beginning of the 1973 Yom Kippur War, in which the Israeli Army deployed land-to-land missile batteries for the Jericho missile after Egypt had deployed two divisions of Scud missiles, more as a warning to Egypt. According to Professor Yuval Neeman, a former senior army intelligence officer, Israeli Army Chief of Staff David Elazar ordered that the missile batteries not be camouflaged in order that Soviet satellites would pick up the intelligence and pass it to Egypt. Similarly, after Saddam Hussein threatened to scotch half of Israel during the 1991 Gulf War Israeli officials deliberately leaked to journalists that Israel would 'reply 100 times greater', a barely disguised reference to the country's nuclear capability. Then Prime Minister Yitzhak Shamir, speaking on CNN in October 1990, at the time said 'somebody threatening you with the most terrible weapons in the world has to think about certain responses to the use of such weapons'. But while a few of the disclosures to the foreign media over the years may be viewed as intentional, these should not be exaggerated; the major dents in the image of ambiguity discussed in this article were unintentional or came from foreign government sources.

Military censorship is integral to the country's ambiguity posture. Thus, in April 1986, journalists were barred by the military censor from reporting remarks made by an army briefing officer about the possibility that Syria might be in a position to use chemical weapons against Israel. By late 1986 military spokesmen began to speak more openly about Syria's possession of chemical weaponry. However, a definite confirmation of Israel's nuclear capability would run the risk of irritating American and international public opinion.

This article examines the extent of military censorship on Israeli nuclear policy. The subject of the role of media exposure and governmental secrecy in the country's nuclear arms policy has been little discussed by researchers. Aronson,[4] Harkabi,[5] and Neeman,[6] for example, emphasize the international aspects in their writings on nuclear policy. Cohen discusses the traditional dilemma which a secrecy posture raises in a democratic society.[7] Goren,[8] Negbi,[9] and Segal,[10] in their writings on military–media relations, focus almost wholly on matters of conventional defence such as access for reporters to the battlefield and the censorship structure in Israel.

The article describes the growth in censorship from the earliest days of the nuclear project in the 1950s until today. It analyzes how the image of total ambiguity was watered down over the years as a result of declaratory statements by Israeli personalities or such technical developments as aerial and satellite photography. It also questions whether suspicions abroad about the programme have been actively exploited by the defence establishment in order to strengthen the country's deterrent posture.

NUCLEAR SECRECY OVER THE YEARS

Throughout the years the media in Israel have faced intensive military censorship regarding Israeli nuclear-related information and commentary—in order to preserve the secrecy factor which is a key ingredient of Israeli nuclear deterrence. While giving testimony at the Vanunu trial Shimon Peres explained:

> All matters dealing with the nuclear subject, from its beginning up to this day, are classified by the ministerial level as 'most secret'. Until today we have avoided publication of everything related to nuclear activities in Israel and we have taken strict steps that these matters should not leak out. The nuclear subject has been accorded a 'preferred secret' status—and we have related to it in this way concerning security clearance procedures. As the Defence Minister I gave an instruction that the nuclear subject should be guarded in the most secretive way.[11]

In the 1960s even indirect mention of Israel possessing a nuclear capability was prohibited by the censor, because it made Israel's nuclear option too visible. In 1968 the Parisian news weekly, *L'Express*, published an article on Israel's nuclear programme. Uri Avnery, the editor of the crusading *Haolam Hazeh* weekly, wanted to reprint the article. Avnery translated the article word for word but the censor refused him permission to reprint the article. A petition to the Supreme Court was rejected. Early in 1967, prior to the Six Day War, Zeev Schiff, *Ha'aretz*'s military correspondent, wrote a series of articles which included Arab perceptions of Israel's nuclear potential. It was banned by the then military censor, Colonel Walter Bar-On, on the grounds that it was based on what the Arabs were saying and not on what the Israelis were saying.[12]

A book manuscript chronicling the nuclear programme, *None Will Survive Us, the Story of the Israeli A-Tomb*, by lawyer Eli Teicher and journalist Ami Dor-On, was banned in its entirety by the censor in 1980, and its authors were warned that they would face fifteen years in prison if they ever revealed its contents.[13] Dan Raviv, CBS Radio correspondent in Israel, who reported the banning of the book, and the book's claim about Israeli–South African nuclear cooperation, became only the second foreign correspondent in Israel's history to have his press credentials cancelled.

An official inquiry into the level of radioactive fall-out in Israel in 1986 from Chernobyl found that 'Israel was totally unprepared and unorganized to deal with a nuclear accident in a distant country. Measures taken to deal with the fallout were ill-organized and unplanned'. The report was banned by the censor lest it arouse public discussion about the consequences of nuclear energy development. According to then Knesset member Mattityahu Peled, 'the Israeli public has a right to know, as do publics in all other democracies, where radioactive waste is stored, how distant this is from populated areas, or in what level at sea it is buried, and what are the levels of danger of radiation reaching places of settlement'. Examination of Israeli agricultural produce by government inspectors after Chernobyl was done only selectively despite high levels of radiation being discovered, the produce even being turned back by the West German authorities. The Israeli customer was not notified nor was it made public that in the week after Chernobyl children, who are five times at risk compared with adults from radioactivity, were exposed to one-tenth the radioactivity they generally absorb during an entire year.[14]

Writing about nuclear and non-conventional warfare was rare, and journalists were discouraged from doing so. 'There is no doubt that this was an error, and I include myself among those responsible for it', said Schiff.[15] The result has been that the majority of writings about nuclear weapons in the Middle East has come from foreign sources, not a few of which were full of basic errors and, what is worse, also written with the intention of harming Israel.

The media's reticence in covering Israeli nuclear policy exists against the background of wide public support for possessing the Bomb. Asked in a 1998 poll by the Jaffee Centre of Strategic Studies whether they favoured development by Israel of the Bomb, 92 percent of Israelis responded favourably. The trend towards non-conventional weaponry in the Middle East raised the level of public support—which reached a climax in the 1991 and 2003 Gulf wars. (By contrast, in 1986 and 1987 54 percent and 78 percent of Israelis polled favoured Israeli possession of the Bomb.) Moreover, willingness to deploy the Bomb increased from 36 percent and 53 percent in 1986 and 1988 respectively to 88 percent and 80 percent.[16]

Partly, the media's subservience on the nuclear issue may be traced to effective official mechanisms of censorship. But much may be explained by an underlying willingness of the Israeli public to accept official defence doctrines. It reflected an attitude that the military knows best, which pervaded Israeli society in the state's earlier years. A framework of cooperation already existed between the Hebrew press and the leadership of the Jewish Yishuv in Palestine during the British Mandate. The so-called Reaction Committee was a framework for the Jewish leaders to brief editors of the Hebrew press, to win the latter's cooperation to raise public morale, and acted as a conduit for the editors to alleviate measures taken against them by the British, such as the closure of newspapers. After independence in 1948, the newly-named Editors Committee continued to function.[17] It was briefed on a variety of classified matters in lieu of agreement not to publish sensitive information. However, the nuclear subject was regarded as so sensitive that it is unlikely that it was raised in this forum.

The media's 'subservience' began to change after the 1973 Yom Kippur War, which was characterized by a failure of Israeli military intelligence to predict the outbreak of the Egyptian–Syrian coordinated attack. Israeli editors had acceded to requests by Prime Minister Golda Meir not to publish reports concerning Egyptian and Syrian military exercises which preceded the war lest the news upset the Israeli population on the eve of the Yom Kippur holy day. Military correspondents have since been more challenging and critical of official military doctrine.

The same trend extended over the years to some other defence-related fields. After the so-called Shin Bet affair—in which a terrorist who hijacked a bus from Ashkelon to Tel Aviv was killed subsequent to his arrest—the Israeli media became more questioning of the operations of the Shin Bet, the country's domestic intelligence agency. In the affair the media played an important role in first disclosing the killing of the terrorist after he was arrested, and secondly, the framing by the Shin Bet of a senior Israeli Army officer for the killing. In the 1990s, media coverage of the Mossad, the country's external intelligence agency, became less glamorous, and a number of Mossad failures were the subject of critical reporting by the media. The difficulty for reporters in gaining complete details of the agency's operations has somewhat limited the media's coverage of the agency. But this new openness did not extend to nuclear policy.

Four schools of thought may be delineated regarding secrecy and nuclear policy. The dominant school is pro-secrecy. Public support for the Bomb has extended to the policy of secrecy in nuclear matters. Since 1987, when the question was first polled by the Jaffee Centre, there has been a consistent trend of between two-thirds to three-quarters of Israelis backing secrecy.

The pro-secrecy school in nuclear matters is mirrored at the parliamentary level where there is bipartisan support both for the nuclear programme and for the policy of ambiguity. Bipartisan support has ensured that nuclear policy has infrequently drawn parliamentary attention. If raised in parliamentary questions, the nuclear subject has invariably been shunted off to the Knesset's Defence and Foreign Affairs Committee which meets behind closed doors. Supervision of nuclear policy by the Defence and Foreign Affairs Committee is undertaken by a small sub-committee, comprising two Knesset members (MKs) from the governing party and two from the opposition, minimizing the possibility of leaks to the media.

While the committee has toured the Dimona nuclear facility more than once—and while the State Comptroller's Office investigates the work of the Atomic Energy Authority, such as safety standards for reactor workers—some MKs have protested at the lack of parliamentary supervision of nuclear policy. It has never been debated in the full Knesset plenum—with one exception in 1999, following an initiative by Communist MK Issam Makhoul. The Speaker of the Knesset attempted to pass the matter to committee but relented after Makhoul threatened to appeal to the Israeli Supreme Court. In the event the somewhat superficial plenum debate lasted less than an hour. In 2002 62 percent of the public supported keeping Israel's nuclear plans concealed, compared to 72 percent in 1999, two-thirds in 1998, to 71 percent in 1993, and 78 percent in 1987.[18]

A third school is against the Bomb, either for ethical or strategic reasons. The former see their campaign against the Bomb as requiring a fully informed public in order to generate public pressure for the dismantlement of the reported nuclear programme. Among its noted backers is Mordechai Vanunu, who disclosed the country's nuclear secrets to the London *Sunday Times*. A fourth school favours confirming the existence of the reported Bomb for economic reasons to limit Israel's total dependence on conventional defence systems which the inclusion of the non-conventional capability in the country's defence deterrent would enable, or for strategic reasons of building a rational deterrent framework. Freedom of information would only be a byproduct.

The second school is the most complicated of the four. On the one hand it accepts that Israel should not confirm whether or not it possesses the Bomb. On the other hand, it has grave misgivings about the dangers of secrecy, about the lack of free public discussion, and about the question of government accountability. For example, an analysis of the content of Israeli media nuclear subjects in 1999 found that 42 percent of the items appeared in the quality daily *Ha'aretz*.[19]

Israeli journalists are particularly to be found in the second school but many are also in the first school. As early as 1964, a serious study of Israeli nuclear strategy, *Nuclear War and Nuclear Peace*, by a former head of Israeli military intelligence, Professor Yehoshafat Harkabi, appeared in Hebrew and went immediately into a second printing. In 1966 it was published in English. Yigal Allon, the Labour minister, articulated his critique of nuclear deterrence in *A Curtain of Sand*. Academics like Professors Shlomo Aronson, Shai Feldman and Yair Evron and journalists like Avraham Schweitzer of *Ha'aretz*, Haggai Eshed of the extinct *Davar*, and Ephraim Kishon have discussed the issue. *Netiv*, the right-wing intellectual review, is also a forum of debate among nationalist thinkers. But discussion has often been wary.

Thus, at the foot of an article by Alan Dowty in the Israeli academic journal, *State, Government and International Relations*, which articulated unambiguously the case for nuclear ambiguity, was appended the disclaimer: 'This article is based entirely on published sources. The author had no access to classified information. He is not linked to the Israeli government nor did he receive official or background guidance in preparing this article'.

It is incorrect to say that there has been no debate about the Bomb within informed circles or that there has been no organized opinion. A number of groups surfaced over the past twenty-five years which campaigned on an anti-nuclear platform. These included a group led by Hillel Schenker of *New Outlook*, Mapam's intellectual review; the Committee for Nuclear Disarmament in the Arab–Israeli region in the 1960s, whose leaders included Hebrew University dons, among them the scientist and philosopher Yeshayahu Leibowitz, the philosopher Professor Gershon Scholem, the Talmudist Ephraim Urbach, and sociologist Shmuel Eisenstadt. In 1983 the Israel League against Nuclear Armament demanded the international inspection of nuclear sites by the United Nations. Israeli Doctors against Nuclear War campaigned concerning the medical effects of nuclear war.

Secrecy lessened considerably during, and in the immediate aftermath of, the 1991 Gulf War. Unprepared to go public with its capability, Israeli officialdom encouraged journalists to write about the deterrent, thereby giving veiled warnings to Baghdad.

Blunt allusions in the media to an Israeli nuclear deterrent, which previously would have been censored, were not. There was probably greater informed discussion in Israel about non-conventional strategy than at any other time in the country's history. Widespread public concern in Israel in 1990 and 1991 over the Iraqi threat stimulated public and media discussion about the threat and the options for an Israeli non-conventional military response. So did missile threats and such related developments as the Bush proposal for regional arms control. But as memories of the Gulf War began to dull, public apathy on the subject returned. In the 2003 Iraq War, the swift success of the US-led coalition, and the failure of the Saddam Hussein's regime to shell Israel, ensured that discussion in Israel of the non-conventional option barely arose.

The above analysis of the content of Israeli media on nuclear subjects in 1999 found that of some 165 nuclear-related items or articles in the Israel media, the two popular mass circulation papers (*Ma'ariv* and *Yediot Aharonot*) accounted for only 35 percent of them, Moreover, the news programmes of Israel's two television channels accounted for 3 percent.[20] Also illustrative was a 2000 piece on the popular talk show 'Po-Politika', hosted by Dan Margalit. When the programme passed to the subject of nuclear weaponry two-thirds of its viewers switched to the other television channel.

CENSORSHIP POLICY

A considerable amount of the material which entered the public domain over the years, such as the Vanunu expose, and satellite photos, has created significant data, albeit unconfirmed, about nuclear arms policy. According to the former censor, Brigadier-General Itzhak Sheni, 'If you take all the stories about the atomic bomb that have appeared in the Israeli press—from its sources and with the approval of the censor—you'll see that the contention that no discourse on the subject exists in Israel is simply incorrect. Anyone who wants to delve into the issue can do so, as long as he goes about in an appropriate manner'.[21] Some military correspondents corroborate Sheni's claim.

An examination of Israel's three main Hebrew dailies and two major TV channels found that during 1999 165 nuclear-related items were published or broadcast, making this issue the most covered after Lebanon and the Palestinians. Broken down, the biggest nuclear-related sub-category concerned Israeli nuclear policy (49 items), the second biggest nuclear theme was arms control and international treaties (24). Another big category concerned Vanunu. By contrast, radioactive waste and safety at the nuclear reactor resulted in only four and seven items.[22] Already in 1986 a Jaffee Centre poll (conducted nine months before the Vanunu expose) found that 92 percent of Israelis questioned believed that Israel possessed nuclear weapons; 54 percent of those asked were sure that Israel possessed nuclear weapons and 38 percent thought that Israel did but were not sure.[23] By contrast, a 1976 poll found that 62 percent of respondents thought that Israel possessed the Bomb, while 33 percent said they did not know.[24] A landmark was the broadcasting by Israel Television's Channel One in 2000 of pictures of the Dimona reactor from 1968 and 1971 (as the pictures were previously published or were available on the Internet website of the Federation of American Scientists they fulfilled the military censor's criterion).

But much of the material published over the years is old. For example, although the Vanunu disclosure had an undoubted significance coming from an insider, it draws on the time he worked there seventeen years earlier. Moreover, the censor's policy of editing journalists' reports in order to leave in doubt whether or not Israel possesses the Bomb makes an intelligent discussion about nuclear policy difficult. By qualifying whatever is written about nuclear policy as 'according to foreign sources', the media, lest it appear to confirm possession of the Bomb, has in fact been recruited as an integral part of the country's deterrent posture. According to senior *Ha'aretz* journalist Hanoch Marmori: 'In other subjects there is black and white, but on the nuclear theme we need to play politicians and use the government's style in nuancing articles against our will'.[25]

The Israeli Atomic Energy Commission has succeeded in avoiding the media spotlight. Most journalistic contact has been with the army spokesperson and the Ministry of Defence. The commission provides no briefings for defence and military reporters or visits to nuclear facilities, and almost no military reporters have gained off the record contacts with figures inside the commission. The commission's spokesman only rarely spoke publicly. These occasions included the scare in 1992 over radioactive spillout from the reactor to the nearby 'Little Crater'. The environment minister, Yossi Sarid, took a well-publicized visit to the reactor to show that the leak did not reflect inadequate safety standards within the reactor. Doctorates prepared by a botanist and a zoologist found radioactive effects on the vegetation and wildlife respectively in the Dimona area. Both doctorates were banned from publication. Another instance where the Atomic Energy Commission addressed the public was at the weekend at the end of the Millennium when the reactor was closed down for safety reasons. Reflecting the sheer cynicism about the public's right to know about nuclear policy, a former commission director-general, Shalheveth Freier, wrote in 1992 that he did not 'know of any instance of official attempts to stifle public discussion of the nuclear issue'. He placed the blame on academics who, in addition to not including in their publications official attitudes to the Bomb, do not share the products of their research with governmental sources.[26]

Foreign correspondents based in Israel are subject to the same legal controls as the local Israeli media and are required to submit material to the military censor for prior clearance. Yet they are less conditioned by historical–cultural pressure towards self-censorship. Thus, after *Time* photographer David Rubinger snapped the Dimona reactor from beyond the perimeter fence, he argued with the censor for hours until he convinced the latter that the American U-2 spyplane had been able to photograph more than he could ever do from the ground. Moreover, foreign news organizations working from their bases outside Israel's national boundaries were not subject to any requirements to submit to the Israeli censor.

GOVERNMENT RESPONSES TO MEDIA DISCLOSURES

All articles or reports dealing with the country's nuclear programme have to be submitted for prior clearance. And, prior to the outbreak of the 2003 Iraq War, the military censor reminded Israeli media websites of this need. Censorship has extended beyond the legal powers of the censor to official pressures of one sort or another. For example, in 1986 after the Peres government heard about the plans of the *Sunday Times* to publish Vanunu's information, Peres hurriedly brought together the Editors' Committee and appealed to the patriotism of attending editors asking them to limit their coverage of the impending expose. While he could not stop them quoting from the London paper, he asked those attending to refrain from extending reporting to local and regional reaction to the story.[27]

In 1961 the Defence Ministry asked Israeli newspaper editors not to publish articles on the subject by journalist and Knesset member Eliezer Livneh of the Mapai Party 'for reasons of national security'.[28] *Ha'aretz* has been subject through the years to various requests not to publish matters relating to the nuclear issue; on one occasion when the censor's guidelines did not allow for a particular item to be banned, a senior Israeli official approached the paper's editorial board arguing that its publication would encourage an 'undesirable' public discussion in Israel. The paper turned down the request.[29]

In 1976 Mabat Sheni (Second Look) Israel Television's flagship current affairs programme, planned a programme entitled 'Israel's nuclear option'. This was banned by the Israel Broadcasting Authority's director-general 'because the subject was delicate and would arouse public discussion much beyond what had been discussed up to that time'. 'The function of television is to report information and not cause public discussion', added the director-general, who is a government appointee. An Israel Television reporter, Shlomi Eldar, who began investigating the radioactive leak to the Little Crater in 1992, was asked to see the environment minister who, according to Eldar, 'discouraged' pursuing the story any further.[30]

Illustrative of the pressures was the case of Avner Cohen, a US-based Israeli-born researcher. Using foreign archives, and the US Freedom of Information Act, Cohen managed to gather many previously unpublished documents about the project. In particular Cohen gathered much material on US–Israeli relations, including the negotiations between Golda Meir and President Richard Nixon resulting in the 1969 US–Israeli understanding. While preparing his book, *Israel and The Bomb*, Cohen was subject to telephone calls with veiled threats from the Ministry of Defence's security wing. In a visit to Israel in 1994 he was taken aside at immigration control at Ben Gurion Airport and informed by a police officer that his work was likely to infringe censorship regulations. Cohen did not submit his book for censorship clearance partly because in 1994 when he submitted a single chapter to the censor, the latter, to Cohen's surprise, sent back the manuscript telling him 'we are returning it without censorship, and we leave it to you to decide how it act'. When Cohen insisted that as an Israeli citizen he was obliged to get the censor's permission, the latter replied that if this was the case, 'the whole chapter is banned'. He then appealed to the courts against this ban but, according to Cohen, the court, sitting behind closed doors, said that if he failed to reach a compromise with the censor it would take a long time for the courts to adjudicate on the matter.

At that point Cohen decided to publish abroad.[31] The dilemma for the Israeli authorities was that it is not illegal to publish information learnt from foreign sources. To suggest that Cohen should not publish information gathered from open foreign archives is to introduce a double standard. Israeli foreign correspondents freely gather information from all sources abroad and do not submit their reports to the censor for prior clearance.

But, in addition to accessing US archives and interviewing US officials, Cohen also interviewed a long list of Israelis who had direct knowledge of the Dimona project. They included Professor Israel Dostrovsky, a former AEC chairman, Shalheveth Freier, Shimon Peres, Zvi Dinstein, a former deputy defence minister, and General Yehoshafat Hakarbi, a former head of military intelligence. Cohen used these interviews to supplement the information that he gathered from the archives.

Cohen refrained from visiting Israel for a long period; when he finally did in 2002 he was subject to a long police investigation, and then released. In another case, the Israeli authorities did arrest Brigadier-General Yitzhak Yaacov. Yaacov had been a source for *Yediot Aharonot* journalist Ronen Bergman. Yaacov had been involved in the early development of the IDF's response to the non-conventional threat in the region. His arrest sent shockwaves through the country's political–defence elite and may have been designed to do exactly that. The Justice Ministry's decision to put him on trial was the subject of discussion by the Knesset's Law and Statute Committee which had been debating the need to revise the laws of espionage and treason, including the need to differentiate between passing classified information to an enemy and passing it to the media. His subsequent acquittal raised the separate question of the heavy sentence imposed on Vanunu for the same offence.

In the wake of the Avner Cohen affair, the Ministry of Defence sought to close the archival materials loophole. Personal papers belonging to Levi Eshkol, Israel's prime minister in the 1960s, including details of the nuclear programe, which Cohen had used in his research, were removed from the property of Eshkol's widow's. The Israeli authorities managed to persuade US official archives to censor documents from the Lyndon Johnson Administration, which included US assessments of the Israeli nuclear capability. Prime Minister Ehud Barak in 2000 appointed Avraham Shalom (a former head of the Shin Bet), to strengthen security around the nuclear reactor and nuclear policy.[32]

Israeli officials have sought to address the threat from commercial satellite photography in disclosing classified information. In the absence of their own spy satellites, Arab states make use of commercial satellite photography. The older satellite systems have less precise resolution—such as the French commercial satellite with a 10 metre resolution and the Indian satellite with a resolution of 5.8 metres—and pose less of a security threat to Israel. But new satellite systems have a resolution of one metre. For example, the latter are able to differentiate between nuclear storage and conventional storage. Future satellites may be able to detect vehicles and weapons in the open as they undergo maintenance or are being used in training.

In the early 1990s the Clinton administration, itself concerned with the dangers which commercial satellite photography posed to US classified defence information, prohibited US satellite companies from producing satellite photos of one metre resolution; these could be no more precise than the pictures produced by the Russian, Indian or French satellites. But as the Russians began to corner the market in commercial satellite photography, the Clinton Administration relented to pressure from US companies to allow photos of even one metre resolution (which Lockheed was able to do by early 1995).

Israel's then prime minister Yitzhak Rabin, however, was able to persuade Clinton of the dangers of the highly precise satellite photos, and under an agreement negotiated between David Ivry, director-general of the Israeli defence ministry and CIA Director John Deutsch, US companies were prohibited from selling satellite photos of Israel of less than 5.5 metre resolution. In 1996 Congress legislated an amendment entitled 'The Prohibition on Collection and Release of Detailed Imagery relating to Israel and other countries and areas', banning US companies from selling satellite photos of Israel with a resolution of less than that which can be obtained from other countries (2 metre resolution at the time) But such controls are a short-term solution because as one metre precise photos become available from other countries, there was nothing to stop American companies from selling such photos of the Dimona reactor and other Israeli defence-related facilities.[33]

THE AMBIGUITY POSTURE AND THE MEDIA

The image of total ambiguity surrounding the Dimona project has weakened as a result of a series of actions involving the disclosure of information, some of which the media have played a role in, so that the total secrecy which surrounded the project in the late 1950s has greatly weakened. In 1976 *Time* disclosed how during a critical period of the October 1973 war Prime Minister Golda Meir gave Defence Minister Moshe Dayan permission to activate nuclear weapons. It occurred after Egyptian forces crossed the Suez Canal and broke through Israeli defensive lines.[34] In 1986, Mordechai Vanunu, a former nuclear technician at the Dimona reactor, gave the *Sunday Times* a detailed description of the reactor and its working process. His description enabled the newspaper to calculate that Israel had produced between 100 and 200 nuclear weapons, a far higher estimate than earlier estimates, most of which were generally 20–30. The story was also important because it came from somebody with direct knowledge of the facility. The paper also disclosed that Israel was producing lithium deuteride and tritium, material used in thermonuclear bombs.[35]

In 1989 the US network NBC reported the joint testing by Israel and South Africa of an intercontinental missile with a range of over 1,500 km as part of the reported nuclear cooperation between the two countries. The possibility was raised that Israel may have given South Africa access to US missile technology. In 1994, two Americans, in *Critical Mass: The Dangerous Race for Superpowers in a Fragmenting World*, detailed how Israel had developed a command, control, communication and technical intelligence apparatus to execute its nuclear doctrine; that Jericho nuclear-capable missiles were stored at Beer Yaacov near Tel Aviv; that nuclear research, and even nuclear explosions, were carried out at the Nahal Soreq nuclear reactor which is under international supervision; that a nuclear weapons design and missile development laboratory was situated at the Raphael arms industry complex at Yodfat in the Galilee region; and that nuclear weapons were housed at the Tel Nof airbase and at bunkers at the nearby village of Zechariah in the Judean Hills. The command base was divided between the Netavim Airbase in the Negev and IDF Headquarters at Hakirya in Tel Aviv.[36] In 2002 *The Bulletin of Atomic Scientists* claimed that the Israeli Airforce fleet of F-16s was equipped to carry nuclear warheads.

In 1998, the *Sunday Times* Tel Aviv corespondent, Uzi Mahnaimi reported that Israel was designing a biological bomb which could ethnically distinguish between Arab and Jewish genes. In 2000 he reported that Israel had deployed nuclear bombs on the Golan Heights. *Der Spiegel* reported the same year that Israeli submarines carried nuclear-capable missiles.

The image of ambiguity was also dented by a number of apparently unintentional statements by senior Israeli officials. In 1974 the President of Israel, Professor Ephraim Katzir (himself a scientist of some international renown and an important figure in Israel's Atomic Energy Commission), told a group of American and European scientific journalists that 'Israel has a nuclear potential'. A reporter followed up Katzir's utterance with a question about the capability and time limit for realizing the nuclear potential, to which Katzir retorted, 'Do you think I'd state a date here in these circumstances?' Another reporter asked him whether Israel's nuclear potential was not a worrisome phenomenon. Katzir replied: 'Why should this matter worry us? Let the world do the worrying.' His remarks set off a chain reaction around the world. The President's office put out a clarifier saying that Katzir was referring only to the 'general potential in Israel of scientists and general scientific-technological experience that objectively could be implemented if so desired'. In 1976, Moshe Dayan, a former defence minister, was criticized for telling French television: 'For Israel, the future should include the option and possibility of possessing nuclear weapons. I think we have the possibility of manufacturing the Bomb now. I believe that if the Arabs introduce an atomic bomb in the Middle East sometime in the future, we ought to have a bomb before they do, yet naturally not in order to use it first.'[37]

The challenge to Israeli secrecy further increased with satellite photography. In 1993 *Aviation Week*, using satellite photos obtained from Russia, appeared to confirm earlier claims regarding nuclear installations. The following year the London-based *Jane's Intelligence Review*, drawing on satellite photos obtained from Russia and from the French commercial satellite 'Spot', printed eight satellite pictures showing Israel's 'nuclear infrastructure'.[38]

Analyzing the photograph of Dimona, Harold Hough, a US analyst of satellite photography, claimed that three features in the photos of the reactor gave away the location of nuclear facilities. First, the reactor is surrounded by a heavy perimeter fence with many patrols and roads; secondly, the reactor is surrounded by heavy vegetation, even though it is arid desert, in order to screen the site from passing traffic; thirdly, there is also an unusual amount of space inside the reactor to give defence in depth. Hough also claimed that nuclear weapons were being tested at the country's second nuclear reactor, at Nahal Soreq, to the south of Tel Aviv. According to Hough, Zecharya, situated in the centre of the country, is the missile base and home of Israel's strategic nuclear deterrent. He said the area of the site, the Judean Hills, was naturally suited to the construction of underground bunkers, because it is composed of limestone and is riddled with caves. By placing the nuclear deterrent in the centre of the country, it would be one of the last parts of Israel to fall to an enemy.

Satellite photography has its limitations. Only after careful study of general ground-level photos are specialists able to identify the precise location of the facility. Nor can satellite photos provide data on the capacities of particular installations or on the specific materials they may be using to produce weapons-grade uranium or how long the nuclear facility had been functioning. Satellite-obtained information revealed only the roofs of hangars.

Public and media concern over the safety standards at the reactor led to more information on the subject entering the public arena. Following the 1992 radioactive leak to the Little Crater, the AEC announced some eight months later, for the first time in Israel's history, that radioactive waste was stored in Dimona. Up to then, nobody had disclosed whether radioactive waste was stored in Israel. The 1990s saw a stream of legal claims by families of workers who had suffered cancer as a result of exposure to radioactive materials. Over 100 law suits are pending, each demanding one million or more shekels. For officials there was a danger that highly sensitive information about work methods inside the reactor would be exposed in court.[39]

Yet the cases which had the greatest diplomatic ramifications for the issue of ambiguity did not come from the media. In December 1960, an American U-2 spyplane photographed the reactor. The CIA revealed to an emergency session of the Nuclear Energy Congressional Committee that what the

Eisenhower administration had been led to believe was a textile plant was a large and tightly guarded nuclear facility. Ben-Gurion then informed the Knesset that a thermal reactor was being constructed in the Negev with French assistance, but said that it would be devoted to peaceful ends.

Surprisingly, then Deputy Defence Minister Peres was still claiming in 1963 that Dimona was a water desalination plant 'intended to turn the Negev into a garden'. In order to verify that the reactor was being used for civilian purposes only, the Kennedy and Johnson administrations insisted on inspecting Dimona, and made weapons sales conditional on the inspections. Another case where ambiguity was dented occurred when the US 'Vela' satellite in 1979 recorded a double flash of light originating from the South Atlantic–Indian Ocean area. The CIA informed the National Security Council that a two- or three-kiloton bomb had been exploded from a joint South African–Israeli testing of a nuclear device. But a scientific panel set up by President Carter suggested that the flash probably resulted from the impact of a small meteorite on a satellite.

CONCLUSION

There is a need to revise official thinking about the value of nuclear secrecy. The implicit contradiction between national security and the principle of the right to know has not been reconciled in the case of nuclear matters in a satisfactory manner. No major news organization has confronted the defence establishment and declared it will no longer comply with ambiguity. One exception where the media have fulfilled their watchdog role concerns the question of adequate safety standards inside the reactor. The secrecy is even costly to official decision-makers who are unable to generate public support through discussing Israel's nuclear programme. Belated steps, like the 2004 decision of Israel's Atomic Energy Commission to establish a website hardly begin to fill the gap in public information about nuclear policy. The increasing dangers of non-conventional wars in the region necessitate public understanding of the dangers and the Israeli response.

The morality of current official practice on nuclear-related information is most questionable. A democracy whose citizens are informed of sensitive national security issues only through that information being published abroad is weak. Notwithstanding the fact that the majority of Israelis favour nuclear secrecy, the minority in a democracy possess basic rights on such fundamental matters. A democracy should be self-contained with a formal mechanism for monitoring sensitive national information, which should be classified, and declassifying the remainder. Among questions which require answers include the cost of the nuclear programme; and which ministers and officials are involved in the decision-making process to deploy the capability if necessary?

The belief that Israel going public would endanger US aid assistance is a diplomatic argument rather than one concerning narrow defence considerations and is thus a danger which cannot be justified on democratic merits. Judge Aharon Barak's ruling in the 1989 *Hair* case, narrowing the censor's criterion for limiting publication to that defence information for which there was a 'near certainty' that its publication would damage the country's security, has not been applied to nuclear-related information. Foreign aid is not included among those matters of which there is a near certainty that they will damage the security of the state. Moreover, the defence establishment's claim that making the nuclear capability public would create pressure in the Arab world to achieve nuclear parity with Israel, creating nuclear escalation, is highly questionable given that Iraq and Iran still went ahead to develop their nuclear programmes.

NOTES

1. Asher Arian, Ilan Talmud and Tamar Hermann, *National Security and Public Opinion in Israel*, Tel Aviv, 1988.
2. Leonard S. Spector, *The Undeclared Bomb*, Cambridge, MA, 1988, pp. 386–387m
3. See Protocols of the Vanunu Trial, No. 260139.
4. Shlomo Aronson, *The Politics and Strategy of Nuclear Weapons in the Middle East*, Albany, NY, 1992.
5. Yehoshafat Harkabi, *Nuclear War and Nuclear Peace*, Tel Aviv, 1983.
6. Yuval Neeman, 'Israel in the Nuclear Age', *Nativ*, Vol. 5, No. 46 (1995).
7. Avner Cohen, 'Nuclear Weapons, Opacity, and Israeli Democracy', in Avner Yaniv (ed.), *National Security and Democracy in Israel*, Boulder and London, 1993.
8. Dina Goren, *Secrecy and The Right to Know*, Ramat Gan, 1979.
9. Moshe Negbi, *Paper Tiger: The Struggle for Press Freedom in Israel*, Tel Aviv, 1985.
10. Zeev Segal, *Freedom of the Press — Between Myth and Reality*, Tel Aviv, 1996.
11. Protocols of the Vanunu Trial, No. 260138.
12. *Politika*, November 1987.
13. *Davar*, 29–30 December 1986.
14. *Alternativa*, March 1987; June 1987.
15. *Politika*, March 1987.
16. Asher Arian, 'Public Opinion in Israel on the Nuclear Subject', *Strategic Update*, November 1998.
17. Goren, *Secrecy and the Right to Know*, Chapters 10, 11.
18. Survey carried put by the Jaffee Centre for Strategic Studies, Tel Aviv University, 1999.
19. *Ha'aretz*, 29 March 2000.
20. Ibid.
21. Ibid., 25 May 2000.
22. Ibid., 29 March 2000.
23. Survey by the Jaffee Centre for Strategic Studies, Tel Aviv University, 1987.
24. *Ha'aretz*, 25 March 1976.
25. Address by Hanoch Marmori at conference on 'Nuclear Weaponry, the Public and The Media', Haifa University, 1995.
26. *Politika*, November 1992.
27. Zvi Lavie, 'The Editors Committee: Myth and Reality', in *1987 Journalists Yearbook*, Tel Aviv, Israel Journalists' Association.
28. *Ha'aretz*, 12 October 1962.
29. *Politika*, March 1987.
30. *Shishi*, 24 February 1993.

31. Avner Cohen, *Israel and the Bomb*, New York, 1998; *Yediot Aharonot*, 12 June 2000; http://www.seas.gwu.edu/nsarchive/israel/history/ltm.
32. *Ha'aretz*, 20 July 2000.
33. Ibid., 17 August 1998.
34. pp. 508–511.
35. *Sunday Times*, 5 October 1986; Yoel Cohen, *The Whistleblower from Dimona: Vanunu, Israel and the Bomb*, Tel Aviv, 2005.
36. William Burrows and Robert Windem, *Critical Mass: The Dangerous Race for Superpowers a Fragmenting World*, NewYork, 1994.
37. *Ha'aretz*, 29 February 1976.
38. Harold Hough, 'Israel's Nuclear Infrastructure', *Jane's Intelligence Review*, November 1994.
39. *Ma'ariv*, 29 April 1994.

The Media and National Security: The Performance of the Israeli Press in the Eyes of the Israeli Public

MARTIN SHERMAN and SHABTAI SHAVIT

'The essence of successful warfare is secrecy, the essence of successful journalism is publicity'
        British Ministry of Defence During the Falklands War, 1982

'Anyone who trades liberty for security deserves neither liberty nor security.'
        Benjamin Franklin

The above quotes underline the inexorable clash between the two inherently adversarial disciplines—that of the media and that of the military. This intrinsic dissonance is especially acute in times of national crisis, when, as Marvin Kalb wrote, in the wake of the 11 September 2001 terror attacks on the United States, the press faces a 'monstrously difficult challenge: how to be sensitive to the feelings of a ... patriotic nation while doing their job of applying proper doses of journalistic skepticism'.[1]

In many ways the disharmonious relationship between those who would expose information and events in the name of 'liberty', and those who resist such exposure in the name of 'security', is a product of modern technology. For, as Kalb points out, 'up until the discovery of the telegraph in 1843, the military could safely accommodate journalists, even on the battle-field, because press dispatches were so slow in getting into print that there was little chance of providing comfort to the enemy or embarrassment to the generals—or the politicians'.[2]

However, in the modern era much has changed and the speed of media dispatches and the span of their reach have dramatically transformed the potential impact the press may have on events and processes that impinge on national security.[3] Over the latter part of twentieth century there has been a sense of disquiet in certain quarters in the democratic world over what they see as a tendency on the part of an overly zealous liberal media elite to take Benjamin Franklin's foregoing *caveat* to imprudent extremes. In many western democracies, the prevailing sentiment in the media world appeared to be that 'liberty' had to be more jealously guarded than 'security'. Organs of state security in democratic societies were perceived to be a greater threat to democracy than external adversaries – however antithetical the latter might have been to democratic values. This prompted a well-known American conservative to complain that liberal elites 'who seized control of America in the late 1960s believed and argued that the CIA was a considerably greater threat to America than the Soviet Union'.[4]

In Israel, among certain leading media personalities it appears to have become an article of faith that infringements of freedom of expression are more deleterious to the public interest than any source of external threat. However it would seem that this heavy media bias (or at least apparent bias) in favour of 'liberty' over 'security' is not necessarily a position shared by the general public, whose interest they purport to safeguard.

The ensuing paper surveys the evolving, and fluctuating, attitudes that leading democracies, such as the US, UK and Canada, have adopted in relation to the "free expression versus national security" dilemma, at the legal, political and philosophical level. It also presents some empirical findings regarding the Israeli public's position on this issue, which are consistent with the results of polls conducted in the US regarding the military/media relationship during the 1991 Gulf War and the post-9/11 operations in Afghanistan.

Overall, the findings of this study seem to indicate that both prevailing practices and public perceptions in democratic societies favour a far sterner approach to freedom of expression in times of national crisis than some of its more vocal self-appointed champions in the Israeli media would have us believe.

FREEDOM OF EXPRESSION AND NATIONAL SECURITY: SOME HISTORICAL, LEGAL AND PHILOSOPHICAL PERSPECTIVES

> When a nation is at war many things that might be said in time of peace are such a hindrance to its effort that their utterance will not be endured so long as men fight and that no Court could regard them as protected by any constitutional right.
> Justice Oliver Wendll Holmes, US Supreme Court, 1919

This almost century-old excerpt from the summation of a US Supreme Court Justice in the well-known and oft-cited case of *Schenck v. United States* (1919) incorporates a clear criterion regarding the exercise of the right to free speech in democratic societies. This criterion implies that while in times of peace, freedom of expression should be largely unfettered, in times of war, it is proper, even in a well-established constitutional democracy, that restrictions be imposed upon such freedom. It should perhaps be pointed out that in spite of the lengthy period of time that has elapsed since this ruling, it has not lost its relevance in the legal discourse in the US. Indeed, the Schneck judgment was cited by Susan Estrich in an article published on September 13, 2001. In her article, Estrich identifies the decision as a valid legal guideline for determining appropriate government response in the wake of the terror attacks that took place in New York and Washington two days previously.[5]

Elsewhere in his judgment, Justice Holmes goes on to elaborate on this principle. He argues that while the First Amendment might indeed protect a speech 'in ordinary times', when there is a 'clear and present danger' that the speech will cause harm it must not only be restricted but also punished. As he explains, 'the character of every act depends upon the circumstances in which it is done. The most stringent protection of free speech would not protect a man in falsely shouting fire in a theatre and causing a panic. It does not even protect a man from an injunction against uttering words that may have all the effect of force.'

In a later ruling (*Abrams* v. *United States*, 1919), Holmes affirmed the position taken in his earlier decision, declaring:

> I do not doubt for a moment that ... the United States constitutionally may punish speech that produces or is intended to produce a clear and imminent danger that it will bring about forthwith certain substantive evils that the United States constitutionally may seek to prevent. The power undoubtedly is greater in time of war than in time of peace because war opens dangers that do not exist at other times.[6]

This statement by Holmes is especially interesting and significant for a number of reasons. Firstly, it was made in spite of the fact that in contrast to his decision in the *Schenck* v. *United States* case, Holmes argued against the prosecution of the plaintiffs. Indeed, in his dissenting opinion in *Abrams* v. *United States*, Holmes (together with Justice Louis Brandeis), specifically upholds his previous ruling, remarking that he 'had never seen any reason to doubt the questions of law in the *Cases of Schenk*'.[7] Thus, although this opinion is commonly cited as a landmark, constituting 'the starting point in modern judicial concern for free expression',[8] it nevertheless recognized the principle that governments have the right—indeed duty—to restrict and even punish certain forms of expression, should they result in 'substantive evils' which merit prevention.

This article will therefore adopt the principle inherent in Justice Holmes' position as a moral yardstick in its ensuing discussion of the role of the media (the principal vehicle for free speech in modern democratic societies) as a major factor impinging on national security in times of conflict. In other words, it will adopt the notion that even the most democratic societies recognize that while in periods of calm and stability freedom of expression should be largely unrestricted, in periods of national peril such freedoms can, and at times should, be constrained, with the degree of constraint being dependent on the degree of peril.

At this juncture it is important to underscore that *raison d'être* invoked for the curtailment of free expression in democratic societies is not founded on the conviction that the incumbent regime has (or needs to create the impression that it has), a monopoly on the truth—and thus all dissenting opinion should be suppressed as inadmissible falsehood. Rather it is based on the concern that freedom may be abused and exploited to harm the democratic collective, and the liberties it stands for.

It is of course true that US judicial attitudes on this matter have waxed and waned over the course of the twentieth century. Indeed the ruling in the 'Pentagon Papers' case (*New York Times* v. *United States*), involving the US government's unsuccessful attempt to halt further publication of Daniel Ellesberg's classified research on Vietnam, has been interpreted by some as indicating that judicial predilections have changed, giving freedom of expression far greater precedence over considerations of national security than was the case in the *Schenck* ruling.[9] However, closer scrutiny of the judgment will reveal it to be, if anything, more a change of prevailing mood than of permanent principle. For not only did three out of the nine judges dissent from the majority position to allow publication of the classified papers, but even some of those concurring with it appear to specifically confirm this.[10]

Nonetheless, there can be little doubt that the general tenor of the prevailing attitudes in the final stages of the Vietnam War and in the immediate post-war period tended toward unrestricted freedom of the media and the exercise of free speech. However, by the time of the Gulf War, this had changed significantly. This trend of change, which will be elaborated on later, was aptly expressed by Christopher Dandeker in his analysis 'Public Opinion, the Media and the Gulf War':

> Desert Shield and Desert Storm were emphatic that the relatively open military/media relationship characteristic of the Vietnam era would not be allowed to become (so it was thought) a source of military weakness by fomenting an erosion of the domestic political will to sustain the war. The power of the media would be integrated into the overall political and military management of the war—in short, the democratic right to know would be subordinated to the military need to know.[11]

Other leading democracies have also shown a willingness to curb freedom of expression in the name of national security. Britain, for example, severely restricted press activity during the Falklands War.[12] Indeed, Peter Preston of *The Guardian* claims that the manner in which the British managed the press hugely impressed the Pentagon, and served as a model for US control of the press during its military operations in Panama and Grenada, and later during the 1991 Gulf War.[13] The dramatic attacks of 11 September 2001 on New York and Washington constituted a turning point for many in the West regarding the conduct of national security affairs. It brought about a marked stiffening of attitudes as to the latitude afforded in the exercise of individual freedoms, including freedom of expression.

However, even before the cataclysm of 9/11, grave misgivings were being felt in Britain regarding the 'promiscuity' of the media's exposure of classified material. Almost six months before the 11 September attacks, the Parliamentary Intelligence and Security Committee, which oversees the work of MI5, MI6 and GCHQ, expressed fears that the existing form of the Official Secrets Act provided inadequate means to protect the secrets of Britain's intelligence services. The committee warned that 'the traditional threat of espionage from hostile and foreign governments has not receded, whilst other threats such as chequebook journalism [*sic*] have increased'.[14]

For the purposes of this essay it is of course significant that 'chequebook journalism' appears to be referred to as a threat comparable to 'traditional espionage' as is the recognition that the media's hunger for ratings (together with technological advances facilitating the dissemination of information) have rendered existing legal arrangements ineffective in preserving state secrets, and thus could undermine national security. In concluding its report on this matter, the committee 'recommend[ed] changes to ensure that the Acts protect secret information' in the future.

THE IMPACT OF 9/11

As noted, the 11 September 2001 attacks were a landmark occurrence for many democratic governments and induced a distinct change in the manner in which they related to the national security/freedom-of-expression equation.[15] The sense of threat and vulnerability generated in the wake of the devastation that they wrought brought an almost across-the-board increase in the stringency of the approaches in most countries—including western democracies—to the exercise of civil liberties, including freedom of expression. This is evident in the following excerpt from a UNESCO review of the situation:

> The events of September 11 and the war against terrorism have given rise to new concerns regarding press freedom. Various legal and legislative measures announced, proposed or adopted in Australia, Canada, Cyprus, France, India, ... the United Kingdom, the United States, ... and the European Union, among others, have been assailed by critics for their negative impact on the work of the media. In some cases also, the climate of insecurity generated by September 11 and the subsequent war on

terrorism, have provided governments with an opportunity to take restrictive measures which had long been in the pipelines.

Some measures, taken or contemplated, restrict the "right to know", with government agencies withdrawing information that had previously been available to the public. According to the Columbia Journalism Review, the rules of war reporting set up by the Pentagon have "never been as tough" as during the campaign in Afghanistan.

Steps have also been taken to restrict privacy on the Internet, including restrictions on the use by private citizens—but also by human rights groups and the media—of encryption software to protect their email traffic, and to facilitate wiretapping by the authorities.

But obstacles to freedom of the press are not limited to legal and legislative measures. According to the UK-based press freedom watchdog organization Article 19, "official actors have taken steps which both directly limit freedom of expression and information".[16]

In Canada, for example, the government passed the controversial Anti-Terrorism Act (Bill C-36) into law on 24 December 2001. This piece of legislation, which was greeted by howls of protest from numerous free speech activists, significantly increased the powers of the security forces, enabled an expansion (and easing) of the use of electronic surveillance, and imposed greater restrictions on access to, and the use of, information relating to national security.[17]

Following 11 September 2001, the US also responded swiftly to increase executive powers at the expense of civil liberties.[18] Measures were also directed towards restricting the media and the availability of information. The White House persuaded US television networks to limit the use of videotapes issued by Osama bin Laden and his aides. National Security Adviser Condoleezza Rice warned network executives that long, pre-recorded statements issued by bin Laden and his spokesmen could be used to 'frighten Americans and inspire supporters, and could even include coded messages to followers that could result in a new attack'.[19]

Interestingly, network officials called the administration's request 'unprecedented' but 'reasonable', and consented not to air such tapes as they were received but to review them first.

According to the *Washington Post*, CBS News president Andrew Heyward responded to the White House's measures in the following terms: 'This is absolutely unprecedented in my experience. The story is unique; the attack on the U.S. is unique. Nobody took umbrage at this [request]. We are all giving the government the benefit of the doubt; the propaganda issue is a legitimate issue.'[20]

CNN, with its broad international audience, was of particular concern to the administration. The network showed that it was sensitive to this, stating that it would not run statements from al Qaeda live and that it would 'consider guidance from appropriate authorities' in deciding what to air.[21]

CBS News anchor Dan Rather was quoted as stating he 'didn't think that [the government's concerns were] inappropriate', while Tom Rosenstiel, executive director of the Washington-based Project for Excellence in Journalism, considered the administration's request 'eminently sensible'.[22]

It would appear that these statements by senior US media personalities captured the mood that prevailed among the American public at the time. For example, a poll taken by Pew Research Centre for People and the Press in mid-October 2001 indicated that six out of ten Americans believed that the military—rather than news organizations—should have more control over the news regarding the US bombings in Afghanistan and over 50 percent thought that news organizations should refrain from airing speeches by Osama bin Laden.[23]

These findings are consistent with polls conducted during the 1991 Gulf War which indicated that the majority of US viewers were satisfied with the restricted information they received concerning fighting. In fact many expressed the fear that 'too much information was being disseminated regarding the conduct of the war by the United States and its allies' and were concerned that 'the information would be found useful by the Iraqis and would somehow be used against our troops in the field'.[24] Indeed the conduct of the US media and its representatives, and its congruence with the domestic public mood, especially in the wake of 9/11, makes for an interesting comparison with Israel in subsequent sections of this study.

THE ROLE OF THE MEDIA IN DEMOCRATIC SOCIETIES: THE INHERENT TENSION BETWEEN A FREE PRESS AND NATIONAL SECURITY

The inherent tension between the demands of the media and the exigencies of national security, particularly in times of crisis, is encapsulated in the previously cited declaration by the British Ministry of Defence during the Falklands War in 1982: 'The essence of successful warfare is secrecy; the essence of successful journalism is publicity.'[25]

This tension between the two spheres—the preservation of democratic values against domestic sources of infringement on the one hand, and the defence of democratic values against external attack, on the other—generates the perennial dilemma for responsible journalists. This dilemma was succinctly described by Dandeker:

> During the Gulf War ... the tension characteristic of all wars fought by democracies became strikingly evident: that between the military operational requirement for information to be made available only on a need to know basis, and the right of the citizens of a democracy to know

about and judge what operations are being planned and conducted in their name.[26]

Following 9/11, Ted Koppel, as quoted by the *Washington Post*, echoed this view, remarking that 'The media ... face the familiar challenge of covering a war without jeopardizing national security and upholding their obligation to inform Americans as fully as possible'.[27]

There is, therefore, an inherent structural potential for mistrust between the military and political elites on the one hand and the media and their publics on the other. As one scholar of media/military relations observed, the former can legitimately ask 'what conspiracies or cover-ups of errors of judgment are being concealed by the phrase "in the interests of national security"'.[28] Conversely, the military can ask 'why the operational need for secrecy (and the chance of military success and minimum casualties on one's own side) should be compromised by scrutiny of the media, which in the guise of serving the public's "right to know" are pursing market share, advertising income and the professional career interests of the journalists themselves'[29]—a fear very reminiscent of the concern over 'increased chequebook journalism' expressed in the Interim Report of the British Parliamentary Intelligence and Security Committee mentioned above.[30]

The ensuing sections of this study will be devoted to an analysis of how the performance of the Israeli media is viewed by the Israeli public, which it purports to serve, both in absolute terms and relative to that of the Israeli military.

THE ISRAELI MEDIA IN TIMES OF NATIONAL CRISIS—PUBLIC PERCEPTIONS OF PRESS PERFORMANCE

In the preceding analysis, the discussion focused primarily on perceptions of the appropriate conduct of the media in times of severe national crisis in which military forces were engaged in on-going operations or poised just prior to doing so. In such a context, particularly in the post-Vietnam era, there 'appears to be little debate in most democratic societies between the media, the military and citizens alike regarding the restriction of information that might, if disseminated, jeopardize or endanger lives by compromising a current or future military operation'.[31]

However, in the Israeli case matters are more complex. In contrast to other democracies like the US and the UK, where there has normally been a relatively clear and distinct divide between times of war and periods of peace, Israel has, for much of its existence, maintained itself under what may be termed 'twilight' conditions. These conditions involve a constant on-going threat to its national security, which at times increases in intensity (and even flares into open warfare) and at times diminishes, igniting the hopes (usually unfounded) of imminent peace.

However, whether the threat has waxed or waned, it has never subsided to negligible levels which allow the nation to enjoy a sense of security akin to that of most other post-World War II western democracies. These conditions of enduring, but fluctuating, levels of threat make for a potentially more problematic set of relations between the security sector and the press than in most other liberal societies.

In an attempt to address this difficult issue several prominent Israeli media specialists met in November 2001 for a two day seminar. The group included practitioners from the electronic and the printed press, theoreticians from various academic institutions, former and then incumbent spokespersons of official state bodies as well as a former head of the Israeli government censor's office.[32] The principal focus of the discussions was on the function of the media and national security in times of national crisis.

These discussions were summarized in a working paper entitled 'Information Management in the Information Age'.[33] The tenor of the opening paragraphs of the paper appears to reveal the sense of discomfort (if not distaste) felt by the Israeli media at their US colleagues 'rallying round the flag' in the wake of 9/11:

> The words "National Strength and the Media" are a highly explosive combination. Those engaged in media industry reject the approach that, because the media is considered to influence—indeed shape—"national strength", it should be called upon to show "national responsibility [sic]".
>
> Even if media personnel, whether practitioners or theoreticians, eventually admit that the press does in fact mold national strength, most of them will repudiate the natural conclusion is implied by this admission.
>
> Here and now, this is the position in Israel.
>
> The attack on the Trade Center on 9/11/2001, threatens to undermine this situation. At a first and superficial glance, it appears that the US media, the birthplace of assertive investigative journalism, independent, open and liberal, is towing the government line, accepting the directives of the US administration and bowing to it wishes.
>
> We believe that his is a matter which must be studied very carefully, lest we leap to hasty and unfouded conclusions. It is in no way clear that it is possible apply the patterns of conduct now occuring the new and unkown the realities in US to the ongoing and enduring realties in Israel, which have been molded by very different dimensions of time and scope. This is a topic that requires profound debate and study, and the time has not yet come to draw any conclusions.

The group then formulated five dilemmas which it was felt broadly epitomize the conflicting considerations with which the Israeli media must contend in its daily functioning—particularly in times of security-related crises. The five dilemmas, as formulated by the task force, are summarized briefly below.

Freedom of Expression vs the Need to Restrict such Freedom

Several reasons can be given to justify restricting freedom of expression, for example, the prevention of incitement. However, the issue is normally raised in times of national emergency, on the grounds of the need to preserve morale, social cohesiveness and military secrets. How are the media to behave when in the name of national security, they are faced with demands for voluntary, self-imposed censorship or legally imposed restrictions?

The Duty of the Media to Criticize Government vs the Need to Preserve the Stability of the Government

This involves the problem of the media's 'dual duty'—the duty to criticize the performance of government on the one hand and the duty to prevent the deterioration of the crisis-situation, on the other. How are the media to behave when in the name of national security they are faced with demands to silence, or to suspend, criticism.

The Media as a Public Asset vs the Media as a Commercial and Profit-Oriented Entity

The growing variety, and privatization, of the communications media raise the question of 'social ownership'. Are the media regular commercial enterprises or are they assets in the public domain even if they happen to be privately owned?

The Journalist as a Loyal Citizen vs the Journalist as an Unbiased Professional

The view of the journalist in a dual capacity as a media professional on the one hand and as a citizen loyal to his country on the other raises conflicting pressures which are particularly acute in times of national crisis. Should journalists place their professional integrity before their civic duties, even if this may jeopardize national security or undermine the national interest?

The Media as a Tool that can be Harnessed for Propaganda Purposes vs Media as an Impartial Vehicle Immune to Propaganda Exploitation

The media if they are to be credible and responsible, must be immune to government manipulation and propagandist exploitation. However should this rule be more leniently applied in times of national crises? Should the principle *A la guerre comme à la guerre* not be adopted and the nation's media channels be harnessed to help in the effort against its adversaries and to bolster national security?

The working group did not broach the task of attempting to resolve these dilemmas but limited itself to their formulation and to placing them on the national agenda for discussion. However, they were presented to the general public. Following the seminar, a country-wide poll was conducted to determine public attitudes towards the above dilemmas.[34] The major findings of the poll are presented below.

In general, public attitudes regarding the media in times of national emergency show overwhelming support for subordinating the principles of free expression to the needs of censorship and considerations of national interest. This tendency was manifested in all the questions posed on this issue in the survey.

- 75 percent of those polled expressed the belief that censorship on security grounds is more important than freedom of speech during a national crisis.
- 62 percent felt that the media should restrain themselves and delay criticism of government authorities during national crises. About 33 percent disagreed.
- 74 percent believed that journalists should also censor themselves in the interest of national security. About 23 percent said professional considerations should be afforded priority by journalists.
- Almost 84 percent felt that the media should give precedence to considerations of the public good and national interest over commercial gain and economic interests of media owners. Only 13 percent held the opposite view.

A large majority of respondents (74 percent) felt that the Israeli media should express greater empathy toward Israel during the period of violent confrontation between Israel and the Palestinians; 15 percent disagreed with this. At the same time, about half of the respondents agreed that the Israeli media must present a balanced and objective account of the conflict. It appears that the polls did not see a contradiction between the need for a more pro-Israeli stance on the one hand and balanced and objective media coverage on the other. This of course may be consistent with the proposition that the media coverage at the time of the poll was perceived as having an *anti-Israel* bias.

In regard to the public's assessment of media credibility, only about 37 percent of those polled agreed that the Israeli media has a credibility rating that is either 'high' or 'quite high'. About 40 percent feel media credibility is 'mediocre' and about 20 percent assert that this credibility is 'low' or 'quite low'. In other words, as of November 2001, about 60 percent did not regard the Israeli media as being highly credible.

In contrast, the Israel Defence Forces (IDF), and the security establishment enjoyed a high level of trust. About 70 percent of respondents ranked the military's credibility as 'high' or 'quite high'. About 20 percent saw IDF credibility as 'mediocre' and less than 8 percent viewed it as 'low'.

The level of credibility accorded to both the media and the military remained consistent across all segments of the public regardless of age, political affiliation or economic standing. The majority of those on both the left and right of the political spectrum assigned the media a 'low' or 'mediocre' credibility rating. On the other hand, 70 percent of those who identified themselves as right-wing and 64 percent of those on the left gave the military a credibility grade of 'high' or 'quite high'.

CONCLUSION

From this analysis of prevailing practices in major western democracies and of the public perception in Israel, several conclusions appear to emerge. Although attitudes toward the degree of inviolability of free speech have waxed and waned over the last century, democracies have seldom, if ever, accorded it absolute sanctity. Even at the zenith of liberal leniency (in the latter stages, and immediate aftermath, of the Vietnam War), there was an awareness that freedom of expression may have to be curtailed to some degree and subordinated to the exigencies of national security when the latter is under threat. Since the post-Vietnam era, particularly since the 1991 Gulf War and even more so in the post-9/11 period, there has been a perceptible hardening across the democratic world as to the freedoms that are considered appropriate in times of national crisis, with a growing realization taking hold that some freedoms will have to be reigned in temporarily if they are not to be lost permanently.

Modern technologies which facilitate rapid (indeed almost instantaneous) and wide-ranging (indeed virtually global) transmission and dissemination of information have radically transformed the potential impact that the media can have on issues pertinent to national security. Modern technologies have also made the task of suppressing potentially deleterious information much more difficult. This has created a qualitative change in the media/military equation, and a commensurate need to prudently reassess, in today's modern hi-tech context, the significance of Benjamin Franklin's dictum that those who would forgo liberty for security deserve neither security nor liberty. The leeway that could be afforded journalists in the past without adversely affecting national security is now not only far more limited but also vastly more difficult to maintain.

In this regard it should be kept in mind that unrestricted freedom may be counterproductive, and its exercise may jeopardize the very socio-political basis upon which any freedom is founded. Awareness of this has brought democratic powers like the US and the UK to impose stringent restrictions on the coverage of military operations (such as in the Falklands in the 1980s, the Gulf in the 1990s and in Afghanistan and Iraq more recently). By and large both the press and public in these countries have accepted these measures with a significant degree of understanding and support.

In Israel the relationship between the media and security-related sectors is somewhat more complex and problematic for a number of reasons: As opposed to the case with most other democracies where there has usually been a reasonably clear distinction between periods of war and of peace, Israel has been compelled to endure a very tangible and continuous threat to its national security for almost its entire existence. It has thus been suspended in 'twilight' conditions between overt war and periods of quasi-calm, which were also imbued with the latent threat of further violence. Thus both the extended period of time and the fluctuating levels of perceived threat to national security set the conditions in Israel apart from those of most other democratic societies.

Against this backdrop an empirical investigation of public perceptions of press performance was studied. The analysis of the results of this investigation seems to indicate that the Israeli press is misperceiving or mis-performing its role in Israeli society. For the public, whose interest the media is purported to safeguard, is highly critical of the latter's performance. Not only does it appear that the general public understands and supports the need for greater restrictions on freedom of expression than is the case among media personnel, but it also strongly disapproves of the manner in which the press covered the current Israeli–Palestinian conflict. For although the Israeli public rejected blatant one-sided reportage, and expressed its preference for a balanced and objective account of events, an overwhelming majority thought that a more positive and supportive representation of Israel would be appropriate.

The Israeli media's stance has seriously undermined its credibility in the eyes of the public, both in absolute terms and relative to the security sector. Barely one-third of the public rated the media's credibility above 'mediocre', whereas almost 70 percent considered the military and the defence sectors to be above this level. Almost three times (2.5) as many citizens considered the media to have been below 'mediocre' credibility compared to the military and the defence sector.

In this regard it should be recalled that, as a general rule, the Israeli population is more familiar with the military and defence sectors than is the case in most other western democracies. This is due to the large size of the defence establishment in Israel (with which many of its citizens are directly or indirectly involved), as well as to the existence of compulsory military conscription in the country and relatively widespread (albeit declining) reserve duty following compulsory service. Thus while only a few are truly familiar with the nation's military secrets, Israelis are comparatively better placed than citizens in most other democracies to make an informed assessment of the defence sector's credibility. This tends to lend added weight to the low rating assigned to the media's relative credibility, making this a finding which should not be lightly dismissed.

The lack of faith in the Israeli press is an ominous sign, for the media have a crucial role to play in ensuring the proper functioning and maintenance of the democratic process. Loss of faith in the nation's media bodes ill for society as a whole. Although it is true that the results of a single study are neither totally conclusive nor incontrovertible, they do appear to constitute a warning light. It seems that the manner in which the Israeli media discharge their duty leaves much to be desired—at least in the eyes of the public for whom they purport to cater. The press should take heed of this dissatisfaction. For if it alienates its audience, and loses its trust, any media establishment that subscribes to freedom of expression will, in effect, lose its *raison d'être*.

NOTES

1. Marvin Kalb, 'Whose Side Are We on?', *Washington Post*, Thursday, 11 October 2001.
2. Marvin Kalb, quoted in Christopher Dandeker, 'Public Opinion, the Media and the Gulf War', *Armed Forces and Society*, Vol. 22, No. 2 (Winter 1995/1996), p. 298.
3. See Richard R. Heppner, 'Electronic Information and the Gulf War', *Journal of Social and Evolutionary Systems*, Vol. 16, No. 1 (1993), pp. 45–97; Brad D. Lafferty *et al.*, 'The Impact of Media Information on Enemy Effectiveness: A Model for Conflict', at http://www.au.af.mil/au/awc/awcgate/readings/media-laf.doc.
4. Balint Vazsonyi, 'Aid and Comfort to the Enemy', at http://www.founding.org/columns/html/shns009.html.
5. Susan Estrich, 'The thin, thin line between safe and free', *USA Today*, September 13 2001. See http://www.usatoday.com/news/comment/2001-09-13-ncguest1.htm
6. *Abrams v. United States*, 1919, at http://www.lectlaw.com/files/case19.htm.
7. Ibid.
8. 'Introduction to the Court Opinion on the New York Times Co. v. United States Case', at http://usinfo.state.gov/usa/infousa/facts/democrac/43.htm.
9. This perhaps may be inferred from the following opinion expressed by Justice White with which Justice Stewart concurred: 'after examining the materials the Government characterizes as the most sensitive and destructive ... [I cannot] deny that revelation of these documents will do substantial damage to public interests. Indeed, I am confident that their disclosure will have that result'. Available at http://usinfo.state.gov/usa/infousa/facts/democrac/48.htm.
10. For example Justice Stewart, with whom Justice White joins, concurring:

    Yet it is elementary that the successful conduct of international diplomacy and the maintenance of an effective national defense require both confidentiality and secrecy.... The responsibility must be where the power is. The Executive must have largely unshared duty to determine and preserve the degree of internal security necessary to exercise...power successfully. It is the constitutional duty of the Executive – as a matter of sovereign prerogative and not as a matter of law as the courts know law – through the promulgation and enforcement of executive regulations to protect the confidentiality necessary to carry out its responsibilities in the fields of inter-national relations and national defense. This is not to say that Congress and the courts have no role to play. Undoubtedly Congress has the power to enact specific and appropriate criminal laws to protect government property and preserve government secrets... We are asked, quite simply, to prevent the publications by two newspapers of material that the Executive Branch insists should not, in the national interest, be published. I am convinced that the Executive is correct with respect to some of the documents involved. < http://usinfo.state.gov/usa/infousa/facts/democrac/48.htm > liberties

11. Dandeker, 'Public Opinion, the Media and the Gulf War', p. 298.
12. Julian Barnes, *The Guardian*, 25 February 2002.
13. Peter Preston, *The Guardian*, 8 October 2001.
14. *Intelligence and Security Committee Interim Report 2000–01*, Presented to Parliament by the Prime Minister by Command of Her Majesty, March 2001. Available at http://www.archive.official-documents.co.uk/document/cm51/5126/5126.pdf.
15. 'After Sept. 11, a Legal Battle Over Limits of Civil Liberty', *New York Times*, 4 August 2002.
16. At http://portal.unesco.org/ci/ev.php?URL_ID=1669&URL_DO=DO_TOPIC&URL_SECTION=201&reload=1024432641.
17. At http://canada.justice.gc.ca/en/news/nr/2001/doc_29513.html.
18. William Safire, 'Seizing Dictatorial Power', *New York Times*, 15 November 2001.
19. *Washington Post*, 11 October 2001.
20. Ibid.
21. Ibid.
22. *Washington Post*, 12 October 2001.
23. 'Public Not Rattled by Anthrax Reports; Six in 10 Say Military Should Exert Control Over War News', *Associated Press*, 16 October 2001.
24. Heppner, 'Electronic Information and the Gulf War', p. 87.
25. At http://www.newseum.org/warstories/essay/secrecy.htm.
26. Dandeker, 'Public Opinion, the Media and the Gulf War', p. 299.
27. *Washington Post*, 12 October 2001.
28. Dandeker, 'Public Opinion, the Media and the Gulf War', p. 299.
29. Ibid.
30. At http://www.archive.official-documents.co.uk/document/cm51/5126/5126.pdf.
31. Heppner, 'Electronic Information and the Gulf War', p. 87.
32. The task force for the Herzliya Conference media group included Nachman Shai, Head; MK Colette Avital; Jeff Barak; Dr. Yariv Ben-Eliezer; Ron Ben-Ishai; Dr. Eva Berger; Dr. Yehiel Limor; Brig. Gen. Israela Oron; Dan Pattir; Dr. Reuven Pedatzur; Col. (Res.) Issac Shani; Dr. Vicki Shiran; Dr. Martin Sherman; Meir Shlomo; Prof. Gabi Weiman; Ruth Yaron.
33. The paper was distributed at the 2001 Herzliya Conference on the Balance of National Strength and Security, December 16–18, 2001.
34. The poll was conducted by telephone interviews on a representative nationwide sample of 500 Jewish Israeli adults aged 18 and above. It was carried out by the Ramat Gan-based *TNS-Teleseker* on 27–28 November 2001.

Competing Land Uses: The Territorial Dimension of Civil–Military Relations in Israel

AMI OREN and DAVID NEWMAN

'Security comes before everything else' has been a slogan which has accompanied the State of Israel throughout its history. Security considerations are the number one national priority in Israel and their influence is felt in almost every walk of life. Research projects have analyzed the problematic military–civilian relationship in a number of areas, but have not dealt with the way in which this national priority has influenced the formation of the human and civilian geographical landscapes. This paper examines the way in which regional and local planning have been influenced by the security discourse and the role of security considerations in the decision-making process concerning land use, zoning and physical planning. The problem is even more acute in Israel than other countries because of the small territorial size of the country, the rapidly growing population and the resultant competition for scarce land resources. There is virtually no region inside Israel where competition between military and civilian land uses and priorities does not take place. Military and civilian land uses are intertwined with each other, creating a complex mosaic which often causes conflicts and tensions.

The debate concerning military–civil relations has become increasingly multi-disciplinary in recent years. Political scientists, sociologists, economists and anthropologists have become involved in an ever-widening, and increasingly critical, debate over the role of the military authorities and defence establishments in western democracies in general and in Israel in particular. Noticeable for its absence, however, has been a discussion of the geographical and territorial dimensions of the civil–military interface. This is all the more surprising given the fact that the defence and military establishment is one of the major consumers of land, with army camps, training grounds, weapons stores and personnel accommodation requiring relatively large tracts of land. Land zoning for military and defence purposes is disproportionate to the size of the country and the amount of available land—the size of the defence establishment is not a function of the size of the country. Thus Israel has a large defence and military establishment, requiring large areas of land in comparison with almost any other western democracy.

Since land is such a scarce resource in Israel, the competition and conflict over competing land uses is much greater than in countries where remote and peripheral regions are available for military land use. Moreover, the intense involvement of the military in almost all walks of Israeli life also means that defence-related land use is much more visible to the public eye, in some cases located in the centre of densely built-up and populated areas. This is in direct contrast to those countries where the major military facilities are located in areas which are more remote and largely invisible to the public eye, and where the army is of little relevance to the daily life of the majority of the population.

This paper examines the role of the defence establishment as a major consumer of land in Israel. In particular, it will focus on the ongoing competition for land between civilian and military authorities, a competition which has become more intense in recent years as civilian and private sector agencies are eager to acquire land for developmental purposes. The paper will discuss the mechanisms through which land zoning and planning permits are issued and the way in which the military and defence establishments are able to influence the decision-making process through the use of the securitization discourse—a discourse which is generally accorded prominence over all other civilian discourses. The paper will also discuss the impact of military land use on the environment and the ecology of the country, an impact which has both destructive and preservative elements.

Finally, the paper will assess the decision-making processes and planning mechanisms that exist in Israel, through which land zoning decisions are made. It will be shown that the defence establishment has special privileges with regard to the normative statutory planning requirements and, in many cases, is enabled to ignore the civilian planning commissions altogether. Within this decision-making framework we will present some of the conflicts that arise over contested land uses between civilian and military consumers of territory as a scarce resource. The growing demand for land, especially in the metropolitan centre of the country, for economic development also raises the issue concerning defence-related land use as a valuable piece of real estate.

With the exception of some comments concerning the role of settlements in wider defence perceptions, the paper focuses only on the area within the pre-1967 borders of Israel. The Occupied Territories are subject to a different set of rules and regulations concerning the use of land for security considerations. This is beyond the scope of the present paper.

SOME CONCEPTUAL COMMENTS

The normal regional and physical planning terminology does not have a category for defensive and security land use. The relative lack of professional literature dealing with the planning implications of the security discourse is due to the fact that much of the relevant data is classified, even in western democracies. The information on military land use in the United States is exceptional in this respect, appearing in official documents,[1] as well as research publications[2] and on US defence department internet sites. The military establishment views territory in general as a land resource for their own use, determined by their own security considerations[3] whether or not they possess formal ownership of the territory in question.

The military–civilian land use interface can be examined from two contrasting perspectives:

1. Territory as a dependent factor whose use is determined by the defence establishment. The geographical, demographic and topographical conditions form the frame within which military decision-making takes place. In this determinist perspective, territory is a given—and largely unchanging—output of the system. This discourse is concerned with the traditional discussion concerning the nature of territory as a strategic and geopolitical resource, requiring topographic advantages, buffer zones and early warning areas.
2. Territory as an independent factor in which the securitization discourse determines the country's land uses with all the associated implications for economic and regional development. The literature discusses the influence of military landscapes on settlement patterns,[4] as well as the process through which military land uses are transformed for civilian usage.[5] Recent research has begun to focus on the environmental and ecological implications of defensive land uses, the preservation of sites of natural beauty, as well as historical and archaeological sites,[6] and the restoration of lands which have been damaged by military-related activities.[7]

CIVIL–MILITARY RELATIONS IN ISRAEL: THE TERRITORIAL DIMENSION

The wider discussion of the territorial and spatial dimensions of civil–military relations is noticeably absent from the literature dealing with civil–military relations in Israel. A survey of the geographical literature on Israel also indicates little research in this area.[8] A number of studies have analyzed the wider geopolitical and geo-strategic aspects,[9] such as the demarcation of the country's borders and the relevance of the size and shape of the country for its security posture.[10] There have been many studies dealing with the connection between the settlement process and the security discourse, some of it by geographers,[11] others by historians.[12] The former studies take a critical approach to the use of lands for civilian purposes aimed at strengthening the territorial control practised by the state, especially in border areas or regions in which there is a large Arab-Palestinian population. The latter group of studies describes the process through which lands were taken over by the state during the early years of statehood. A recent historical geographical study[13] has analyzed the role of the Israel Defence Forces (IDF) in the early years of Israel and its role in the formation of spatial patterns of development.

Other studies have focused on traditional notions of strategic depth and security borders, or have dealt with regional security and scenarios for future spatial configurations as part of a peace agreement in the West Bank[14] and the Golan Heights.[15] The history of Israel's borders has been discussed by Israeli political geographers Moshe Brawer[16] and Gideon Biger.[17] The 'Green Line' and the issue of frontier areas have been the subject of other research.[18]

The first studies to deal directly with defence-related land uses as a scarce resource were written in the 1980s, following the Israeli withdrawal from Sinai and redeployment to the Negev region of southern Israel. This raised a whole series of new problems relating to civilian land use in this region and the potential for conflict with the military authorities.[19] Within the framework of Project Israel 2020, the long term regional planning and dispersal of the army was examined.[20] A more critical school of thought studied the conflicts for territorial control at the micro level in the Galilee,[21] in the Nazareth region,[22] the mixed Arab–Jewish cities,[23] in Lod,[24] the Adjami neighbourhood[25] in the city of Tel Aviv-Jaffa, and the role of tree planting as a means of ensuring territorial control in border areas.[26] This academic discussion has itself been the subject of political argumentation and controversy, focusing on contested interpretations of the nature of land control between Jewish and Arab populations, especially in areas of dense Arab residence such as the Galilee, the northern Negev, and Jerusalem.[27]

DEFENSIVE LAND USES AND THE CONTROL OF SPACE

In Israel, the defence establishment has direct and indirect control over half the country's land surface, while its 'standing' with respect to the way that lands are used and zoned encompasses the entire country. According to data provided by the Planning Authority in the Ministry of Agriculture, 10.5 million dunams out of a total 22 million dunams (48 percent) are areas reserved for military camps and training grounds. The types of defence-related land uses are diverse and can be categorized according to a number of functional criteria:

- According to general criteria, such as fenced-in land to which entry is forbidden, or open spaces lacking clear borders between military and civilian uses.
- According to functional criteria based on defensive needs—strategic, operational or tactical.
- According to spatial criteria, based on the size and shape of the area under military control, ranging from large tracts of land for training purposes, to micro spaces which include single buildings within the urban environment or even single antennas which are fenced in within a few square metres.
- According to statutory definitions based on military planning considerations, such as a closed military area, a munitions factory, and so on. Some of these may be formally marked on civilian maps or in planning outlines.

A temporal analysis of defensive land uses since the establishment of Israel in 1948 demonstrates the impact of strategic considerations on the one hand, and the changing internal discourse within the defence establishment on the other. These have taken into account changing strategic priorities in terms of the location of troops, army camps, weapons and tanks in relation to the country's border regions and the technological change in the art of warfare—particularly in the era of electronic communications and ballistic missiles. The changing logistics of military organization have also affected the way in which land is used for defensive purposes, as too the gradual transition from the use of old British army bases from the pre-state era, to modern and more advanced defence-related facilities.

Notwithstanding, the initial dispersion of many of the major military areas has remained in the same location throughout the past fifty years, if only because of the relative advantages of an existing presence and the inertia of the defence system to make changes which were not directly related to immediate strategic needs.

The territorial demands of the army also underwent change according to the influence of external factors, not least the redeployment of the country's security forces following the cessation of warfare, as a result of the implementation of peace agreements and the withdrawal from territories, as well as the shift in focus from traditional warfare against neighbouring states to the battle against terrorism activity within state confines. Other external factors which have become of greater importance in recent years have been the growing empowerment of civil society which has placed pressure on the military establishment to evacuate land areas which are located in the urban heartland of the country and which have been transformed into spaces contested between civil and military requirements.

Defensive land uses occur at almost all spatial levels—ranging from large territorial tracts of land for training purposes, army camps and military headquarters in both rural and urban environments, to the personal defence spaces of individual families in their houses and apartment blocks. Figure 1 shows the diverse types of locations and functions which fall under the definition of security land uses. It includes many affiliated land uses, which are not normally immediately identified as being defensive in nature, especially the construction of urban neighbourhoods and other housing projects within a civilian environment, but for the exclusive use of military personnel. Given the often secretive nature and precise location of defence-related installations, large tracts of land in the wider vicinity are often fenced off so as to keep the prying eyes of the civilian population well away. Thus the multiplier effect of the defence-related land use activities is far greater than direct military usages alone. Defence-related land uses can be divided into a number of categories.

Army Camps and Bases

Army bases and other fixed military installations are the major form of physical infrastructure requiring land reserves. These consist of a wide

Closed areas which have defence industries	Peripheral areas in which there is security activity	Open areas which have military training areas or army camps	Large cities with army bases in the vicinity	Location · · · · · · · · · Function
Along the coast; in the Negev and the Galilee regions	–	Negev, Golan Heights, Lakhish region, Wadi Ara, etc.	The Kiryah defence headquarters in Tel Aviv; the Tzrifin, Tel hashomer, and Glilot military areas; army camps in Beer Sheva, Haifa areas	**Economic impacts**
	Borderlands along the Green Line, Lebanon, Jordan Valley and Aravah, the border with Egypt			**Preventing land use for civilian development purposes**
Negev and Galilee regions		Negev and Galilee regions	Negev and Galilee regions	**Creating access and/or settlement development**
–		–	Everywhere in Israel— within neighbourhoods and housing complexes	**Private spaces**
Along the coast; in the Negev and the Galilee regions		Negev, Golan Heights, Lakhish region, Wadi Ara, etc.	Throughout the country	**Ecological and environmental impacts**
Along the coast; in the Negev and the Galilee regions		Galilee and Negev regions, the Golan Heights	The Kiryah defence headquarters in Tel Aviv; the Tzrifin, Tel hashomer, and Glilot military areas; army camps in Beer Sheva, Haifa areas	**Impact on the visual landscape**

FIGURE 1
TYPOLOGY OF DEFENSIVE–SECURITY LAND USES IN ISRAEL

range of facilities, including regular army bases with their living accommodation; training camps; logistic centres; food, ammunition and transportation stores; air fields; electronic and communication facilities; the military industries; national and regional army headquarters; non-designated offices and houses for the intelligence and secret service agencies. While many of these facilities are located in the country's open areas, some of them are to be found within the heart of the urban areas, not least the national military headquarters, known as the Kiryah, occupying prime real estate in the heart of Tel Aviv. Given the small territorial extent of the country, the majority of these bases and installations are part of the public domain and, although they are not marked on civilian maps, can normally be seen by anyone travelling on the country's roads. One of the largest such areas in the centre of the country is the Tzrifin army base just outside of Tel Aviv, occupying thousands of dunams of land.

Training Grounds and Test Areas

The zoning of land for test areas is an important use of relatively large tracts of land in the country's open and peripheral regions, mostly in the Negev. But, unlike the case of army bases, this does not necessarily require the construction of buildings. Neither are they used on a permanent or continuous basis. By definition, these areas are located in regions where there is the least amount of civilian activity because it often necessitates the use of live ammunition and the testing of new weapons. These areas are demarcated on tourist and hiking maps published by the Nature Preservation Authority, based on a survey of Israel's open spaces which was undertaken in October 2000. The evacuation of the Sinai Peninsula as part of the Camp David Peace Accords necessitated a major relocation on the part of the army of its air force bases, camps and training areas. Although the Negev is constantly presented as the 'empty' half of the country, requiring future development and populating, the fact remains that almost half of this region is closed for private developmental and/or hiking purposes by army fences and restrictions.

Building Restrictions

The defence establishment imposes a wide range of building restrictions in areas of close proximity to military installations, bases and training grounds. The reasons for this are varied. There is a desire to keep civilians away from secret installations. This is more difficult to carry out in the centre of the country, but applies to army camps, air force bases and nuclear installations in peripheral regions. In some cases, civilian development will be kept away because of the safety implications of accidents taking place in munitions stores and affecting a wider area. Restrictions on construction—especially the height of buildings—are imposed in areas where the army requires communication fields which are not affected by extraneous noises.

This is particularly the case around airfields and around the military headquarters in the Kiryah complex in central Tel Aviv. The high rise development which has been taking place within the metropolitan area over the past decade has been limited in terms of location and height by the requirements of the defence authorities. In some cases, tower blocks, such as the Azrieli office and commercial complex, had to make do with fewer floors than had originally been planned because of these military restrictions.

Infrastructure in Border Areas

Given the potential for future armed conflict between Israel and its neighbours, the country's border regions are taken up with defensive infrastructure which can be employed where deemed necessary by the military authorities. Such infrastructure includes fences, trenches, patrol roads, quick access arteries and so on. Its infrastructure is to be found along almost all of Israel's border regions, especially the Lebanese and Syrian borders.

Emergency Spaces

In reality, almost the entire country is part of the emergency space which has potential for use by the army in times of crisis. Many of these spaces are under civilian control and ownership but can be taken over by the military authorities during times of emergency. Major public institutions, such as the country's universities, are sometimes taken over for emergency procedure training within the framework of Shelach. During both Iraq wars (1991 and 2003), areas in the metropolitan centre of the country were used for the positioning of anti-ballistic Patriot missiles. Public buildings can be appropriated for emergency recruitment of reserve troops or vehicles, while prior to the Six Day War, some areas were prepared as emergency cemeteries. Given the fact that these areas may be needed at any point in the future, the military authorities often intervene in the planning and development of these places so that, should the need arise, they will be accessible and readily usable.

Areas for Daily Security Activities

In order to facilitate what is termed 'ongoing' security functions, certain areas—particularly along the borders, frontier regions and in other zones of potential conflict—are closed to all civilian activity, thus enabling their use by the army if, and when, required. During the first three decades of statehood many areas were designated as closed as a means of establishing state control and authority in regions deemed as problematic, especially those of major Arab population concentrations. Such areas included large parts of the Galil, Ramot menashe, the east Sharon Plain (the Triangle), the Beer Sheva valley and the Northern Negev. This included all those places which were under the military administration prior to their abolition in 1966.

Civilian Functions—Control Landscapes and Settlements
Even with the abolition of the military administration, the desire to strengthen the territorial control of the state in regions of Arab population continued to be carried out in the name of national security. This follows on the state expropriation of most of the lands evacuated by Palestinian refugees in the wake of the War of Independence in 1948–1949 and the erasing of most of the physical remnants of the villages. This land was taken over by the Israel Lands Authority, which retains its ownership of over 90 percent of the country's lands (including those under military usage) as a means of preserving state control over contested territories. The zoning of land, the granting—or the non-granting—of expansion and construction permits through the normal planning mechanisms, based on the stated preferences of the defence establishment, have proved to be an effective way of controlling land on behalf of the state. Similarly, the demarcation of municipal and local government boundaries, separating Jewish and Arab municipalities, is another effective means of land control at the local level.

In his analysis of the Nazareth metropolitan region, Palestinian geographer Ghazi Falah has shown how the Arab town of Lower Nazareth has been virtually prevented from any further expansion despite the rapid demographic growth of the city, while the Jewish town of Upper Nazareth extended over a far larger jurisdiction area with a smaller population.[28] Falah further argued that planning policy in this region was aimed at preventing the spontaneous expansion of Arab settlements, through the mechanisms of jurisdictional demarcation and the creation of settlement 'wedges' in between the existing Arab townships and villages.

The establishment of new settlements for the Jewish population has always been seen as fulfilling an ideological and security function at one and the same time, thus extending the effective spatial control of the state over contested territories.[29] This policy has taken place throughout the past hundred years, prior to the establishment of the state, during the first twenty years of statehood in the border and peripheral regions, and as part of the post-1967 West Bank settlement policy.[30] Much of the settlement development has been couched in terms of the securitization discourse, with civilian settlements being seen as an adjunct of defence policy. This policy was rooted in the role of pre-state settlements in defending peripheral regions, and the role of individual settlements during the 1948 War of Independence in holding up the rapid advance of Arab armies. It was later translated into military policies through the establishment of the Nahal corps—soldiers who divided their army duty between combat tasks and the creation of new settlement outposts.[31]

This policy also lay at the heart of the immediate post-1967 Allon Plan to establish a line of settlements along the new eastern line of 'defence' in the Jordan Valley, as well as throughout the Golan Heights. The need to evacuate these settlements during the Yom Kippur war of October 1973 resulted in questions as to whether the policy linking settlement to defence-related activities was still relevant in a modern era of warfare technology. Moreover, the West Bank settlements require large soldiered garrisons to ensure the safety of their residents and have now become controlled by the hostile environment, rather than acting as the control agent they set out to ensure in the first place.

Protecting the Home Front

The home front is an important part of the defence landscape in Israel, as are the border regions of the country. This has become even more true during the past decade with the establishment of the Home Front as an equal part of the defence hierarchy, following the uncertainty caused by the firing of Iraqi missiles into the heart of Tel Aviv during the Gulf War of 1990–1991. The use of space for defence-related activities on the home (civilian) front touches upon many dimensions of daily practices at the most local and micro of activity spaces. At the level of housing, the personal and family space of almost every individual in Israel is affected by security-space considerations. Houses and apartments must have security rooms or concrete shelters within close proximity, space which could otherwise have been used for other purposes particularly within the densely populated Israeli urban environments.

The authorization for moving into a new house requires a permit from the local defence authorities that the safety room has been constructed in accordance with the defence-determined criteria. Space is also controlled in such a way that the entry to almost all public institutions, commercial centres, places of entertainment, universities, government offices, shops and even cafes, is limited to a single controlled and guarded entry point in an attempt to maintain safety through personal checks. This has become even more marked during the past few years with the growth of suicide bombers operating inside the heart of the country's civilian facilities, such as restaurants, shopping centres and buses, thus necessitating the provision of additional security barriers, check-posts and defence-related activities in the functional backyard of almost all of the country's citizens.

Transportation Arteries

All major highways and inter-urban transportation arteries are constructed by the Israel Roads Authority (Ma'atz) only after approval and, in some cases, after an initial recommendation from, the defence establishment. Access routes from the centre of the country to the southern, northern and eastern boundaries are not only intended to improve access for tourism, access to employment and other commuting functions, but are also seen as points of speedy access to the country's borders in times of war or other threats.

THE SECURITIZATION DISCOURSE, LAND ZONING AND THE PLANNING MECHANISM

Israel has an orderly and hierarchical system of physical and regional planning, consisting of three tiers of statutory authorities. The National Master Plan is drawn up by the Planning Authority of the Ministry of Interior (TAMA 35). This sets the national guidelines for planning and construction activity, based on demographic and socio-economic forecasts and projections. At the next level, the country is divided into six regional planning authorities which have to approve local plans from the lower level but which must ensure that such plans fit into the wider regional and national priorities. At the third level, municipal authorities—normally grouped together at sub-regional levels—approve and authorize the development plans of specific settlements, developers and housing contractors.

Each level of the planning committee has representatives of various public agencies, some of them on a permanent basis, others participating depending on the particular project being discussed. These agencies include the Lands Authority, and the infrastructural agencies (such as electricity, roads, communications), the military authorities, economic agencies, the environmental lobby and municipal authorities.

At the national level there are three types of plans. The first of these are broad guidelines for the spatial development of the country over a given period of time, consisting of all relevant civilian functions but with a major focus on the construction and expansion of the settlement network to meet growing population demands. The second type of plan is thematic in nature with each major authority—the Electricity Corporation, the Roads Authority, Education and Health Ministries—producing their own national master plans for development. The third types are specific infrastructural plans focusing on heavy infrastructural projects such as the establishment of power stations, desalination plants and so on. All of these master plans require prior coordination with the military authorities.

Despite the fact that the army is such a major user of land, there is no national master plan, even taking into account different security and strategic scenarios ranging from conflict to peace, for security land uses in their broadest sense. The defence establishment works on a case by case basis, depending on specific needs (as self-defined within the system), making the problem of national coordination very difficult. The Physical Planning Authority of the IDF is part of the General Command. This body is responsible for dealing with all matters relating to planning and construction. Its work is divided into three main areas of activity:

- internal army plans for construction and development and the coordination of these plans with the relevant land 'consumers' and contractors;
- preparation for the plans according to the statutory requirements which are demanded from the military authorities (as compared to the normal requirements within the civilian sector), and
- coordination with, and between, all relevant civilian agencies in respect of specific plans on an ad hoc basis.

The statutory requirements derive their authority from Section 6 of the Planning and Construction law which deals with the special status of 'defence-related facilities', enabling the defence establishment to preserve land for its own use, to prevent non-defence-related use where necessary and to have formal representation on all local and regional planning authorities.

As in all such statutory authorities throughout the world, conflicts of interest often arise between representatives, and this is exacerbated in the case of Israel owing to its small size, and the growing empowerment on the part of civilian and economic development groups in the ongoing civilian–military dialogue during the past decade. Within the civilian planning authorities, decisions are made on a majority vote basis, normally following an intensive period of discussion and lobbying by interest groups for particular projects. Coalitions can take place between groups which are not normally known for their common interests.

In Israel, in particular, there are three powerful interest groups—the defence establishment, the economic developers and, in recent years, the environmental lobby. Any two of these may often link up together (along with other public authority interests) to push a decision through (or to oppose the ratification of a permit). The defence establishment (the army or the Ministry of Defence) rarely becomes involved in this process because the normal planning legislation is not incumbent upon the defence establishment. In most cases, any area of land deemed necessary for defensive purposes, however defined, is not subject to the normal scrutiny or veto power of the civilian planning authorities.

But in cases of civilian development, planning permission has to be coordinated with the defence authorities and they have a veto power over all civilian-related development if, as they often argue, such development is detrimental to security interests. At the same time, all regional and national plans have to be submitted to the defence authorities prior to their being tabled before the relevant committees. At the local and regional levels, the Defence Ministry has automatic power of veto, while at the national level it is rare for decisions to be made which negate the defence establishment's position.

This ability to use the defence–securitization discourse as a national discourse overriding all other civilian and economic development interests means that the defence establishment maintains a monopoly over almost all spatial development throughout the country. This is not always in opposition to civilian purposes. The position of environmental groups is interesting in this respect. In some cases, where the military takes over land—such as for the purposes of military camps, or the construction of the separation fence between Israel and the West Bank—it can have a serious detrimental effect on the physical landscape and the ecological balance and will be opposed by the environmental lobby. In other cases, the army insistence on leaving land for training purposes, and thus preventing its alternative use and despoliation by economic developers, is in the interests of the green lobby which will, in such cases, promote the securitization discourse as a means of preventing other forms of development from taking place in these areas. By linking into the securitization–defence discourse, the relatively weak environmental lobby has a greater chance of succeeding against the stronger economic interests of developers and the construction industry.

The securitization discourse is also linked with a broader discourse of 'national interest', even where the specific purpose is not always directly related to matters of military security or defence. Two of the most important projects of the past decade which have been promoted by Israeli governments without being subject to the decision-making process have been, respectively, the mass construction activity which occurred in the 1990s in order to provide sufficient accommodation for the arrival of nearly one million new immigrants from the former Soviet Union, and the construction of the fence separating Israel from the West Bank along huge tracts of land from the north to south of the region. In both of these cases, the use of the 'national imperative' and 'securitization' needs of the country, as well as the immediacy of the projects, have enabled government to undertake emergency procedures which have not necessitated the authorization, even retroactively, of the planning authorities.

This has had major implications with respect to the conversion of land uses from one function to another (particularly from rural and agricultural to housing and developmental), which otherwise would have taken a great deal of time, discussion and bureaucracy within the normal statutory authorities. In the case of the mass construction for the Russian immigrants, the then minister of national infrastructure, Ariel Sharon, succeeded in gaining emergency powers for the construction of new housing developments without the need to get normal planning authorization from either the Israel Lands Authority or the statutory planning commissions on the grounds of 'national emergency requirements'—thus opening the way for the beginning of land privatization in Israel. The military and defence authorities are thus able to use the argument of 'national interest' as a means of promoting or opposing many projects relating to infrastructural development or land use, a power which is not possessed by any of the civilian planning agencies.

SECURITY LAND USES AS REAL ESTATE

In November 2003 *Ha'aretz* reported that the Ministry of Defence had requested the sum of US$750 million from the Ministry of Finance in lieu of the future evacuation of two prime sites in the centre of the country.[32] One of these sites, the Sdeh Dov airfield, is considered to be one of the last major sites for potential development in the metropolitan area. At the same time, the Defence Ministry demanded that the long term leasing rights for this land remain under their control. Just a few weeks prior to this, the Defence Ministry announced its intention to evacuate other sites in the centre of the country as part of a long term plan to raise financial resources in an era of stringent budgetary cuts.

Much of the land controlled by the defence establishment has substantial real estate value in a country which is undergoing rapid commercial and housing development. The fact that the defence establishment is able to evacuate such areas for commercial gain would suggest that the primary reason for controlling these lands, namely the security needs of the state, are not necessarily legitimate. Moreover, the Defence Ministry and the army have never paid the state or the Israel Lands Authority for the right to these lands in the first place. They were handed over to defence establishment control on the basis of their claims that these areas were required for future security needs.

The single most valuable piece of available real estate for future development in the heart of the metropolitan centre of the country in Tel Aviv is the defence headquarters in the Kiryah complex. Over the years there has been an intense discussion concerning the need to evacuate this area for a mixture of strategic (it is dangerous to have your main headquarters in the heart of the most densely civilian populated area of the country, an argument which was strengthened following the firing of the Scud missiles from Iraq during the Gulf war of 1991) and economic (the army would stand to gain major funding for other developmental purposes if it were to agree to evacuate this area for civilian requirements). But the defence establishment has maintained its hold on this important piece of real estate and it is unlikely that it will agree to evacuate this area in the immediate future.

CONCLUSION

This paper has set out to describe the almost monopolistic control of land by the defence establishment in Israel. Approximately half of the country's land surface falls under the different defence-related categories, whether they are used on a daily basis or whether they have potential use in the future. The normative planning mechanism which is applicable to the civilian sector does not apply to most defence-related land uses and, as such, the competition for this scarce territorial resource is not decided on an even playing field. The civilian pressures for land, especially in the metropolitan centre of the country, are increasing, while the army itself is prepared to consider disposing of some of its territorial real estate for monetary compensation. This is indicative of the changing nature of civil–military relations in Israel, a relationship in which civilian empowerment is beginning to raise questions and break the monopoly which has been held by the defence establishment for the past fifty years.

NOTES

1. See US Department of Defence, *Base Structure Report: A Summary of DoD's Real Property Inventory*, Fiscal Year 1999 Baseline, Office of the Deputy under Secretary of Defence, Installations and Environment, 1999; US Department of Defence, *Base Structure Report: A Summary of DoD's Real Property Inventory*, Fiscal Year 2002 Baseline, Office of the Deputy under Secretary of Defence, Installations and Environment, 2002.
2. D. Cragg, *Guide to Military Installations*, 6th edition, Mechanicsburg, PA, 2000.
3. For some general discussions of the use of land by the defence establishment in Israel, see A. Derman, 'Criteria for the Determination of Military–Strategic Space', in *The Physical Infrastructure of Israel*, Tel Aviv, 1984, pp. 11–26; S. Yanai, 'The Land Policy of the Israel Defence Forces', *Karka*, Vol. 50 (2000), pp. 32–42; A. Oren, 'Military Spaces in Israel: The Use of Land by the Army from the War of Independence until the Sinai Campaign (1948–1956)', Unpublished Ph.D thesis, Haifa University, 2003; A. Soffer and J. Minghi, 'Israel's Security Landscapes: The Impact of Military Considerations on Land Uses', *The Professional Geographer*, Vol. 38 (1986), pp. 28–41.
4. S. Conway, 'Locality, Metropolis and Nation: The Impact of the Military Camps in England during the American War', *History*, Vol. 82, No. 268 (1997), pp. 547–562.
5. C.M. Corcoran, 'Rehabilitation of Former US Military Lands Bordering the Panama Canal', *Journal of Sustainable Forestry*, Vol. 8, No. 3–4 (1999), pp. 67–79.
6. M. Blacksell and F. Reynolds, 'Military Training in National Parks: A Question of Land Use Conflict and National Priorities', in M. Bateman and R. Reily (eds.), *The Geography of Defence*, London and Sydney, 1987, pp. 215–227; D. Doxford and J. Savage, 'The Proposed Development of Otterburn Military Training Area in Northumberland National Park: A National Perspective', *Journal of Environmental Planning and Management*, Vol. 38, No. 4 (1995), pp. 551–560; R. Woodward, 'Gunning for Rural England: The Politics of the Promotion of Military Land Use in the Northumberland National Park', *Journal of Rural Studies*, Vol. 15, No. 1 (1999), pp. 17–33; G. Brown, 'Salisbury Plain Training Area—The Management of an Ancient Landscape', *Landscape History*, Vol. 17 (1995), pp. 65–76; D. Doxford and T. Hill, 'Land Use for Military Training in the UK: the Current Situation, Likely Developments and Possible Alternatives', *Journal of Environmental Planning and Management*, Vol. 41, No. 3 (1998), pp. 279–297.
7. E.L. Etnier, J.F. King and A.P. Watson, 'Chemical Warfare Material: Unique Regulatory Issues', *Environmental-Management*, Vol. 25, No. 4 (2000), pp. 347–356.
8. Y. Gradus and S. Krakover (eds.), *Israeli Scholar's Publications in Human Geography and Development Studies*, Beer Sheva, 2000; Y. Bar-Gal, 'The "Tribal Elders": Continuity and Change in Israeli Geography', *Horizons in Geography*, Vol. 51 (1999), pp. 7–39.
9. D. Newman, 'The Geographical and Territorial Imprint on the Security Discourse', in D. Bar-Tal, D. Jacobson and A. Klieman (eds.), *Security Concerns: Insights from the Israeli Experience*, JAI Press, London, 1998, pp. 73–94.

10. For differing perspectives on this see A. Soffer, 'Geography and National Security', in Offer and A. Kover (eds.), *Quality and Quantity*, Tel Aviv, 1985, pp. 321–330; Newman, 'The Geographical and Territorial Imprint on the Security Discourse'. Soffer's analysis represents the traditional securitization discourse which has remained largely unchanged since the 1940s and 1950s, while Newman argues for changing understandings of the territorial and spatial factor in the securitization discourse as a result of changing political, military and security realities.
11. D. Newman, 'The Role of Civilian and Military Presence as Strategies of Territorial Control: The Arab-Israel Conflict', *Political Geography Quarterly*, Vol. 8, No. 3 (1989), pp. 215-227; O. Yiftachel, 'Settlement vs Sumud: The Territorial Restructuring of Israel/Palestine', in G. Bennet (ed.), *Tension Regions of the World*, Iowa, 1997, pp. 105–126; See also A. Oren, 'The Geographer in the Service of Military Physical Planning', *Ma'archot*, Vol. 385 (2002), pp. 60-67.
12. For a traditionalist analysis of the relationship between pre-state settlement policy and securitization objectives, see Z. Tzur, *Settlement and the Country's Borders*, Tel Aviv, 1980; O. Shiran, *Points of Strength: Settlement Policy in Relation to Political and Security Objectives in the Pre-State and Early-State Periods*, Tel Aviv, 1998; E. Oren, *Settlement in the Period of Struggle, 1936–1947*, Jerusalem, 1978.
13. Oren, *Military Spaces in Israel*.
14. Newman, 'The Geographical and Territorial Imprint on the Security Discourse'; see also G. Falah and D. Newman, 'The Spatial Manifestation of Threat: Israelis and Palestinians Seek a "Good" Border', *Political Geography*, Vol. 14, No. 8 (1995), pp. 689–706; D. Newman, 'The Geopolitics of Peacemaking in Israel–Palestine', *Political Geography*, Vol. 21, No. 5 (2002), pp. 629–646.
15. A. Shalev, *Peace and Security in the Golan Heights*, Tel Aviv, 1993.
16. M. Brawer, 'The Green Line: Functions and Impacts of an Israeli–Arab Superimposed Boundary', in C. Grundy-Warr (ed.), *International Boundaries and Boundary Conflict Resolution*, University of Durham, 1990, pp. 63–74; M. Brawer, 'The Making of an Israeli–Palestinian Boundary', in C. Schofield, D. Newman and A. Drysdale (eds.), *The Razor's Edge: International Boundaries and Political Geography*, London, 2002, pp. 473–492.
17. G. Biger, 'Israel's 1949 Armistice Lines', in M. Naor (ed.), *The First Year of Independence, 1948–1949*, Jerusalem, 1988, pp. 201–212.
18. Brawer, 'The Green Line: Functions and Impacts of an Israeli–Arab Superimposed Boundary'; See also D. Newman, 'The Functional Presence of an "Erased" Boundary: The Re-emergence of the "Green Line"', in C.H. Schofield and R.N. Schofield (eds.), *World Boundaries: The Middle East and North Africa*, London, 1993, pp. 71–98; D. Newman, 'Boundaries in Flux: The Green Line Boundary between Israel and the West Bank Past, Present and Future', Monograph Series, *Boundary and Territory Briefings*, Vol. 7, England, 1995; A. Kartin, 'A Geographical Analysis of the Threat of Hostile neighbours on the Settlement of Israel's Frontier Zones', Unpublished PhD thesis, Tel Aviv University, 1995.
19. A. Vachman and R. Lerman, *Masterplan for Negev Development*, Interim Report No. 1, 1979; A. Derman, 'Is there a Conflict between Civilian and Military Planning in the Negev?', *Conference Abstracts, Israel Geographical Association*, 1982, pp. 46–48; A. Derman, 'The Negev after the Evacuation of Sinai: Space for Army Redeployment or for Regional Development?', *Nofim*, No. 17 (1983), pp. 55–70.
20. E. Sverdlov and A. Derman, *Planning Policy for the Defence Establishment*, part of the National Masterplan for the year 2020, Faculty of Architecture and Town Planning, University of Haifa, 1996.
21. O. Yiftachel, 'State Policies, Land Control and an Ethnic Minority: The Arabs in the Galilee, Israel', *Environment and Planning D: Society and Space*, Vol 9 (1991), pp. 329–362.
22. G. Falah, 'Land Fragmentation and Spatial Control in the Nazareth Metropolitan Area', *Professional Geographer*, Vol. 44, No. 1 (1992), pp. 30–44.
23. G. Falah, 'Living Together Apart: Residential Segregation in Mixed Arab–Jewish Cities', *Urban Studies*, Vol. 33, No. 6 (1996), pp. 823–857.
24. H. Yacobi, 'Urban Ethnocracy and the Deconstruction of Identity: The Case of Lod', Unpublished PhD thesis, Ben-Gurion University, 2003.
25. J. Portugali, *Implicate Relations: Society and Space in the Israeli–Palestinian Conflict*, Netherlands, 1996.

26. S.E. Cohen, 'The Politics of Planting: Israeli–Palestinian Competition for Control of Land in the Jerusalem Periphery', *Geography Research Paper*, Chicago, 1993, p. 236.
27. For a debate on the Galilee's 'Judaization' settlement activities, see the following exchange of articles: G. Falah, 'The Facts and Fictions of Judaization Policy and its Impact on the Majority Arab Population in the Galilee', *Political Geography Quarterly*, Vol. 10, No. 3 (1990), pp. 297–316; O. Yiftachel and D. Rumley, 'On the Impact of Israel's Judaization Policy in the Galilee', *Political Geography Quarterly*, Vol. 10, No. 3 (1990), pp. 286–296; A. Soffer, 'Israeli "Judaization" Policy in Galilee and its Impact on Local Arab Urbanization', *Political Geography Quarterly*, Vol. 10, No. 3 (1991), pp. 282–285; See also O. Yiftachel, *Planning a Mixed Region in Israel: The Political Geography of Arab–Jewish Relations in Israel*, Aldershot, 1992.
28. Falah, 'Land Fragmentation and Spatial Control in the Nazareth Metropolitan Area'.
29. For a long term analysis of Israeli settlement policies, see B. Kimmerling, *Zionism and Territory: The Socio-Territorial Dimensions of Zionist Politics*, Berkeley, 1983; A. Kellerman, *Society and Settlement: Jewish Land of Israel in the Twentieth Century*, Albany, NY, 1993.
30. For an analysis of the relationship between political objectives and urban and regional planning policy with respect to the West Bank settlement process, see S. Reichman, 'Policy Reduces the World to Essentials: A Reflection on the Jewish Settlement Process in the West Bank since 1967', in D. Morley and A. Shachar (eds.), *Planning in Turbulence*, Jerusalem, 1986; D. Newman, 'The Territorial Politics of Exurbanisation: Reflections on Thirty Years of Jewish Settlement in the West Bank', *Israel Affairs*, Vol. 3, No. 1 (1996), pp. 61–85; D. Newman, 'Colonization as Suburbanization: The Politics of the Land Market at the Frontier', in P. Misselwitz et al. (eds), *City of Collision*, Birkhauser Publishers, Basel, 2006.
31. Newman, 'The Role of Civilian and Military Presence as Strategies of Territorial Control'.
32. See A. Harel, 'The army considers the evacuation of bases in the centre of the country as a means of raising funds', *Ha'aretz*, 30 September 2003; A. Barzilai, 'The army requests 3.5 billion shekel in consideration for future sales of army bases', *Ha'aretz*, 11 November 2003; Z. Meir, 'If there isn't any money, let them give us land', *Ha'aretz*, 16 November 2003; M. Basok, 'The Defence Ministry will evacuate army bases in Rishon Letziyon and in the Sharon region', *Ha'aretz*, 6 February 2004.

Defending Territorial Sovereignty Through Civilian Settlement: The Case of Israel's Population Dispersal Policy

MATT EVANS

Israel's population dispersal policy is one of the longest ongoing attempts to defend territorial sovereignty by directing population settlement to areas of strategic national importance. Although civilian population settlements have been used in many places throughout the world in order to maintain control of strategic regions, the case of Israel's population dispersal policy is unique in its longevity and durability, and is also unprecedented among modern democratic countries.

During the course of the country's existence the objectives and methods of implementation for this policy have varied with socio-economic, demographic and political changes. Yet population dispersal policy has become so far-reaching in Israeli governance that it has been characterized by Shachar and others as a planning doctrine.[1]

Such doctrines are tantamount to paradigms and provide heuristic constructs that are used to organize a variety of different policies.[2] Hence, population dispersal policy represents a strategic framework that comprises and coordinates a number of different policies and has affected the movement of large numbers of people and resources.

This article will review the development of population dispersal policy over the course of the country's history. It will also examine the policy's strategic importance in defending Israel's border regions and its impact on the country's civilian population. As will be shown, this policy has proven very versatile, remaining relevant despite major geo-political and socio-economic changes that have occurred over the past six decades.

PRE-STATE CONDITIONS

Competition for land between Jews and Arabs began long before the founding of the state. Jews, preparing for the ultimate founding of a Jewish state, spread agricultural settlements throughout British-controlled Palestine. Although most of the land purchased by Jews was far from the major Arab concentrations, frequent clashes did arise, leading to hundreds of deaths. During the approximately 70 years prior to the establishment of the state, Jews settling in Palestine tried to establish as many agricultural settlements as possible. The establishment of agricultural settlements served several purposes. First, it was in line with Zionist ideology, which promoted getting Jews out of cities and onto the land. Working the soil, instead of the urban professions which the Jews had traditionally occupied, was meant to rebuild the Jewish people on both an individual and a national level.[3]

Second, there were strategic defence objectives. The Jews were in competition with the Arabs for control of the area, with each pursuing nationalist interests in the struggle for control of the land. Establishing settlements provided a way of defending territorial claims. In fact, however, during the British mandatory era, up until the formation of the state, the Jewish population became highly concentrated along a narrow coastal strip, especially in Tel Aviv and Haifa, and within the city of Jerusalem. This concentration was due to British restrictions on Jewish settlement, the inability of agricultural settlements to provide economic opportunities on the scale found in large cities and tensions with Arabs living in the inland hill regions.

1948—THE WAR OF INDEPENDENCE

Following the armistice at the end of Israel's War of Independence, the new nation was beset by a number of pressing strategic problems.

Hostile Neighbouring Countries

Following the United Nations brokered cease-fire none of the four neighbouring countries was willing to recognize Israel or sign a peace treaty. Subsequently, these countries enabled terrorist groups to use their territory to launch strikes against Israeli towns and villages.

Narrow Borders

The centre of the country was defined by a narrow coastal strip. The distance between the West Bank territory held by Jordan and the Mediterranean Sea was only about 15 kilometres (approximately 10 miles) wide at its narrowest point. In the south of the country, the distance between the Egyptian-controlled Gaza Strip and Jordan's West Bank was less than 40 kilometres. In the far north, in the Galilee panhandle, the fertile Hulda valley was sandwiched between Lebanon and Syria in a five-kilometre-wide basin. Finally, Israel's only outlet to the Red Sea was an unpopulated ten-kilometre shoreline between Jordan and Egypt's Sinai desert.

The Arab Majority in Peripheral Regions

Another major strategic problem for the new state was the fact that northern Galilee and the southern Negev, which together comprised approximately 80 percent of the country's land, both had an overwhelming Arab majority. Most of this Arab population had sided with the neighbouring countries in the War of Independence and many had actively fought against Israel. Although they were recognized as citizens most of them were perceived to be hostile to the state's security interests. In the north, Arabs accounted for 63 percent of the population. In the Beer Sheva sub-district in the south, which comprises about 60 percent of the nation's land, more than 91 percent of the population were Bedouin Arabs[4] (see Table 1).

A Jewish Population Densely Situated in a Small Area

An additional defence liability for the new state was the fact that 80 percent of the Jewish population was concentrated along the coastal strip between Tel Aviv and Haifa. This region constituted only 10 percent of the country's land. Also, it was the narrowest part of the country and closest to the Jordanian front lines in the West Bank.

In addition to the challenge posed by defence needs, Israel had to manage a host of other problems during its first years. Foremost among these were settling a large influx of immigrants, creating a proper infrastructure and stimulating economic development.

Immigrant Settlement

Between 1948 and 1951 Israel's population doubled. This was primarily due to the influx of impoverished Jewish refugees from Europe and the Arab world. Although the number of immigrants subsequently decreased, significant immigration continued until the mid-1960s.[5] During the first few years after the state's establishment tens of thousands of immigrants were housed in abandoned Arab towns and former British Army bases in the centre of the country, thus adding to the over-concentration in the central region.[6]

Infrastructure Creation

Since the vast majority of the immigrants were destitute refugees, it was left to the government to house them. At first this was done in a crisis atmosphere, wherever housing could be found or easily created. However, once the number of immigrants started to decline and the security situation eased, the government began to create housing and infrastructure according to national needs.

Economic Development

The concentration of the country's population in the centre of the country created an imbalance in the economy. The vast majority of industry and

TABLE 1
ISRAEL'S POPULATION—1948

	Area (sq. km) *	% of State's Land	Jews	%	Arabs	%	Total	% of Population	% Jewish
Jerusalem District	627	2.9	84,200	12.0	2,900	1.9	87,100	10.2	96.7
Northern District	4,501	20.9	53,400	7.6	90,600	58.1	144,000	16.8	37.1
Haifa District	854	4.0	147,700	21.1	27,400	17.6	175,100	20.5	84.4
Central District	1,242	5.8	106,200	15.2	16,100	10.3	122,300	14.3	86.8
Tel Aviv District	170	0.8	302,100	43.2	3,600	2.3	305,700	35.7	98.8
Southern District	14,107	65.6	6,000	0.9	15,400	9.9	21,400	2.5	28.0
Ashqelon Sub-District	1,272	5.9	4,800	0.7	2,400	1.5	7,200	0.8	66.7
Beer Sheva Sub-District	12,835	59.7	1,200	0.2	13,000	8.3	14,200	1.7	8.5
Total	21,501	100.0	699,600	100.0	156,000	100.0	855,600	100.0	81.8

* Includes the Golan Heights in the north and East Jerusalem, which were annexed after the 1967 war.

Source: Central Bureau of Statistics, (1985-2001) Statistical Abstract, Government Press, Jerusalem.

commerce was located in the two port cities of Tel Aviv and Haifa. The concentration of employment there reinforced the tendency of the population to cluster in these areas.[7]

PLANNING TO MEET DEFENCE AND CIVIL NEEDS

After the formation of the state, government decision-makers decided that one of the first issues that had to be addressed was the country's highly polarized settlement pattern. Approximately three-quarters of the Jewish population lived in the three large cities (Tel Aviv, Haifa and Jerusalem), and while there were many small rural villages, there existed very few mid-sized towns in the country.[8]

In 1949 Prime Minister Ben-Gurion presented the Defence Service Law to the Knesset. This had several civilian components, including absorbing immigrants and population dispersal throughout the country, important strategic goals intended to address demographic liabilities in key areas and in hostile border regions.[9]

One of the main elements of this doctrine was populating frontier communities along the state's borders. Part of the implementation of this policy was a mix of military training along with Zionist agricultural ethics in the new settlements that were established.[10]

During the War of Independence a committee had been established to determine the location of new agricultural settlements. The committee comprised representatives from the army, the Jewish National Fund (JNF), the Jewish Agency, the Ministry of Agriculture, and the Histadrut. In order to coordinate efforts in this area the army established a Settlement Branch which would focus on planning and implementation of settlement development. Establishment of settlements was carried out by the army's Engineering Corps and the Planning Department of the Jewish Agency. The military was also involved in settling soldiers in these areas to further protect border areas.[11]

Toward the end of the War of Independence there were approximately 100,000 soldiers who were to be gradually demobilized. In order to utilize this reserve to bolster peripheral settlements the Culture and Welfare Department of the IDF established a unit called the 'Department for the Soldier's Future'. The main objectives of this unit were to direct soldiers to settlement areas according to national priorities and to provide agricultural and vocational training before their discharge.[12]

The operations of this unit were in accord with the Defence Service Law, which designated agricultural/pioneering training as a part of basic military training for new recruits. One of the stated aims of this training was to shore up frontier settlements for the good of state security.[13] Between 1948 and 1949, 39 agricultural settlements were established by Palmach soldiers. In 1952 demobilized soldiers founded another 14 agricultural settlements.[14]

The direction of demobilized soldiers to frontier agricultural settlements was in keeping with the traditional Zionist principles of Israel's political leaders, of settling Jews in rural areas rather than cities. During this period the government was also forced to provide for hundreds of thousands of immigrants pouring into the country. Despite the Zionist agricultural ideal, it soon became clear that they could not all be placed in small rural settlements. Government planners soon proposed a new strategy for large-scale settlement.

They began working on policy solutions for the various problems facing Jewish settlement before the state's founding. According to one of the state's senior planners at that time, Eliezer Brutzkus, a group of planners and architects had been active as early as 1938, creating plans for changing the country's regional development patterns.[15] The type of large-scale planning proposed by this group represented a break with existing patterns and sought to create new types of settlements.

Planners recommended dividing the country into 24 regional units. Each unit was planned according to a regional hierarchy concept, with the population divided between agricultural villages, small towns and regional centres, in an area of between 300 and 500 square kilometres.[16] Eventually, many of the regional units were combined and their number reduced to 14. When a new administrative division of the country into six districts took place, in 1953,[17] these regional units were incorporated according to planners' classifications and were designated sub-districts.[18]

Government planners sought to develop a hierarchy of settlements, with small and medium-sized towns designed to serve peripheral agricultural settlements. Towns were to provide a local or regional market for agricultural produce; non-agricultural jobs (in case of a crisis in the agricultural sector); jobs for rural youth who did not want to work in agriculture; and a way of distributing regional services, including health and education.[19]

The population dispersal plans promoted by the newly formed Planning Department were not unanimously accepted. Some private architects urged that development should be concentrated in a chain of cities along the coast for reasons of economy and efficiency.

In 1949 Prime Minister Ben-Gurion appointed the Hofein Committee to examine the settlement issue.[20] The decentralist view of government planners who promoted the creation of dozens of new towns throughout the country was compared with an alternative approach for the establishment of a relatively small number of large cities along the coast. The latter strategy would have provided for strong transportation and economic development. However, the approach promoted by government planners received the backing of the army, a powerful force in policy-making, which opposed increasing coastal density for defence reasons.

The committee ultimately decided to support the population dispersal policy promoted by planners and the army.[21]

IMPLEMENTING THE DISPERSAL POLICY

The implementation of population dispersal policy was based on four main elements:

1. The establishment of new towns on the periphery.
2. Construction of housing and infrastructure in designated areas.
3. Spurring the development of industry on the periphery.
4. Settlement of immigrants according to national priorities.

NEW TOWNS

The establishment of development towns was one of the keys to population dispersal during the 1950s and 1960s. The towns were located, established and built according to the designs of government planners. The plans developed during this period designated regional hierarchical patterns of cities, towns and rural settlements.[22]

Establishment of the towns was facilitated by the fact that following the War of Independence approximately 90 percent of the country's land was under state ownership. Most of the land had been inherited from the British Mandate, was abandoned Arab property, land that was previously unclaimed (especially in the southern desert) or land under the ownership of organizations associated with the pre-state Yishuv (such as the Jewish National Fund).[23] Hence, an abundance of land was available for establishing new towns in accord with national strategic objectives.

Security priorities played an important role in choosing the location for many of the new towns. One noteworthy case is Kiryat Gat in the Lachish region, between Tel Aviv and Beer Sheva. The Lachish region connects the coastal plain to the Negev, and maintaining control of this territory was strategically vital in order to separate Egyptian-held Gaza from Jordan's West Bank.[24] Kiryat Gat developed as an industrial base and regional centre for the surrounding agricultural settlements.

Development towns helped populate and stabilize remote rural areas and served as manpower reserves for agriculture and industry.[25] Of the 29 development towns[26] established during the 1950s and 1960s, all but five were in the periphery, with 11 in the north and 13 in the south. The towns grew rapidly, and by the mid-1960s more than 300,000 people lived in development towns, representing approximately 50 percent of the north's Jewish population and 80 percent of the south's.[27] Establishment of these towns was key to the successful implementation of dispersal policy.

HOUSING AND INFRASTRUCTURE

Creating and populating the new towns in remote peripheral areas required massive government investment in housing and infrastructure. According to Lichfield, the government's housing investments in development towns were 'the biggest contribution to dispersal'.[28]

During the decade from 1958 to 1967, government-sponsored housing accounted for approximately 55 percent of total housing starts.[29] Of the publicly built housing units during this period, a combined 40 percent were built in Israel's northern and southern districts, despite the fact that only about 17 percent of the Jewish population lived in those two peripheral districts. Meanwhile, the Tel Aviv district, with more than 35 percent of the population, was the recipient of approximately 20 percent of government-sponsored housing.[30]

Government initiative was vital due to a lack of interest by the private sector. Incentives and loans provided by the government proved effective, as the private sector increased its share of construction from less than one percent in the two peripheral districts to more than 18 percent by 1967.[31]

DEVELOPING EMPLOYMENT ON THE PERIPHERY

In order to stimulate economic development in peripheral areas, to support population dispersal policy, the government adopted the Capital Investment Encouragement Law in 1950. One of the stated principles of the law was, 'Planned dispersal of the population across the nation's territory'.[32] The inter-ministerial committee to determine which areas should be given preference as development areas naturally included a representative of the Defence Ministry.[33]

Although there were a few cases of direct government investment in industry in peripheral areas, such as in the case of the establishment of heavy mining in the south, the main goal of this policy was to induce private investors to establish industries in new towns.[34] The main incentives used to lure industrial development to areas that had no economic advantages at all were generous land allocations, income tax reductions and government loans at very favourable rates. In the areas of highest priorities, such as the Negev and Galilee, the government took care of 70 percent of development costs.[35]

In establishing new towns there were sometimes periods of several years between the town's establishment and the development of industry there. These gaps were often partially filled by temporary employment created by the government, the Jewish Agency or the JNF, such as development and construction work, forestation and seasonal agricultural labour.[36]

The government's incentives had the desired effect, and by 1965 industrial construction in the south and north combined reached more than 50 percent of the nation-wide total.[37] Growth in new towns on the periphery continued and by the early 1970s unemployment had virtually disappeared in development towns, and in some areas there was even a manpower shortage.[38]

IMMIGRANT SETTLEMENT

From 1948 to 1967 more than 1.2 million immigrants entered the country comprising close to half the population. Government decision-makers saw this influx as an important resource to be used to achieve national objectives, foremost among them population dispersal.[39] Consequently, immigrant settlement was geared toward populating development towns and rural settlements on the periphery. To this end, government direction of immigrants to these areas was an integral part of national plans for population dispersal.[40]

The government sometimes used heavy-handed methods to bring immigrants, who like the rest of the population preferred the centre of the country, to settlement areas on the periphery. Immigrants who refused to move to the designated areas faced the possible loss of housing and employment benefits. With few options and resources the immigrants usually complied.[41]

The use of immigrants for national objectives was clear in the settlement patterns that emerged. By 1960, while close to 70 percent of Israel's Jewish population lived in the major cities, only 38.9 percent of immigrants were found there. Conversely, 40 percent of immigrants were settled in rural towns (usually development towns), four times the rate of veteran citizens. In agricultural settlements, too, immigrants were found at about twice the national rate.[42]

1967—THE SIX DAY WAR

By the mid-1960s Israel's population dispersal policy had made significant progress toward achieving the strategic objectives of increasing the population on the periphery. In the 20 years since the state's establishment the population of the two peripheral districts had grown from 8.5 to 21.2 percent of the Jewish population. The change was especially dramatic in the south of the country, where the population increased from 0.9 percent of the Jewish population in 1948 to 11.2 percent in 1967. In addition, the goal of having a Jewish majority in northern and southern districts in order to prevent territorial claims by Arabs in those areas who might want a confederation with neighbouring states was also realized. By 1967 Jews were a majority in peripheral districts, comprising 56 percent of the northern district's population and 91 percent of the south (see Table 2).

However, during the next two decades several circumstances altered the strategic importance of population dispersal policy and the impetus to implement it. Israel's victory in the 1967 Six Day War meant that the territory under the state's control expanded greatly. As a result, national security

TABLE 2
ISRAEL'S POPULATION—1967

	Area (sq. km)	% of State's Land	Jews	%	Arabs	%	Total	% of Population	% Jewish
Jerusalem District	627	2.9	225,700	9.5	70,700	18.1	296,400	10.7	76.1
Northern District	4,501	20.9	238,600	10.0	186,700	47.8	425,300	15.3	56.1
Haifa District	854	4.0	378,200	15.9	64,300	16.5	442,500	16.0	85.5
Central District	1,242	5.8	459,500	19.3	35,900	9.2	495,400	17.9	92.8
Tel Aviv District	170	0.8	814,000	34.2	7,600	1.9	821,600	29.6	99.1
Southern District	14,107	65.6	267,600	11.2	25,100	6.4	292,700	10.6	91.4
Ashqelon Sub-District	1,272	5.9	127,800	5.4	400	0.1	128,200	4.6	99.7
Beer Sheva Sub-District	12,835	59.7	139,800	5.9	24,700	6.3	164,500	5.9	85.0
Total	21,501	100.0	2,383,600	100.0	390,300	100.0	2,773,900	100.0	85.9

Source: Central Bureau of Statistics (1985–2001) Statistical Abstract, Government Press, Jerusalem.

concerns changed. The southern and central parts of the country were no longer in danger of attack from the West Bank, Gaza and Sinai. Similarly, the danger that Arabs living in the Galilee might try to forge an alliance with Jordanian forces in the West Bank no longer existed. Thus, Jewish settlement in the north and south became less crucial to the state's security.

Following the victory in the Six Day War, the territory under the state's control increased three-fold. Holding this territory required a great deal of military and civilian resources. In addition, the establishment of new settlements in the Golan Heights, the West Bank, Gaza and Sinai in the early 1970s also required funding. Consequently, budgeting priorities for other policies, including population dispersal, had to change.

Another factor affecting the implementation of this policy was a reduction in the number of immigrants. In the mid-1960s the number of immigrants to Israel dropped sharply. From a high of 240,000 in 1949, the number of immigrants fell to a mere 14,000 in 1967.[43] This diminished the state's ability to implement dispersal policy, since the main source of population of peripheral development towns was new immigrants. Although the number of immigrants increased briefly for a few years during the early 1970s, immigration remained low and dropped below 10,000 per year for the only time in the country's history in the mid-1980s.[44]

Several geo-political events during this period impacted on Israel's defence stance, and with it the priority given to population dispersal policy. Following the 1967 war, the Palestinian guerrilla groups which had operated against Israel from the West Bank were forced to relocate east of the Jordan River in Jordan. The Palestinian forces soon came to threaten the Jordanian monarchy and after an extended military conflict the Palestinian Liberation Organization (PLO) was driven from Jordan in 1971. This further secured Israel's eastern border.

In 1978, Israel relinquished the Sinai peninsula in a peace treaty with Egypt. Under the terms of this treaty Egyptian troops were to be kept out of the Sinai and far from Israel's southern border. To the north, the PLO had regrouped in Lebanon and frequently launched attacks against Israel from the territory it controlled. The expulsion of the PLO to Tunis in 1982 during Israel's Lebanon war removed the last strategic threat from Israel's borders.[45]

During this period a lack of immigration and investment stunted growth in the peripheral areas. By 1988 high Arab birth-rates and Jewish migration had once again led to a Jewish minority in the northern district. In the south the Jewish share of the population had fallen below 90 percent, and in the Beer-Sheva sub-district (which comprises 60 percent of the state's land) it had dropped below 80 percent (see Table 3).

TABLE 3
ISRAEL'S POPULATION—1988

	Area (sq. km)	% of State's Land	Jews	%	Arabs	%	Total	% of Population	% Jewish
Jerusalem District	627	2.9	399,900	10.9	144,300	17.6	544,200	12.2	73.5
Northern District	4,501	20.9	360,000	9.8	386,500	47.3	746,500	16.7	48.2
Haifa District	854	4.0	476,100	13.0	128,900	15.8	605,000	13.5	78.7
Central District	1,242	5.8	870,700	23.8	78,700	9.6	949,400	21.2	91.7
Tel Aviv District	170	0.8	1,018,800	27.8	13,400	1.6	1,032,200	23.1	98.7
Southern District	14,107	65.6	467,200	12.8	65,800	8.0	533,000	11.9	87.7
Ashqelon Sub-District	1,272	5.9	219,600	6.0	1,600	0.2	221,200	4.9	99.3
Beer Sheva Sub-District	12,835	59.7	247,600	6.8	64,200	7.9	311,800	7.0	79.4
Territories	–	–	66,300	1.8	200	0.0	66,500	1.5	99.7
Total	21,501	100.0	3,659,000	100.0	817,800	100.0	4,476,800	100.0	81.7

Source: Central Bureau of Statistics (1985–2001) Statistical Abstract, Government Press, Jerusalem.

1990s—THE OSLO PEACE PROCESS

In the late 1980s and early 1990s several major events occurred to affect the strategic importance of Israel's borders and peripheral areas. In late 1987 the first Intifada started and led to continued rioting and attacks on Israelis in the West Bank and Gaza strip over a five-year period. The Intifada drew fresh attention to the Palestinian issue and was one of the main factors leading to the Oslo treaty in 1993. Subsequently, Israel signed a peace treaty with Jordan in 1994. The reduced threat to Israel's borders and hopes for a permanent peace with the Palestinians led some analysts to discuss a new defence paradigm which emphasized the threat of missiles and non-conventional weapons from countries located farther away rather than from Israel's neighbours.[46] Consequently, many policymakers began to reassess the importance of building settlements in the periphery to protect the country's borders.[47]

While defence objectives were still a factor in dispersal policy in the 1990s, the real impetus for continued implementation of this policy came from environmental and other considerations. Planners and environmentalists drew the attention of policymakers and the public to the fact that Israel had become one of the most densely populated countries in the world and that unchecked development in the centre of the country threatened land reserves.[48]

During this period an important event occurred to revive population dispersal policy. In 1989 the Cold War ended and a flood of immigrants poured into the country. In 1990 approximately 200,000 immigrants came to Israel. The following year another 176,000 entered the country. This was the highest two-year total since 1949–1950 and it increased Israel's population by 10 percent.[49] The sudden demographic shift required the Israeli government to become involved in developing housing, as the private sector was unable to make the adjustment and unwilling to gamble that the supply of immigrants would continue.[50]

The influx of immigrants revived dispersal policy and the hopes of populating peripheral areas with Jews. During the initial two-year period in which close to 400,000 immigrants arrived, the number of housing units initiated by the Ministry of Housing grew by approximately 2,000 percent, from an annual average of 3,000 units in 1989 to a total of 120,000 units in this two-year period.[51] In addition, the number of housing units planned by the Ministry of Housing increased from 50,000 to 450,000.[52] A very large percentage of these units were in the periphery due to both population dispersal goals, and the fact that these were the only areas that had enough available land to build on the scale needed to house immigrants.[53]

The flow of immigrants continued and during the decade between 1990 and 2000 approximately one million arrived in Israel.[54] The settlement of immigrants during the 1990s was different than during previous periods in the state's history. Social and political changes did not allow for the direct transfer of immigrants to development towns, as had been done in the 1950s.⁵⁵ Instead, attempts were made to lure immigrants to peripheral areas using financial incentives. The new immigrants of the 1990s, like the bulk of Israeli citizens, preferred the economic and cultural advantages of the centre of the country. Yet the government's massive building in the periphery did have the desired effect. More than 35 percent of new immigrants in the 1990s settled in the periphery, approximately 50 percent higher than the share of Israel's total Jewish population.⁵⁶ The added population spurred growth and development in many development towns and this has continued even after the number of immigrants declined.

In addition to building in the periphery, several new towns were built along the areas that border the West Bank. These towns were supported by both the Likud and Labour governments during the early 1990s. The towns, such as Modiin, Shoham, Katzir, Harish and the expansion of Rosh HaAin, had strategic value in preserving Israeli sovereignty in important border areas.⁵⁷

2000—THE SECOND INTIFADA

Prospects for a peaceful settlement with the Palestinians were dimmed with the outbreak of the second Intifada in September 2000. More than four years of violence left the majority of Israelis with the impression that it would be quite some time before the country's borders were quiet and peaceful. Although Palestinian bomb attacks have often targeted Israel's main cities, areas bordering the West Bank have come under frequent attack by snipers and infiltrators, while areas bordering the Gaza Strip have suffered from rocket and mortar fire.

Not only have defence priorities refocused on dangers from the Palestinians during this period, but the concern of alliances between Palestinians and Israeli Arabs were revived. A week after the start of the Intifada, in October 2000, rioting broke out in Israeli Arab villages. Rioters waved Palestinian flags and mimicked the tactics of masked Palestinian rock throwers.

This event, however, was the culmination of Israeli Arabs developing closer ties with the Palestinians over the course of the decade since the start of the Oslo process.⁵⁸ During this period many started referring to themselves as Palestinians with Israeli citizenship rather than Israeli Arabs. Israeli Arab politicians during the 1990s also began to support openly the Palestinian conflict with Israel.⁵⁹ Following the start of the latest Intifada there were numerous incidents of Israeli Arab involvement in Palestinian terror attacks.⁶⁰

The closeness between Palestinians and Israeli Arabs was not only political. A few villages on either side of the 1948 'Green Line' had physically grown together to form a single municipal entity. The most apparent case is Baka-al-Garbia (Israeli) and Baka-al-Sharkia (Palestinian) which have been linked to form a contiguous settlement.[61] In addition to the security risk, this phenomenon also presents a territorial liability.

In the south of the country there has been increasing attention given to the demographic problems presented by the Bedouin. While less boisterous than the Arabs in the north, here too the Bedouin rioted and waved Palestinian flags in October 2000. The Bedouin present additional sovereignty problems to the state. First they have among the highest natural growth rates in the world, approximately three times that of the Jewish population.[62] Second, approximately 50,000 Bedouin live in scattered settlements across the Negev, defying the government's attempts to settle them in towns.[63] In many cases the illegal settlements are on government land. The struggle for control of land on the periphery has intensified in recent years and one government minister referred to the massive illegal building by Israeli Arabs as a 'construction Jihad'.[64]

All these issues began to receive more attention following the outbreak of the Intifada in 2000. While avoiding direct mention of the security threat posed by Arab citizens, Israeli leaders have taken a number of measures in dealing with perceived threats by Israel's Arab population. For instance, in August 2003 a law was passed barring Palestinians from attaining Israeli citizenship by marrying Israelis. Although the stated rationale was to prevent terrorists from entering the country, it was clear that one of the main motives was to limit the growth of the Arab population within Israel.[65] In addition, the number of illegal Bedouin homes outside legal settlements that have been demolished has increased significantly since 2003.[66]

In dealing with this security issue the Israeli government has once again turned to population dispersal policy. The massive immigration of the previous decade had ended by this time. Although the inflow of immigrants from the former Soviet Union had helped infuse new life into many towns on the periphery, there was little demographic change in the composition of peripheral districts. High Arab birth rates nullified any potential changes from the immigration of the 1990s. By the year 2000 Jews still only comprised 49 percent of the population of the north. In the Beer Sheva sub-district in the south, the proportion of Jews actually decreased, to 76.7 percent, despite the settlement of tens of thousands of new immigrants (see Table 4).

With no new supply of immigrants to settle in the periphery the government has had to attract Jews to these areas through incentives and the creation of more affluent, smaller suburban-type communities. In 2002 the government approved more than a dozen new towns to be established in the north and south of the country.[67] The aim of these communities is to increase the share of the Jewish population in these areas and to prevent Arab settlement on open land. In addition, the government continues to provide financial incentives to encourage people to move from the centre of the country to the periphery. In August 2003 the government decided

TABLE 4
ISRAEL'S POPULATION—2000

	Area (sq. km)	% of State's Land	Jews	%	Arabs	%	Total	% of Population	% Jewish
Jerusalem District	627	2.9	542,303	10.5	215,975	18.2	758,278	11.9	71.5
Northern District	4,501	20.9	530,940	10.2	552,355	46.5	1,083,295	17.0	49.0
Haifa District	854	4.0	643,241	12.4	175,261	14.7	818,502	12.9	78.6
Central District	1,242	5.8	1,342,670	25.9	115,042	9.7	1,457,712	22.9	92.1
Tel Aviv District	170	0.8	1,139,474	22.0	14,297	1.2	1,153,771	18.1	98.8
Southern District	14,107	65.6	783,775	15.1	115,618	9.7	899,393	14.1	87.1
Ashqelon Sub-District	1,272	5.9	405,325	7.8	733	0.1	406,058	6.4	99.8
Beer Sheva Sub-District	12,835	59.7	378,450	7.3	114,885	9.7	493,335	7.7	76.7
Territories	–	–	198,212	3.8	103	0.0	198,315	3.1	99.9
Total	21,501	100.0	5,180,615	100	1,188,651	100	6,369,266	100	81.3

Source: Central Bureau of Statistics, (1985-2001) Statistical Abstract, Government Press, Jerusalem.

to offer special grants to people choosing to buy homes in border regions and development areas. Similarly, the government continues to try to offset the private sector's preference for the Tel Aviv area by investing in infrastructure on the periphery.[68]

CONCLUSION

Thus, Israel's policy of population dispersal continues to be an integral part of the government's strategic effort to bolster the population of border areas and peripheral regions and secure territorial sovereignty against a perceived threat of an alliance between Israeli Arabs and Palestinians. The tactics employed in implementing this policy have varied over the state's existence in accordance with socio-economic and political changes, as well as fluctuations in the number of immigrants arriving in the country. Yet, the policy of encouraging civilian settlements in peripheral regions in order to protect territorial sovereignty continues to serve Israel's defence interests while affecting Israel's demography, economy and environment.

NOTES

1. A. Shachar, 'Reshaping the Map of Israel: A New National Planning Doctrine', *Annals of the American Academy of Political Science*, Vol. 555 (1998), pp. 209–218. Also, G. Golan, 'Physical National Planning in Israel: The Evolution of a Planning Doctrine', PhD dissertation, Jerusalem, 1998.
2. Andreas Faludi, 'Patterns of Doctrinal Development', *Journal of Planning Education and Research*, Vol. 18 (1999), pp. 333–344.
3. A. Shachar, 'Israel's Development Towns', *Journal of the American Institute of Planners*, Vol. 37, No. 6 (November 1971), pp. 362–372.
4. The division of districts and sub-districts was not created until several years later.
5. See Central Bureau of Statistics, *Statistical Abstract*, Jerusalem, 1950–2003.
6. E. Brutzkus, *Physical Planning in Israel*, Jerusalem, 1964.
7. Ibid.
8. N. Lichfield, *Israel's New Towns: A Development Strategy*, Tel Aviv, 1971.
9. Moshe Lissak, 'The Civilian Components of Israel's Security Doctrine: The Evolution of Civil–Military Relations in the First Decade', in S. Troen and N. Lucas (eds.), *Israel the First Decade of Independence*, Albany, 1995, p. 580.
10. Ze'ev Drori, 'Utopia in Uniform', in Troen and Lucas (eds.), *Israel the First Decade of Independence*, p. 595.
11. Ibid., p. 604.
12. Ibid., p. 605.
13. Ibid., p. 606.
14. Ibid. p. 606.
15. Brutzkus, *Physical Planning in Israel*, p. 17.
16. S. Reichman and M. Yehudai, *A Survey of Innovative Planning 1948–1965*, Jerusalem, 1984, p. 48.
17. The six districts defined by planners in 1953 are still the main administrative divisions used by government ministries today.
18. Brutzkus, *Physical Planning in Israel*, p. 19.
19. Reichman and Yehudai, *A Survey of Innovative Planning 1948–1965*, p. 47.
20. Ibid., p. 52.
21. Ibid., p. 54.

22. Brutzkus, *Physical Planning in Israel*, p. 22.
23. Ruth Kark, 'Planning, Housing and Land Policy 1948–1952', in Troen and Lucas (eds.), *Israel the First Decade of Independence*, p. 478.
24. R. Feasey, *Israel: Planning and Immigration in Relation to Spatial Development*, University of Durham, Durham, England, 1976, p. 47.
25. E. Brutzkus, *Regional Policy in Israel*, Jerusalem, 1970, p. 41.
26. Various researchers have compiled different lists of development towns. The ones referred to here are comparable to those used by Ruth Zilverberg, *Population Dispersal in Israel 1948–1972*, Jerusalem, 1973, and do not include some towns in the centre that have appeared elsewhere, such as Lod or Ramle.
27. Central Bureau of Statistics, *Statistical Abstract*, Jerusalem, 1969.
28. Lichfield, *Israel's New Towns: A Development Strategy*, p. 312.
29. Housing starts were not recorded by district until 1958.
30. Central Bureau of Statistics, *Statistical Abstract*, Jerusalem, 1959–1968.
31. Ibid.
32. Zilverberg, *Population Dispersal in Israel 1948–1972*, p. 34.
33. Development Areas (1954) Inter-ministerial committee's proposal on development areas, 26 December 1955, Israel State Archives, File G 5513.
34. Brutzkus, *Physical Planning in Israel*, p. 33.
35. Ibid., p. 34.
36. Ibid., p. 22.
37. Central Bureau of Statistics, *Statistical Abstract*, 1966.
38. Borukhov and Werczberger, *Factors Affecting the Development of New Towns in Israel*, Tel Aviv, 1980, p. 10.
39. Brutzkus, *Physical Planning in Israel*.
40. A. Sharon, *Physical Planning in Israel*, Tel Aviv, 1952.
41. R. Dower and A. Stungo, *Regional Planning and Housing in Israel*, London, 1964, p. 26.
42. Central Bureau of Statistics, *Statistical Abstract*, 2001.
43. Central Bureau of Statistics, *Statistical Abstract*, 2003.
44. Ibid.
45. Although Israel remained in a state of war with Syria, that border was kept quiet and hence did not present an immediate threat.
46. U. Bar-Joseph, 'Towards a Paradigm Shift in Israel's National Security Conception', *Israel Affairs*, Vol. 6 (2000), pp. 99–114.
47. Shachar, *American Academy of Political Science*.
48. A. Mazor, 'Land Reserves in Spatial Planning', in *Israel 2020—Master Plan for Israel in the 21st Century*, Stage A Report, Volume B, Haifa, 1993.
49. Central Bureau of Statistics, *Statistical Abstract*, 2003.
50. S. Eldor and M. Evans, 'Housing Policies for Immigrant Absorption', in Y. Golani, S. Eldor and M. Garon (eds.), *Planning and Housing in Israel in the Wake of Rapid Changes*, Tel Aviv, 1992, p. 150.
51. Eldor and Evans, 'Housing Policies for Immigrant Absorption', p. 149.
52. Ibid., p. 151.
53. R. Lerman and E. Lerman, 'A Comprehensive National Outline Plan for Construction Development and Absorption of Immigrants - N.O.S. #31', in Golani *et al.* (eds.), *Planning and Housing in Israel in the Wake of Rapid Changes*, pp. 29–48.
54. Central Bureau of Statistics, *Statistical Abstract*, 2003.
55. M. Evans, 'Social Change and Policy Implementation: Population Dispersal in Israel', *Israel Studies Forum*, Vol. 18, No. 1 (2003), pp. 83–106.
56. Central Bureau of Statistics, *Statistical Abstract*, 2001.
57. N. Dunsky and Y. Golani. '"The Stars Plan"—"The Hills Axis"', in Golani *et al.* (eds.), *Planning and Housing in Israel in the Wake of Rapid Changes*, pp. 19–28.
58. E. Rekhess, 'The Arabs of Israel After Oslo: Localization of the National Struggle', *Israel Studies*, Vol. 7, No. 3 (2002), pp. 1–44.
59. N. Gilbert, 'MKs to Fight Arab Lists' Registration', *Jerusalem Post*, 12 November 2002. Also D. Izenberg, 'High Court overturns CEC disqualifications of Tibi, Bishara', *Jerusalem Post*, 10 January 2003.

60. M. Gutman, 'Terror and Israeli Arabs', *Jerusalem Post*, 30 July 2003. Also D. Rudge, 'Hizbullah, Hamas recruiting Israeli Arabs', Jerusalem Post, 26 June 2001.
61. These two villages have been separated once again by the security fence, built to reduce terrorist infiltrations.
62. Central Bureau of Statistics, 2003.
63. J. Ben-David, 'The Land Conflict between Negev Bedouin and the State-Historical, Legal and Topical Aspects', *Karka*, Vol. 40 (1985), pp. 220–246. Also S. Krakover, 'Demographic Assessment of the Negev Bedouin Settlement Program and its Linkage to the Land Dispute Issue', *Studies in the Geography of Israel*, Vol. 16 (2002), pp. 220–246.
64. Y. Ettinger, 'A war of bricks and mortar fire', *Ha'aretz*, 17 August 2003.
65. G. Alon, 'Law approved barring citizenship from Palestinians', *Ha'aretz*, 14 August 2003.
66. Ibid.
67. G. Hoffman, 'Government to build 16 new towns, rebuild Jerusalem's Hurva Synagogue', *Jerusalem Post*, 22 July 2002.
68. M. Bassok and A. Georgi, 'Three rail projects on fast track', *Ha'aretz*, 13 August 2003.

INDEX

A Curtain of Sand (Allon) 170
"A Guy in the *Gahal*" 102
A Lovely War (Dahn Ben Amotz) 86
Abie Nathan's Peace Ship 157
Abrams v. United States (1919) 183
Adan, A. 104
Afghanistan 2002 war 143
Agranat Commission 1, 5, 85, 128
agricultural communities; security belt 53
al-Aqsa Intifada 7, 66, 70
aliya 98
aliya bet (clandestine immigration) 115
Allon Plan 205
Alon, Y. Foreign Minister 17, 87
Alterman, N. 99, 102
ambiguity and the media 176
America 183, *see also* United States
Amit, M. 18
anti-ballistic Patriot missiles 204
anti-hegemonic behaviour 76–8
anti-politics 26
Anti-Terrorism Act (Bill C-36) 187
anti-victim discourse 78
Arab birth-rate 224, 228
Arab infiltration into Israel 54
Arab and Jews competition for land 214
Arab population in the occupied territories 45
Arab-Israeli war 32
Arafat, Y. 8, 141
armed forces and conscription 123
armistice lines (1949) 43
Arms Control Steering Committee 4
army 1, 2, 3, 6, 10; an instrument of integration 109–16; distrust 5, *see also* Israel's Defence Forces; war
Ashkenazi, M. 89
Ashkenazim 17
Atomic Energy Authority 170

Atomic Energy Commission 173
Avidar, J. 57

Baghdad 141
Bar-Ilan University 84–5
Bar-Lev, H. Major General 33
Bar-On, M. 41
Barak, A.; Judge's ruling 180
Barak, E. 8–10, 137
Barlev, H. 18
Basic Law: The Army 1, 2, 3, 6, 10
Basic Law: The Government 2, 4
BBC 155
Bedouin 228
Beersheba 53
Begin, M. 22, 31, 87; Likud's leader 157
Ben-Eliezer, B. 17, 20, 25
Ben-Eliezer, U. 13
Ben-Gurion, D. 10, 32, 55, 99, 154
Ben-Meir, Y. 10
bereaved families; establishment's attitude 93
bereaved parents 76
bereavement 75; bastions of memory 93; blame and victimology 88–91; individualization of 85; nationalizing 78–80; as protest 84–5; public parameter 92; in service of politics 86–8; as "social fact" 76
Bible land 42
Biger, G. 200
biological bomb 177
Border Guard 55
Brawer, M. 200
British Mandate 169, 215
Brutzkus, E. 219
Burg, A. 25

cable television 157
Camp David Peace Accords 203
Camp David peace conference (1997) 88
Canada 183, 187
Capital Investment Encouraging Law 221
Carmel, M. 17
CBS News: Dan Rather 188; president Andrew Heyward 187
censorship policy 154, 172–3
central coastal plain 52
centre party Dash 22
CGS: guardian of democratic values 9; role of 6
Chandeli, Y.110
changes in media maps 132
Channel Ten 158
Channel Two 158
"chequebook journalism" 186
Chernobyl 168
civil society 136; empowerment of 201
civil supremacy; according to Ben-Gurion 11
civilian settlement 214–32
Clinton; President; "bridging plan" 8
Clinton Administration 176
Closed Space military-media relations 139
Cohen, A. 174–5
Cohen, S. 14
Cold War 226
competing land uses 197–213
congressional Symington Law 165
conscription 110, 123
control of information 152
Control Landscapes and Settlements 205
control of space 200–207
Council for Cable and Satellite TV 157
courted relations 126
coverage of military operations 194
Creveld, M. 44
cultural alienation 107–9

Dash; centre party 22
Dash (the Democratic Movement for Change) 157
Dayan, M. 17, 20, 31, 32, 84, 87, 176, 177
Deactivation Model 39, 120
decision-making; system of 44
defence and civil needs 218–20
Defence Scene as Hegemonic Site 92
Defence Service Law 218

"defence-related facilities" 208
defensive-security land uses in Israel 202
demilitarized zone 45
democratic peace 152
demographic change 49
Department for the Soldier's Future 218
detachment of *olim* from homeland 102
development towns 220
Diaspora Jewry 98
Dimona 165, 173, 178
direct elections 28
distrust; the army 5
divine judgment 78
Dor-On, A. 167

Eban, A. 34, 87
editor's committee 154, 169
education and instruction 103
Egypt 32, 166, 224
Egyptian army 39
Eilat 53
Eisenstadt, S 171
Eitam; National Religious Party 23
Eitan, R. 18, 19, 22
Elazar, D.; Army Chief of Staff 38, 166
Emergency (Defence) Regulations (1945) 154
emergency spaces 204
emotion, expression of 81–82
employment, developing 221
Eshkol, L. Prime Minister 31, 45
evacuation of Sinai Peninsular 203
Even-Zohar, I. 76
executive power; civil liberties 187
Exodus 108

Face to Face (Kovner) 107
Falah, G.; Palestinian geographer 205
Falklands War 140; press activity 185
fate; inevitability of 78
France 165
freedom of expression and national security 183–6
Freier, S. 173
Frontier Corps 54
frontier settlements 52; abandonment of 54–6
funerals, restrained 83

Gadera 52
Gadna 58
Gahal 17, 103–6, 104, 107

Galili, Y. head of Haganah National Command 108
Gamal Abd al Nasser 155
Gaza Strip 35, 42, 45, 135, 224, 227
General Odd Bull; chief UN observer 42
ghetto uprisings 108
goal setting 31–47
Golan Heights 177, 200
governance and communication 149–53
government as supreme commander 2
"Green Line" 227
Gulf of Aqaba 45
Gulf War (1990–1) 27, 120, 129, 206
Gur, M. 18

Hadari, Y. 90
Hadera 52
Hafez Al-Assad 137
Haganah 98, 102, 110; High Command 109
Haifa 24
Haim Hazaz's story 'The Sermon' 79
Hanna Senesh 108
Harkabi, Y; Professor 170
Harshav, B. (Hrushovski) 99
Hazan, Y. 40
He Walked in the Fields (Shamir) 107
Hebrew 58, 62
Hebrew language education 60
Hebrew newspapers 154
Hebron; pull out of PA territory 8
Hebron withdrawal plan 4
Hegemonic Bereavement Model 75
Hegemonic Bereavement model; key element 78
Helicopter Disaster 162
Herut party 22
Hillel, S. 83
History of the Haganah (Yehuda Slutzky) 107
Hofein Committee 219
Holmes, O. W. Justice 183–4
Holocaust 49, 80; bereavement 80; as personal catastrophe 108; survivors conscription 102; survivors in army 98–119
home front morale 124
housing and infrastructure 221
Hussein; King of Jordan 137

IBA's Plenum and Public Council 156
identification blame 77
ideological mentality 25
Israeli Defence Force (IDF) 2, 6, 48, 55, 100, 193; company framework 62; erosion of public image 14; infantry 61; operational capability of 64; role in reduction process 15; strength 56–60
immigrants: educational level of 50; population 50–1; settlement 222
In the Fields of the Philistines (Uri Avneri) 106
In the Negev Prairies (Mosenson) 107
indicators; social integration 113
infiltration; rise in 60
'Information Management in the Information Age' 190
information services 131
infrastructure in border areas 204
inter-party competitiveness 24
interocular auma test 77
Intifada: first (1987–1993) 69, 129, 226; second (2000) 141, 227–30
Iraqi missiles 206
Israel: democratic character 13; garrison state 13
Israel Broadcasting Authority (IBA) 156
Israel Educational Television Network 156
Israeli Arabs and Palestinians 230
Israeli bereavement 80
Israeli media dilemmas 191
Israeli National security 147–64
Israeli "Political Bereavement Model" 75–97
Israeli political system; militarization of 13–30
Israeli press 182–96
Israeli reserves 66–74
Israeli-Egyptian relations 32, 45
Israel's nuclear policy 165
Israel's population 217, 223, 225, 229
Israel's War of Independence 32
Ivri, D; Maj. General (Res) 4

Jaffee Centre of Strategic Studies 168
Jane's Intelligence Review 178
Jenin refugee camp 130
Jericho Missile 166
Jericho nuclear-capable missiles 177
Jerusalem 63; old city of 42
Jewish migration 224
Johnson, L. B. US President 34
Jordan 35

Jordan River 224
journalism 135

Kahalani, A. 19; founder The Third Way 22
Kalb, M. 182
Katzir, E. Professor 89, 177
kibbutz: Beit Hashita 83; Givat Hayim Ichud 82
kibbutzim 60, 82
Kimmerling, B. 14
King Hussein of Jordan 42, 137
Kiryab; military headquarters 203
Kiryah complex 210
Kiryat Gat 220
Kiryat Shaul cemetery 83, 86
Kissinger, H. 88
Knesset 17
Kol Yisrael (Voice of Israel) 155
Korean War 31

Lachish region 220
Lahat, S. 23
land, competition for 214
land uses, defensive 200–207
land zoning and planning mechanism 207–10
Latrun; battle of 113
Lebanon War (1982) 6, 67, 75, 91, 123, 128, 224
Leibowitz, Y. 171
Likud 23, 87
Lipkin-Shahak, A. 19
Lissak, M. 14

Madurat Shabbat (the *Saturday Edition*) 156
Margalit, D. 27
market or regulatory model 156–9
Mass Media Concentration 132
media: credibility in Israel 192–5; in democratic societies 188–9; and Military 120–46; the mixed model 158–62; and national security 182–96; restrictive policy towards 127; as a weapon 124
media changes: functional level 135–6; structural level 132–4
media disclosures 173–6
media maps; changes in 132
Meir, G. Prime Minister 21, 85, 92, 169, 174, 176

memorial books (Gvilei Esh) 86
methodology 76
militarization of Israeli political system 13–30
militarization of politics; index of 24
military; headquarters 203; power 48–65; resistance 48; public relations 124
military action; public support 123
military and media 120–46
military operations in Panama and Grenada 186
military-media: mutual interests 122–4; relations in Israel 127–32; relations in open space 141
military role expansion 15
Mitzna 23, 24
Mizra, K. 82
Mofaz, Lt. Gen. S. 3, 19, 20
Moledet 22
Mordechai, Y.; defence minister 4, 19, 20
Moscow 141
Mossad 169
multi-channel media environment 133

Nahal Soreq nuclear reactor 177
Narkis, U. Major General 38
nation-building 69
national crisis; press performance 189
National Identification among Mass Media 133
National Religious Party Eitam 23
national security 149
National Security Advisory Staff 2
National Security College 5
National Security Council 4, 6
National Unity Government 18
national-patriotic meaning 81
Nazareth metropolitan region 205
Negev 228
Netanyahu, B. Prime Minister 3–4, 19, 93
New Outlook (Shenker) 171
New Settlement; routine security measures 51
New Towns 220
news around the clock 134
Nir David; air base 43
Nixon, R. President 174
None Will Survive Us 167
normality; search for 69
nuclear ambiguity and the media 165–81

nuclear secrecy 166, 167–73; value of 179
Nuclear War and Nuclear Peace 170

Occupied Territories 129, 198
October War 81
olim 101
olim's past 112
Operation Defensive Shield 67, 130; (2003) 71
Operation Sabha 63
operational areas failure 60–3
Oriental countries; absorption 59
Oriental Jews 49
Oriental soldiers; operative capability 63
Osama bin Laden 187
Oslo; agreement 27; peace process 5, 226–7

Palestine 7, 44; and Israeli Arabs 227; refugees 52; suicide terrorism 6
Palestinian Authority 130
Palestinian Liberation Organization (PLO) 224
Palma Village; beside Kalkilya 61
Palmach 110
parachutists; operational capability of 64
parchment of fire 86
party politics; dislike 26
patriotism theories 69
patterns; working through loss 93
'Peace for Galilee Operation' 86
Peled Commission's report (1997) 158
Peled, M.; Knesset member 168
Peled, M. Major General 38
'Pentagon Papers' case (*New York Times v. United States*) 185
Peres, S. 25, 91, 166
Peri, Y. militarization of Israeli politics. 15–18
Perry, Y. 68
Planning mechanisms in Israel 198
pogroms 80
Poland 104
policy of retaliation 60
political bereavement 90–2
political control of the media 147
political-control model 153–6
political-military relations 1–12
politics: local 16; the media and national security 159–621; personalization of 27

politics as continuation of military service 13
politics and the mass media 147–64
population dispersal policy 214–32
post-9/11 operations in Afghanistan 183
post-Vietnam era 193
power of society 49
Press Ordinance issued by the British Mandate 155
prime minister status 5
privatization 150
Project Israel (2020) 200
protecting the home front 206
Psycho-Political approach; history 75–7
Public Broadcasting 133
public criticism 5
public good 149
public support: military action 123; military system's status 123

Rabin, I. 2
Rabin, Y. 18, 20, 25, 32, 56, 87; first retired officer 19
radioactive leak (1992) 178
Ramallah 135, 141, 162
Ramon, H. 25
Raphael arms industry complex 177
Reaction Committee 169
refugee issue 45, 52
regular army; unit commands in 64
reserve personnel motivation 68
retaliation policy 55, 60
retired officers 16; Defence Ministers 20–2; head of large cities 23–4; ministers 17–19; party heads 22–3; Prime Ministers 19–20
right to know 187
Ron, M. 116
Russia 37
Russian immigrants 209

Sad, Y. 111
Sadeh, Y.; commander Palmach 98
Sapir, J. 31
Sarid, T. from Kibbutz Beit Hashita 84
satellite photography 178
satellite television 158
Scholem, G. 171
Scud missiles 166, 210
second intifada 29

securitization discourse 207–10
security 51; crises 75–97; daily 204; objective 160; problems 27; salience of 27
Security Council 35
security loss; abandonment of the frontier settlements 54–6
Self-Mobilization Model 120
separation fence 209
settlements *see* West Bank
Shahak, Lt. General; chief of staff 5
Shaltiel, D. General 54
Shamir, I. 2
Shamir, Y. Prime Minister 166
Shapira, S. Justice Minster 40
Sharett, M. Prime Minister. 79
Sharon, A. Prime Minister 1, 6, 7, 18, 19, 20, 22, 23, 38, 209
Shayetet disaster 93
Shenck v. United States (1919) 183
Sheni, I. Brigadier-General 173
Sheni, M. (Second Look) 174
Shin Bet affair 169
Shir ha-re'ut (Song of Comradeship) 100
Shlomzion Party 22
Shomron, D; Chief-of-Staff 70
Shub, B. 116
Simcha Rotem (Kazik) 109
Sinai Campaign (1956) 128
Sinai Peninsular 224; evacuation 88, 203
Sinai status 45
Six Day War (1967) 31–47, 82, 128, 167, 222–5; results of 41
Sneh, E. 17
social detachment 101–6
social-cultural processes and military-media relations 136–8
society in the 1950s 49
society strength 48–65
South Africa 177
Soviet Union 183
state and media 121
station (7) 157
statutory authorities; tiers of 207
Straits of Tiran; Red Sea 34
strategic defence objectives 215
strategic problems; War of Independence 215
Suez Canal 43, 45
Supreme Court 7; role of 29

survivor-recruits 105
Syria 35, 137

tactics; role of 44
Tal, I. Maj. General.(res) 10
Teicher, E. 167
Tel Aviv 23
territorial defence; concept of 52
territorial dimension 199
terror; motivation in the face of 71
terror attacks; United States 138; impact of 9/11 186–8
terror outbreak 66
The Generation of '48 (Sivan) 107
The 'Green Line' 200
The Physical Planning Authority of IDF 207
The Silver Platter (Alterman) 99
thermal reactor 179
Third Way 22
Threat of Terrorism 66–74
transportation arteries 206
tsidook hadin 78
Turkey 28
Tzrifin army base 203

unit commands in the regular army 64
United Kingdom (UK) 183
United Nations (UN) 35, 114
United States of America (USA) 4, 35, 126, 174, 177, 183, 199
universal conscription 67
Urbach, E. 171

Vanunu expose 172, 173
Vanunu, M. 176
Vanunu trial 167
Vatican 42
Vietnam War 120, 126, 185
volunteer cultural initiators 76

Wallach, Y. Colonel 61
war 5; Afghanistan 120; against infiltration 64; Iraq (2003) 120, *see also* Lebanon; Six Day; Yom Kippur
War of Independence (1948) 50, 53, 64, 79, 81, 100, 205, 215–18
Warsaw ghetto 108, 109
Washington 160
water problem 45
Weizman, E. 17, 20, 32, 40

Weizmann, C. first president 99
West Bank 41, 43, 45, 200, 205, 206, 209, 224
Western Wall 5
Wircberg, B. 110

Yaacov, B. 177
Yaacov, Y. Brigadier-General 175
Yad Labanim House 87
Yad Labanim organisation 79
Yadin, Y. Lt. General 10, 18, 22
Yariv, A. General 18, 32, 49, 131
Yemen civil war 32
Yiddish 104
Yishuv 98, 101

Yom Kippur War (1973) 18, 46, 69, 75, 80–1, 83, 85, 89, 128, 157, 166, 169

Zechariah; village 177
Ze'evi, R. founder of Moledet 18, 22
Zeitgeist 44
Zemer, H. 32
Zionism 60
Zionist fulfilment 100
Zionist ideology 215
Zipori, M. 18
Zomet 22
Zuckerman Commission; 1988 report 158

For Product Safety Concerns and Information please contact our EU
representative GPSR@taylorandfrancis.com
Taylor & Francis Verlag GmbH, Kaufingerstraße 24, 80331 München, Germany

www.ingramcontent.com/pod-product-compliance
Lightning Source LLC
Chambersburg PA
CBHW062138300426
44115CB00012BA/1973